Sunset
COOK
TASTE
SAVOR

----

16 INSPIRING INGREDIENTS FOR DELICIOUS DISHES EVERY DAY

Oxmoor House®

Sunset

ISBN-10: 0-376-02810-6
ISBN-13: 978-0-376-02810-5
Library of Congress Control Number: 2012953109
First Printing 2013
Printed in the United States of America.

OXMOOR HOUSE, INC.
Editorial Director: Leah McLaughlin
Creative Director: Felicity Keane
Brand Manager: Fonda Hitchcock
Senior Editor: Heather Averett
Managing Editor: Rebecca Benton

TIME HOME ENTERTAINMENT INC.
Publisher: Jim Childs
VP, Brand and Digital Strategy: Steven Sandonato
Executive Director, Marketing Services: Carol Pittard
Executive Director, Retail & Special Sales: Tom Mifsud
Director, Bookazine Development and Marketing: Laura Adam
Executive Publishing Director: Joy Butts
Finance Director: Glenn Buonocore
Associate General Counsel: Helen Wan

SUNSET PUBLISHING
President: Barb Newton
Editor-in-Chief: Peggy Northrop
Food Editor: Margo True
Photography Director: Yvonne Stender

CONTRIBUTORS TO THIS BOOK
Editor: Tori Ritchie
Production Manager: Linda M. Bouchard
Copy Editor: Gloria Geller
Senior Imaging Specialist: Kimberley Navabpour
Photo Editor: Sue B. Smith
Photo Coordinator: Danielle Johnson
Project Editor: Lacie Pinyan
Proofreader: Lesley Bruynesteyn
Indexer: Ken DellaPenta

To order additional publications, call 1-800-765-6400
For more books to enrich your life, visit oxmoorhouse.com
Visit Sunset online at sunset.com
For the most comprehensive selection of Sunset books, visit sunsetbooks.com
To search, savor, and share thousands of recipes, visit myrecipes.com

SPECIAL THANKS

Associate Food Editor Elaine Johnson, Recipe Editor Amy Machnak, Test Kitchen Manager Stephanie Spencer, former food editors Jerry Anne DiVecchio and Sara Schneider, and writers, including Linda Lau Anusasananan, Jessica Battilana, April Cooper, Jerry Anne Di Vecchio, Charity Ferreira, Julia Lee, Adeena Sussman, Amy Traverso, Kate Washington, and Molly Watson; plus the Sunset recipe retesters—Kevyn Allard, Angela Brassinga, Dorothy Decker, Sarah Epstein, Lenore Grant, Doni Jackson, Melissa Kaiser, Marlene Kawahata, Eve F. Lynch, Rebecca Parker, Bunnie Russell, Laura Shafsky, Vicki Sousa, Linda Tebben, and Sue Turner

We would also like to thank Erika Ehmsen, Trina Enriquez, Mark Hawkins, Stephanie Johnson, Megan McCrea, Kitty Morgan, Marisa Park, Marie Pence, and Alan Phinney.

COVER

Rainbow carrot, pea shoot, and chicken salad (see page 172 for recipe). Photograph by Annabelle Breakey (food styling by Karen Shinto; prop styling by Emma Star Jensen).

PHOTOGRAPHY CREDITS

Iain Bagwell: 3, 46, 55, 67, 78, 128, 144, 192, 195, 253, 257, 264; **Iain Bagwell/Getty Images:** 110, 164, 177, 178, 269, 270, 273; **James Baigrie:** 228; **Leigh Beisch:** 25, 72, 87, 88, 181, 226; **Aya Brackett:** 93, 199; **Annabelle Breakey:** 4 2nd row #3, 17, 26, 50, 52–53, 58, 62, 64, 79, 80, 83, 108, 112, 132, 137, 153, 188, 261, 262; **Annabelle Breakey/Getty Images:** 11, 18, 30, 35, 38, 47 both, 48, 60, 63, 68, 73, 84, 98, 106, 117, 123, 152, 160, 187, 198, 203, 206, 209, 210, 213, 222, 223, 234, 238, 239, 243, 244, 249, 266; **Rob D. Brodman:** 12; **James Carrier:** 116, 140, 191; **Maren Caruso:** 107; **Harrison Eastwood/Getty Images:** 115; **Alex Farnum:** 32, 34, 77, 111, 186 both, 190 all, 147, 219, 229, 245; **Funkystock/Getty Images:** 37; **Sheri L. Giblin/Getty Images:** 44; **Dan Goldberg:** 99, 121, 143; **Dan Goldberg/Getty Images:** 224; **Leo Gong:** 29, 96, 145, 157, 173; **Thayer Allyson Gowdy:** 167; **Jim Henkens:** 97, 214; **Yunhee Kim:** 39, 233; **Erin Kunkel:** 4 (all except 2nd row #3), 7, 8–9, 13, 14, 22–23, 33, 40–41, 43, 45, 49, 56, 74–75, 90–91, 100, 102–103, 105, 118–119, 124, 127, 134–135, 148, 154–155, 159, 163, 168–169, 174, 182–183, 200–201, 205, 216–217, 225, 240–241, 246, 258–259; **Jennifer Martiné:** 59, 139; **Gary Moss Photography/Getty Images:** 71; **Lauri Patterson/Getty Images:** 197; **Victoria Pearson:** 275; **David Prince:** 21; **Lisa Romerein:** 185; **Thomas J. Story:** 61, 95, 129, 131, 151, 171, 221, 227, 250, 265; **E. Spencer Toy:** 268 both; **Luca Trovato/Getty Images:** 237; **Rachel Weill:** 230, 254

*Caprese skillet eggs
(see page 55 for recipe)*

CONTENTS

INTRODUCTION

Next time you're at the farmers' market or in the produce section of your supermarket, listen in on the conversations around you. What you will hear are people talking about ingredients. Where did this grow? How do I cook it? What will it taste like?

Those ingredient-based conversations are what frame this book. In these pages, you'll learn about 16 essential *Sunset* ingredients and the freshest, most vibrant ways to cook them. Whether it's Meyer lemons or mushrooms, Colorado lamb or Dungeness crab, Oregon hazelnuts or California tomatoes, these are the foods we talk about and that inspire us, both at home and in the *Sunset* test kitchen. They are our local ingredients; after all, no city or town in the West is very far from the ocean, mountain, meadow, valley, orchard, or desert where these things grow or are raised. But these are not just Western ingredients, these are also ingredients you can find anywhere. The West is known as the "grocery basket" of the nation because it provides so much of the produce, meat, and seafood eaten in the United States.

The West is also a place of migration, with waves of settlers bringing recipes and techniques from home and adapting them to what they found here. As a result, these pages are filled with the dynamic, diverse flavors of Latin America, Asia and the Pacific, the Mediterranean, North Africa, and the Middle East. There are also special sections that zero in on six iconic foods and drinks brought by these immigrants, which in turn have become so ingrained in our culture that we can't imagine daily life without them: beer, bread, chocolate, coffee, olive oil, and wine.

Let this book inspire you to join the conversation. Use it to learn about the signature ingredients throughout the growing season, from spring's first artichokes to winter's year-end citrus. Thumb through it for new ideas for parties, picnics, or holidays. Turn to it again and again for weeknight dinners, delicious desserts, healthful snacks, summer grilling, and autumn braising. With these essential ingredients—artichokes, berries, avocados, tomatoes, chiles, onions, dried beans, apples, cheese, lamb, chicken, crab, mushrooms, nuts, dried fruit, and citrus—you can cook, taste, and savor your way to great meals every day.

Ancho-marinated steak with warm black bean salad (see page 105 for recipe)

ARTICHOKES

ARTICHOKES

The artichoke, native to the Mediterranean, is one of the oldest known foods. Whether cooked or raw, it is a go-to ingredient, versatile and unique, that came West with migrants from Italy in the late nineteenth century. It eventually found its ideal growing environment along the cool California coast south of San Francisco.

At farmers' markets and well-stocked stores, you can find both classic green and stunning purple artichokes in a range of sizes—from walloping jumbos to 1½-inch-diameter "baby" artichokes. Unlike most other produce, the little ones aren't juveniles, but fully mature artichokes grown low on the stalk. Shaded by the plant's large, serrated leaves, the small artichokes are more tender and without a fuzzy choke, so once trimmed (see page 20), you can eat the whole thing.

SEASONAL AVAILABILITY While artichokes are available at some grocery stores all year long, they peak in spring, followed by a short second season in fall-winter. Frozen artichokes are available year-round and are an easy-to-use ingredient that we turn to for dips, pastas, and more.

SELECTING AND STORING Choose an artichoke that is heavy for its size and has a compact head with tight leaves. Surprisingly, if there are brown splotches on the leaves, it won't affect flavor, so don't turn away from artichokes that have been "frost-kissed." Store artichokes, unwashed, in a plastic bag in the refrigerator for up to one week. You can freeze artichokes from the market or your garden: Trim them down to the hearts, blanch them in boiling water for 7 minutes, then drain, plunge into cold water to cool, and drain again. Pack in resealable plastic freezer bags, leaving no headspace, then seal and freeze.

USING Large artichokes are nature's perfect single serving when steamed or boiled and offered with mayonnaise or melted butter as a dip for the leaves and heart. While that's the iconic Western method, artichokes can also be fried, roasted, stuffed, grilled, sautéed, and even sliced thinly and served raw with olive oil and parmesan shavings (a dish popular in Italy). Also, if a stem is attached, it can be eaten: Just pare away the tough green outer portion until you reach the pale center, which is essentially an extension of the heart. And have a lemon handy when working with artichokes because artichokes oxidize as they are cut; rubbing the cuts with lemon can help prevent them from turning brown.

Artichoke bruschetta

SERVES 4 to 6 | **TIME** 25 minutes

Ciabatta—or "slipper bread"—is a good choice for these appetizers because of its wide surface area; if you can't find it, use another kind of Italian bread. Slice the loaf thinly and toast in a 350° oven until crispy, then spread with the ricotta. Use fresh, whole-milk ricotta if it's available.

3 tbsp. vegetable oil
2 large trimmed artichokes (about 1½ lbs.; see "Trimming Artichokes," page 20), sliced thinly
½ tsp. kosher salt
5 slices toasted ciabatta bread, cut in half diagonally
¾ cup ricotta cheese
½ tsp. pepper
2 tsp. lemon zest
6 fresh basil leaves, thinly sliced

1. Heat oil in a large frying pan over medium heat. Cook artichoke slices, stirring occasionally, until softened and browned, about 4 minutes. Sprinkle with salt.

2. Put toasts on a plate and spread each with ricotta, dividing it evenly. Sprinkle with pepper and zest. Spoon some artichokes onto each slice and top with a bit of basil.

PER SERVING 356 CAL., 29% (103 CAL.) FROM FAT; 14 G PROTEIN; 12 G FAT (4 G SAT.); 53 G CARBO (4.7 G FIBER); 632 MG SODIUM; 17 MG CHOL.

Sesame fried artichokes

SERVES 4 | **TIME** 30 minutes

We don't normally think of pairing Asian flavors with artichokes, but this easy recipe uses the venerable Roman method of frying, then adds sesame oil and sesame seeds.

About 2 cups vegetable oil for frying
⅓ cup mayonnaise
1 tbsp. toasted sesame oil
3 lbs. baby artichokes
1 lemon, cut in quarters
1 tsp. toasted sesame seeds
Kosher salt

Artichoke bruschetta

1. Heat oil in a medium pot over medium heat until it reaches 350° on a deep-fry thermometer; when oil is hot, reduce heat to low. Mix mayonnaise and sesame oil; set aside.

2. Use a paring knife to shave stem ends of artichokes to a point like a pencil. Trim artichokes (see page 20), squeezing juice from the lemon quarters into the bowl of soaking water and dropping in the peels. Cut each artichoke in half.

3. Drain artichoke halves and blot dry with a towel. Working in 2 batches, cook artichokes until browned and crispy, about 8 minutes. Use a slotted spoon to transfer to paper towels to drain. Sprinkle with sesame seeds and season to taste with salt. Serve with mayo.

PER SERVING 265 CAL., 69% (184 CAL.) FROM FAT; 4.8 G PROTEIN; 21 G FAT (2.6 G SAT.); 19 G CARBO (7.4 G FIBER); 267 MG SODIUM; 5.1 MG CHOL.

Creamy artichoke dip

Artichokes with mint and lemon

SERVES 6 to 8 | **TIME** 30 minutes

Yes, artichokes can be eaten raw—in fact, the Italians have long done so. Raw artichokes are especially good with roasted spring lamb (see page 165 for a recipe). Shave paper-thin and dress with the best olive oil and parmesan you can find (see "Parmesan 101," page 15). Chris Cosentino, chef at San Francisco's Incanto restaurant, gave us this simple salad recipe.

10 baby artichokes
½ lemon plus 3 tbsp. juice
5 tbsp. extra-virgin olive oil
½ tsp. sea salt (see "Sea Salt 101," below)
¼ tsp. pepper
8 oz. wild or baby arugula
¼ cup torn mint leaves
Wedge of parmigiano-reggiano cheese

1. Trim artichokes (see page 20), squeezing juice from ½ lemon into the bowl of soaking water. Cut artichokes crosswise.

2. Mix remaining 3 tbsp. lemon juice, the oil, salt, and pepper in a bowl. Working with 1 artichoke at a time, blot dry, then shave lengthwise with a mandoline or a vegetable peeler into the oil mixture. Add arugula and mint to artichokes; toss to coat. Divide salad among plates; shave cheese over each.

PER SERVING 150 CAL., 69% (104 CAL.) FROM FAT; 6.2 G PROTEIN; 12 G FAT (3.6 G SAT.); 7.3 G CARBO (3.6 G FIBER); 242 MG SODIUM; 9.5 MG CHOL.

Creamy artichoke dip

MAKES 1½ cups | **TIME** About 15 minutes

Go back to the glory days of party dips with this gooey, mayonnaisey 1960s classic. Spread on crackers or crostini, use as a dip for crudités, or serve this sauce with grilled fish or chicken.

8 oz. cream cheese
2 oz. (about ½ cup) thawed frozen artichoke hearts
⅓ cup grated parmesan cheese
1 tbsp. chopped flat-leaf parsley
2 tsp. lemon juice
½ tsp. *each* **salt and pepper**
¼ tsp. lemon zest
1 small garlic clove, finely chopped

Whirl all ingredients in a food processor until blended and artichokes break into small pieces. Transfer to a bowl to serve as a dip, spread, or sauce.

PER TBSP. 40 CAL., 83% (33 CAL.) FROM FAT; 1.3 G PROTEIN; 3.7 G FAT (2 G SAT.); 0.7 G CARBO (0.2 G FIBER); 108 MG SODIUM; 11 MG CHOL.

Sea salt 101

Made from evaporated seawater, sea salt adds a clean, minerally flavor that can't be matched by table salt. Sea salt is available in fine to coarse grains. Refined or unrefined fine-textured sea salt works well for all-purpose cooking and seasoning. Unrefined medium- to coarse-grain sea salt adds texture and flavor when sprinkled on dough, fish, and meat. Connoisseurs particularly prize snowy white French *fleur de sel* ("flower of salt"), delicate crystals that form on top of evaporation ponds, and coarser *sel gris* ("gray salt"), from the lower layers, especially as a finishing salt on dishes, such as the salad above.

Artichokes with
mint and lemon

Spring lamb loin roasted
with mint and garlic (see
page 165 for recipe)

Italian chicken sausage and artichoke soup

Italian chicken sausage and artichoke soup

SERVES 4 to 6 | **TIME** 40 minutes

Light, clean, and green, this soup is particularly good with the fennel flavor of Italian sausage, but any chicken sausage will work. Save the stems from the Swiss chard to use in another soup or stir-fry. To make your own chicken broth, see page 276.

2 tbsp. olive oil
1 lb. Italian chicken sausage, casings removed
    and meat broken into chunks
3 cans (15 oz. each) reduced-sodium chicken broth
1 lb. frozen artichoke hearts, thawed and halved
1 lb. chard, stemmed and chopped
Parmesan cheese (see "Parmesan 101," below)
Warm ciabatta bread

1. Heat oil in a large pot over medium-high heat. Cook sausage until browned, stirring often, 10 minutes. Add broth, artichokes, and 2 cups water and bring to a boil.

2. Reduce heat to low and simmer. Add chard and cook, covered, until wilted, about 3 minutes. Ladle soup into bowls and serve with freshly grated cheese and bread.

PER 1¹/₂-CUP SERVING 225 CAL., 51% (114 CAL.) FROM FAT; 20 G PROTEIN; 13 G FAT (2.8 G SAT.); 8.6 G CARBO (5.2 G FIBER); 611 MG SODIUM; 81 MG CHOL.

Parmesan 101

Parmesan cheese is widely available in the United States and is usually sold in wedges cut from a whole wheel; look for "Parmigiano-Reggiano" stamped into the wax rind. The stamp guarantees that you are buying the real deal, which is expensive, but worth it. If you buy shredded parmesan, the flavors will be diminished; grate or shred parmesan just before serving.

Farfalle with artichokes, peppers, and almonds

SERVES 6 | **TIME** 45 minutes

Baby artichokes are great eaten raw, cooked, or, as in this recipe, macerated in lemon juice and oil. Because it is sprinkled with ground almonds instead of the usual parmesan, it's a good vegan choice. This recipe came to us from Clifford A. Wright, who has written more than a dozen cookbooks, including many on Italy and the Mediterranean.

Zest of ¹/₂ lemon and juice from 2 lemons, divided
2 garlic cloves, finely chopped
³/₄ tsp. pepper
About ³/₄ tsp. kosher salt
¹/₄ cup extra-virgin olive oil
1 jar (16 oz.) roasted red bell peppers, rinsed and chopped
³/₄ lb. baby artichokes (about 5)
12 oz. farfalle pasta
¹/₂ cup chopped flat-leaf parsley
1 cup toasted almonds (see "Toasting Nuts," page 224), coarsely
    ground, divided

1. Combine lemon zest and juice from 1 lemon in a large bowl with the garlic, pepper, ³/₄ tsp. salt, the oil, and roasted peppers.

2. Trim artichokes (see page 20), squeezing juice from remaining lemon into the bowl of soaking water.

3. Slice 1 artichoke at a time paper-thin lengthwise, using a mandoline or knife, and stir into pepper mixture. Let stand about 30 minutes.

4. Meanwhile, cook pasta as package directs. Drain, saving 1 cup pasta water. Toss pasta with pepper mixture, then with parsley and ¹/₂ cup almonds. Mix in a little pasta water if needed for a looser texture. Serve with remaining almonds and season to taste with salt.

PER 1¹/₂-CUP SERVING 461 CAL., 43% (199 CAL.) FROM FAT; 14 G PROTEIN; 23 G FAT (2.5 G SAT.); 56 G CARBO (6.8 G FIBER); 409 MG SODIUM; 0 MG CHOL.

Garlicky steak salad with chickpeas and artichokes

SERVES 6 to 8 | **TIME** 45 minutes, plus 3 hours to marinate

Despite lots of garlic, the dressing in this salad is actually quite mellow with the citrus and soy.

About 1½ tsp. *each* kosher salt and pepper, divided
1 cup reduced-sodium soy sauce
10 tbsp. orange juice, divided
1 flank steak (1½ lbs.), silverskin trimmed
    (see "Grilling Steak," right)
12 garlic cloves, thinly sliced
2 oranges, sliced crosswise
1 lb. thawed frozen artichoke hearts
10 tbsp. extra-virgin olive oil, divided
2 tsp. orange zest
2 tbsp. red wine vinegar
2 qts. *each* mixed baby greens and baby arugula
2 cans (about 14.5 oz. each) chickpeas (garbanzos),
    drained and rinsed
8 green onions, thinly sliced
1 cup shaved parmesan cheese

1. Whisk together 1 tsp. *each* salt and pepper, the soy sauce, and 6 tbsp. juice in a small bowl.

2. Make deep slices ½ to ¾ in. apart across the grain into one side of flank steak, making sure not to cut all the way through and leaving a ¼-in. uncut edge around steak. Stuff slices evenly with garlic. Arrange half the orange slices in a 9- by 13-in. baking dish and set steak, garlic side up, on top. Arrange remaining orange slices over meat and pour soy marinade over them. Cover dish and chill steak at least 3 and up to 24 hours; let stand at room temperature during the last 30 minutes.

3. Heat grill to high (450° to 550°). Skewer artichokes on two 10-in. metal skewers, brush with 2 tbsp. oil, and sprinkle with a little salt and pepper.

4. Oil cooking grate with a wad of oiled paper towels, using tongs. Lay steak on grate, garlic side up (discard oranges); grill, covered, carefully turning over once (some garlic will fall out), 6 to 8 minutes total for medium-rare. Transfer steak to a board, tent loosely with foil, and let rest 5 minutes.

5. Meanwhile, grill artichokes, turning them over once, until lightly browned, about 6 minutes total. Transfer to a plate and remove from skewers.

6. In a small bowl, whisk together remaining ½ tsp. *each* salt and pepper, ¼ cup orange juice, ½ cup oil, the zest, and vinegar. Thinly slice steak diagonally across the grain.

7. Toss baby greens, arugula, chickpeas, green onions, and cheese in a large bowl with about half the dressing. Transfer to a platter or plates, top with steak and artichokes, and drizzle with remaining dressing.

PER SERVING 451 CAL., 54% (244 CAL.) FROM FAT; 29 G PROTEIN; 28 G FAT (6.5 G SAT.); 24 G CARBO (8.7 G FIBER); 801 MG SODIUM; 35 MG CHOL.

Grilling steak

Choose the right meat. Inexpensive, meaty flank steak is the best choice for the recipe above, but New York strip is another option that isn't too costly. Both are boneless and on the thinner side, so they slice up well for salads.

Give it a trim. With a sharp paring knife, trim off any silverskin (the thin, shiny connective tissue on the outside of the meat that gets tough when it cooks), or ask a butcher to do this. You can also cut a few slashes in the meat and insert garlic for extra flavor.

Marinate—if you have time. For the best results, plan ahead to marinate the steak; the marinade will penetrate the meat with flavor and make it more tender. If you're in a rush, just salt and pepper the meat before grilling.

Take the chill off. For the most even cooking, let cold steak, marinated or not, sit at room temperature for about 30 minutes before cooking.

Oil it. If there is no oil in the marinade or you aren't using a marinade, coat the steak with oil so it won't stick to the grill.

Be patient. Let the steak brown on one side before you turn it. It should release easily from the grill when you lift it with tongs.

Let it rest. Put the steak on a board and tent it with foil for a few minutes before slicing so the juices go back into the meat.

Garlicky steak salad with
chickpeas and artichokes

Shrimp and artichoke linguine Alfredo

Shrimp and artichoke linguine Alfredo

SERVES 4 | **TIME** 30 minutes

Shrimp and artichokes get the "Alfredo" treatment and transform a first-course pasta into a complete meal. Reader Aysha Schurman, of Ammon, Idaho, who contributed this recipe, adds even more personality with a flash of herbs, garlic, and chile flakes. To make your own chicken broth, see page 276.

8 oz. linguine
½ cup frozen artichoke hearts, thawed and chopped, divided
1 cup sour cream
½ cup reduced-sodium chicken broth
½ cup chopped celery
¼ cup chopped red onion
⅓ cup grated parmesan cheese
1 tbsp. *each* chopped parsley and minced garlic
1 tsp. *each* chopped fresh rosemary and basil leaves
½ tsp. *each* red chile flakes, salt, and pepper
½ lb. (about 20) peeled, deveined shrimp

1. Cook linguine as package directs.

2. Meanwhile, reserve ¼ cup artichokes. In a food processor, whirl remaining ingredients except shrimp until blended but still chunky. Pour sauce into a medium saucepan. Stir in shrimp and reserved artichokes; cook over medium heat until sauce begins to boil. Reduce heat and cook until sauce thickens, about 10 minutes. Drain pasta, put in a bowl, and pour sauce on top.

PER SERVING 416 CAL., 30% (124 CAL.) FROM FAT; 24 G PROTEIN; 14 G FAT (7.2 G SAT.); 49 G CARBO (4 G FIBER); 603 MG SODIUM; 120 MG CHOL.

Lamb and artichoke daube

SERVES 4 | **TIME** 3¼ to 3½ hours

A *daube* is a French braise, and this is a simplified version of the braised lamb shanks chef Reed Hearon created at San Francisco's LuLu restaurant. Serve over hot couscous.

4 lamb shanks (about 1 lb. each), bones cracked and fat trimmed
Salt and pepper
15 garlic cloves
1 onion (about 10 oz.), cut into ½-in. pieces
2 carrots (about 6 oz. total), peeled and cut into ½-in. pieces
1 bottle (750 ml.) Côtes-du-Rhône or other dry red wine
1 can (about 15 oz.) crushed or diced tomatoes
6 canned anchovy fillets, drained and minced
1 tbsp. minced fresh thyme leaves or 1 tsp. dried
1 tbsp. minced fresh savory leaves or 1 tsp. dried
1 tsp. orange zest
8 oz. thawed frozen artichoke hearts
½ cup pitted kalamata or Niçoise olives

1. Preheat oven to 450°. Rinse shanks and pat dry. Sprinkle lightly all over with salt and pepper, and place in a 12- by 17-in. roasting pan. Bake, uncovered, until meat is beginning to brown, about 20 minutes. Using tongs, turn over shanks. Add garlic, onion, and carrots to pan around shanks, mix to coat with fat in pan, and spread level. Bake until shanks are well browned and vegetables are beginning to brown, about 20 minutes longer.

2. Add wine, tomatoes and their juices, anchovies, thyme, savory, and zest to pan; stir carefully to mix and scrape browned bits free. Cover pan tightly with foil.

3. Lower heat to 325° and bake until meat is very tender when pierced, 2 to 2½ hours.

4. Uncover pan. Spoon off and discard fat from sauce. Gently stir artichokes and olives into sauce around shanks and bake until heated through, about 10 minutes.

5. Use tongs to transfer shanks to a rimmed platter or plates; pour sauce over lamb. Season to taste with salt and pepper.

PER SERVING 686 CAL., 34% (234 CAL.) FROM FAT; 82 G PROTEIN; 26 G FAT (8.5 G SAT.); 29 G CARBO (6.8 G FIBER); 1,001 MG SODIUM; 242 MG CHOL.

Trimming artichokes

Here are instructions for trimming both full-size and baby artichokes.

FULL-SIZE ARTICHOKES

1. Fill a large bowl halfway with cold water and squeeze in juice of ½ lemon.

2. Working with one artichoke at a time, snap off thick green outer leaves down to yellowish core. Cut off thorny tips. If there is a stem attached to the artichoke, trim off about ½ in. and use a vegetable peeler to remove tough outer skin from remaining stem.

3. Cut artichoke in half lengthwise; use a spoon or the point of a knife to scoop out fuzzy, red-tipped choke. As you work, put trimmed artichokes in the bowl of lemon water to prevent them from oxidizing and turning brown. Set aside until you're ready to use.

BABY ARTICHOKES

1. Cut off the stem at the base of the artichoke for a neat presentation. If you want the stem on, use a sharp knife to trim away the tough, dark green outer surface of it.

2. Peel back and snap off the leaves all around the base of the artichoke until you reach the tender inner leaves that are yellow at the bottom and green at the top (you'll remove a lot of leaves).

3. Cut off the top third of the remaining leaves. With a sharp paring knife, trim off any remaining fibrous material from around the base of the artichoke.

4. Drop the trimmed artichokes in a bowl of water mixed with lemon juice to keep them from turning brown, especially if you are using the artichokes raw.

Sautéed baby artichokes

SERVES 4 | **TIME** 1½ hours

It's said that California has a Mediterranean climate, and it's true that many of the ingredients grown there are also grown here. In this recipe, two Roman favorites, artichokes and mint, mix it up in a stylish side dish that's very Californian.

36 baby artichokes
2 tbsp. *each* lemon juice and olive oil
About 1 tbsp. salt
1 oz. pancetta, chopped
2 garlic cloves, sliced
¼ cup dry white wine
¼ cup mint leaves, chopped
Pepper
Shaved or grated parmesan cheese

1. Trim artichokes (see box at left), adding the lemon juice and oil to the bowl of soaking water.

2. Bring a large pot of water to a boil and add salt. Drain artichokes from ice water and add to boiling water; simmer until tender, 10 to 20 minutes. Drain artichokes and let stand until cool enough to handle. Cut larger ones in half, removing any fuzz at the heart.

3. Set a frying pan over medium-high heat. Add pancetta and stir until fat is rendered. Add garlic and stir until golden. Add wine and artichokes and cook until wine is almost evaporated. Add mint and season to taste with salt and pepper. Serve topped with cheese.

PER SERVING 117 CAL., 17% (20 CAL.) FROM FAT; 7.3 G PROTEIN; 2.3 G FAT (0.6 G SAT.); 22 G CARBO (11 G FIBER); 473 MG SODIUM; 3.1 MG CHOL.

Sautéed baby artichokes

BERRIES

BERRIES

If there's one fruit you should savor in season, it's berries. Don't fall for the imports you see at other times of year; it's worth waiting for spring when just-plucked, full-flavored berries begin appearing at farmers' markets and U-pick berry farms.

Berries thrive in the West, especially on California's Central Coast and in Oregon's Willamette Valley (known as America's berry bowl). And healthwise, berries are a terrific source of vitamin C and fiber, plus their red, blue, and purple colors signal their high antioxidant levels.

SEASONAL AVAILABILITY The tastiest strawberries are found near where they're grown, as they are picked at their ripest (peak season is April through June). April is also when you'll begin to find blueberries (Oregon is the third largest producer in the nation). Red raspberries (grown along the coast from California to British Columbia) and delicately flavored golden raspberries (mostly from Washington) ripen from May to September. At the same time, look for blackberries and their kin, including boysenberries (a cross between raspberry and wild blackberry); red-black loganberries (another raspberry–wild blackberry cross); long, slender, olallieberries (a cross of about one-third raspberry and two-thirds blackberry); and the queen of blackberries, tangy-sweet marionberries.

SELECTING AND STORING Avoid bruised or pale berries and berry cartons that are leaky or damp. Ripe berries are delicate and require care. Sort through and remove any squashed, overripe, or moldy ones. Gently blot any moisture with a paper towel (dampness hastens spoilage) and chill them, unwashed, in an airtight container. Wait to wash berries until just before you use them, and use as little water as possible. For strawberries, hull after you wash them to keep the berries from absorbing moisture. Dry completely after rinsing. If you have extras that you won't eat within two days, preserve them: Spread rinsed, dried fruit in a single layer on a baking sheet and freeze until firm; transfer to freezer bags and freeze up to one year.

USING Eating a ripe berry plain, right from your fingertips, may be the best recipe there is. However, we can't resist them in pies and cakes, with cream and sugar, for breakfast and lunch, even in cocktails. We love roasting strawberries (a great topping for ice cream): Toss halved berries with a little brown sugar and a bit of ground cardamom; bake in a buttered pie dish at 400° until softened and a little darker, about 15 minutes. Berries also offer a tangy counterpoint to savory foods, like goat cheese and cooked poultry.

Blueberry–cream cheese coffee cake

SERVES 10 to 12 | **TIME** 1 hour

Who doesn't love blueberries for breakfast—especially when they're baked into coffee cake made rich with cream cheese, yogurt, and a crown of almonds? This recipe, from Elaine Wing Hillesland, owner of Alegria Oceanfront Inn & Cottages in Mendocino, California, is wonderful in the afternoon with coffee or tea. To make your own yogurt, see page 278.

1 cup fresh or frozen blueberries
¼ cup apple juice
1 tsp. cornstarch
2 cups flour
1 cup sugar, divided
½ cup cold butter, cut into chunks
½ tsp. *each* baking powder and baking soda
¼ tsp. salt
1 tsp. lemon zest
¾ cup plain low-fat yogurt
1 tsp. vanilla extract
2 large eggs
6 oz. cream cheese, at room temperature
1 tsp. lemon juice
½ cup sliced almonds

1. Preheat oven to 350°. Butter a 9-in. round cake pan with a removable rim.

2. Bring blueberries and apple juice to a boil in a 1- to 2-qt. pan over medium heat. Lower heat and simmer, stirring occasionally, until blueberries have released their juices, about 3 minutes. In a small bowl, blend cornstarch and 2 tsp. water. Add to blueberry mixture; stir until it simmers and thickens, about 1 minute. Let cool to room temperature.

3. Mix flour and ¾ cup sugar in a medium bowl or a food processor. Add butter and cut in with a pastry blender or pulse until mixture resembles coarse crumbs. Reserve ½ cup; pour remaining mixture into a large bowl and stir in baking powder, baking soda, salt, and zest.

4. Mix yogurt, vanilla, and 1 egg in a small bowl until blended; stir into flour-lemon mixture until incorporated. Spread batter in pan.

5. In a medium bowl, beat with a mixer on high speed, or whirl in a food processor (no need to wash from step 3) cream cheese, remaining ¼ cup sugar, remaining egg, and the lemon juice until smooth. Spread over batter in pan, leaving a ½-in. border bare. Gently spread blueberry mixture over cream cheese mixture, leaving some visible. Stir almonds into reserved flour mixture and sprinkle over cake, concentrating most around edge of batter.

6. Bake until center of cake barely jiggles when pan is gently shaken and top of cake is golden brown, 30 to 40 minutes. Let cool on a rack 15 minutes, then remove pan rim. Serve warm or at room temperature.

PER SERVING 316 CAL., 46% (144 CAL.) FROM FAT; 5.9 G PROTEIN; 16 G FAT (8.7 G SAT.); 37 G CARBO (1 G FIBER); 266 MG SODIUM; 73 MG CHOL.

Sauceless-in-Seattle ribs

Sauceless-in-Seattle ribs

SERVES 4 | **TIME** About 1½ hours

Give your ribs a unique, summery taste by basting with a sauce made from blackberries, ketchup, honey, brown sugar, and spices in this recipe, from Dan Peters, of Federal Way, Washington, which was a grand-prize winner in a *Sunset* recipe contest. The sauce thickens to a sticky glaze while the slab cooks. Garnish ribs with blackberries and mint sprigs for extra flair.

1 slab pork spareribs (about 4 lbs.)
Blackberry Sauce (recipe follows)
³/₄ cup blackberries, rinsed
Mint sprigs (optional)

1. Rinse ribs and pat dry. Trim and discard excess fat. Remove the membrane from underside of ribs: Slide a screwdriver tip along each bone and under one end of membrane to loosen, then grab membrane with a paper towel and pull off (it's okay if membrane breaks and bits remain).

2. Heat grill to medium-low (300° to 350°), leaving an area clear for indirect heat. Set a drip pan in cleared area. Lay ribs on grill over drip pan and cook until meat is starting to pull away from edges of bones, about 1½ hours; if using charcoal, add about 10 briquets to fire every 30 minutes.

3. Baste 1 side of ribs with half the sauce. Set ribs sauce side down on grill and cook until sauce browns and forms a thick, sticky glaze, about 15 minutes. Baste top of ribs with remaining sauce, turn over, and cook until sauce browns and forms a thick, sticky glaze, about 15 minutes longer.

4. Transfer ribs to a platter and garnish with blackberries and mint if you like. Cut between bones to separate portions.

PER SERVING 878 CAL., 55% (486 CAL.) FROM FAT; 52 G PROTEIN; 54 G FAT (20 G SAT.); 45 G CARBO (3.8 G FIBER); 383 MG SODIUM; 214 MG CHOL.

BLACKBERRY SAUCE

In a food processor or blender, combine 1¼ cups rinsed **blackberries**; ¼ cup *each* **ketchup**, **honey**, firmly packed **brown sugar**, and **minced fresh ginger**; 1 tsp. **pepper**; and ½ tsp. **salt** (optional). Whirl until berries are puréed.

Add 1 to 2 tsp. **hot sauce** to taste. Pour into a 1-qt. glass measure. Cover loosely with microwave-safe plastic wrap, leaving vents for steam. Microwave on high, stirring occasionally, until berry mixture is reduced to 1⅓ cups, about 8 minutes.

PER ⅓ CUP 161 CAL., 1.7% (2.7 CAL.) FROM FAT; 0.8 G PROTEIN; 0.3 G FAT (0 G SAT.); 42 G CARBO (2.5 G FIBER); 218 MG SODIUM; 0 MG CHOL.

Cucumber, *soju*, and blueberry shrub cocktail

SERVES 4 | **TIME** 10 minutes, plus about 4 hours to cool and chill

Refreshing vinegar-based drinks are very popular in Korea—and, curiously, they're a lot like "shrubs," the vinegar-spiked fruit drinks of colonial America that are having a revival. Both inspired this sweet-tart cocktail by Rachel Yang and Seif Chirchi, chef-owners of Joule and Revel restaurants in Seattle. It's good as a mocktail too, with club soda instead of *soju*.

¼ cup unseasoned rice vinegar
¼ cup sugar
1 cup blueberries
12 English cucumber sticks (about 3 in. long)
2 cups (about 500 ml.) chilled Korean *soju* or Japanese *shochu**
Club soda (optional)

1. Make blueberry shrub: Bring vinegar, sugar, and ½ cup water to a boil in a small saucepan. Stir in berries. Let cool, then chill airtight at least 4 hours and up to 1 week.

2. Fill 4 tall glasses one-third full with ice; arrange cucumber sticks in them. Pour ½ cup *soju* into each, followed by ⅓ cup shrub (liquid and fruit). Taste, then add more shrub and a splash of club soda if you like.

*****A liquor traditionally made from rice, *soju* can also be distilled from wheat, barley, tapioca, and sweet potatoes. The Japanese style (*shochu*) is generally smooth, clean, and subtle; the Korean (*soju*) tends to have a fuller, stronger flavor. Find it at well-stocked grocery stores and liquor stores.

PER SERVING 343 CAL., 0.3% (1.1 CAL.) FROM FAT; 0.3 G PROTEIN; 0.1 G FAT (0 G SAT.); 29 G CARBO (0.9 G FIBER); 1.2 MG SODIUM; 0 MG CHOL.

Grilled goat cheese and strawberry sandwiches

MAKES 2 sandwiches | **TIME** 15 minutes

A sandwich from Half & Half, a former cafe in Portland, Oregon, inspired reader Sarah Van Winkle to try this combo at home. Van Winkle cooks hers in a panini press, but we found that a frying pan keeps the strawberry juices from running so much.

2 tbsp. softened butter
4 slices *pain au levain* **or other hearty, rustic bread**
3 oz. fresh goat cheese
6 large strawberries, sliced thinly
8 to 12 fresh basil leaves

Butter 1 side of each bread slice. Generously spread goat cheese on unbuttered side of 2 slices and cook them in a frying pan over medium heat, cheese side up, until golden underneath, about 2 minutes. Layer with strawberries and basil on top of cheese. Top with remaining bread slices, buttered side up; turn over and cook until golden, about 2 minutes.

PER SANDWICH 360 CAL., 58% (207 CAL.) FROM FAT; 14 G PROTEIN; 23 G FAT (14 G SAT.); 28 G CARBO (4.4 G FIBER); 573 MG SODIUM; 51 MG CHOL.

Thai shredded chicken and strawberry salad

SERVES 4 | **TIME** 1 hour

The secret ingredient in this salad is fish sauce, a salty, savory element that unites the herbs and fruit without tasting "fishy." For a shortcut, use 4 cups shredded meat from a 2½-lb. rotisserie chicken instead of poaching the chicken.

1½ lbs. boned, skinned chicken breasts
¾ cup unsweetened flaked coconut*
¾ cup lime juice
2 tbsp. sugar
1½ tbsp. Thai or Vietnamese fish sauce
2 tbsp. minced, seeded jalapeño chiles
2 tsp. canola oil
1½ cups *each* **lightly packed mint and basil leaves**
½ cup lightly packed small cilantro sprigs
1 qt. strawberries, hulled and quartered

1. Bring 4 qts. water to a boil in a 5- to 6-qt. pan. Add chicken, cover, and remove from heat. Let stand until the chicken is no longer pink in center, 20 to 30 minutes. Transfer chicken to a plate and let cool.

2. Preheat oven to 350°. Toast coconut in a pan until light golden, 4 minutes. Let cool.

3. Combine juice, sugar, fish sauce, chiles, and oil in a large bowl. Tear chicken into bite-size shreds; toss with dressing. Just before serving, gently mix in herbs and berries. Pile on plates and top with coconut.

*Find in the baking aisle or at natural-foods stores.

PER SERVING 401 CAL., 37% (150 CAL.) FROM FAT; 38 G PROTEIN; 17 G FAT (9.9 G SAT.); 28 G CARBO (7 G FIBER); 616 MG SODIUM; 94 MG CHOL.

Blueberry and prosciutto salad

SERVES 4 | **TIME** 15 minutes

Serve this summery salad from reader Marlene Kawahata, of Palo Alto, California, as a light first course or casual lunch dish.

8 slices (4 oz. total) prosciutto
¼ cup olive oil, divided
1 tbsp. Champagne vinegar
1 tbsp. honey
½ tsp. kosher salt
3 qts. (4½ oz.) lightly packed mixed baby greens
1 cup blueberries
6 oz. fresh goat cheese, divided into 4 portions

1. Lay 2 slices prosciutto on each of 4 dinner plates. In a large bowl, whisk together 3 tbsp. oil, the vinegar, honey, and salt. Add greens and blueberries and toss gently to coat. Arrange a quarter of salad mixture on each serving of prosciutto.

2. Heat remaining 1 tbsp. oil in a small nonstick frying pan over medium heat. Put cheese in pan, leaving 1 in. between portions. Cook until warm and starting to brown on the bottom, about 4 minutes. Use a wide spatula to transfer cheese to the top of each salad.

PER SERVING 412 CAL., 68% (280 CAL.) FROM FAT; 19 G PROTEIN; 31 G FAT (11 G SAT.); 20 G CARBO (4.9 G FIBER); 1,000 MG SODIUM; 34 MG CHOL.

Blueberry and prosciutto salad

Raspberry fool

Marionberry pie

SERVES 8 | **TIME** 1¾ hours, plus 3 hours to cool

Anjou Bakery, in Washington's eastern Cascades, makes this amazing pie, which has a shortbread-like crust and a filling of marionberries—a luscious strain of blackberry.

Crust

2 cups flour
¼ tsp. salt
2½ tbsp. plus 1 cup granulated sugar
14 tbsp. (1¾ sticks) cold unsalted butter, cut into 2-tbsp. chunks

Filling

¼ cup cornstarch
1¾ lbs. (6½ cups) fresh or frozen marionberries or other blackberries (for frozen, measure, thaw until somewhat softened, and use all juices)
Coarse white sparkling sugar*

1. Make crust: Combine flour, salt, and 2½ tbsp. granulated sugar in the bowl of a stand mixer. Add butter and beat with the paddle attachment on low speed, scraping bowl as needed, until pieces of dough are raisin-size. With mixer still on low speed, drizzle in 1 tbsp. ice water and beat until dough comes together, 1½ to 3 minutes. Form 1¼ cups dough into a disk and the rest into a small disk.

2. Preheat oven to 375° with a rack on lowest rung. On a lightly floured board, roll large disk of dough into a 12-in. circle. Loosen dough with a long metal spatula, gently roll around rolling pin, then unroll into a 9-in. pie pan (if dough cracks, press back together). Fold edge under, so it's flush with pan rim; then crimp. Chill 15 minutes.

3. Roll remaining dough into an 11-in. circle. With a cookie cutter, cut out enough shapes (such as squares) to cover most of pie. Set cutouts on a baking sheet and chill 15 minutes.

4. Make filling: In a large bowl, stir together cornstarch and 1 cup granulated sugar. Add berries with their juices and toss to coat. Arrange evenly in pie shell. Lightly brush pastry cutouts with water and sprinkle with coarse sugar. Arrange cutouts over filling, sugar side up.

5. Bake pie until filling bubbles and pastry is golden in center, 55 to 60 minutes (up to 1½ hours if berries were frozen). If edge starts to darken, cover with foil; if pie starts to bubble over, put a rimmed pan underneath it.

6. Let cool on a rack to room temperature, at least 3 hours.

*Find in the baking aisle.

PER SERVING 487 CAL., 37% (182 CAL.) FROM FAT; 4.7 G PROTEIN; 21 G FAT (13 G SAT.); 72 G CARBO (5.7 G FIBER); 77 MG SODIUM; 53 MG CHOL.

Raspberry fool

SERVES 8 | **TIME** 20 minutes

A fool is an Old English term for the simplest of desserts—whole or puréed fruit and sugar folded into whipped cream. Frozen berries work too: Use 12 oz. thawed berries and garnish with fresh mint leaves instead of fresh berries.

18 oz. fresh raspberries (about 4½ cups), divided
½ cup plus 2 tbsp. sugar
2 tbsp. raspberry liqueur (optional)
1 pt. heavy whipping cream

1. In a medium bowl, use a fork to mash 12 oz. of the raspberries (about 3 cups), 2 tbsp. sugar, and the liqueur, if using. Set aside.

2. In a large bowl, whip cream with remaining sugar using a mixer or whisk until firm peaks form. With a spatula, fold in raspberry-liqueur mixture. Divide fool among 8 glasses or bowls and top with remaining raspberries. Serve immediately or cover and chill for up to 2 hours.

PER ¾-CUP SERVING 297 CAL., 67% (198 CAL.) FROM FAT; 1.8 G PROTEIN; 22 G FAT (14 G SAT.); 25 G CARBO (3 G FIBER); 23 MG SODIUM; 82 MG CHOL.

Lemon berrymisu

Lemon berrymisu

SERVES 8 | **TIME** 30 minutes

Baskets of summer berries go into this speeded-up version of tiramisu. You can make a nonalcoholic variation by using lemonade concentrate in place of the limoncello (a lemon liqueur), and you can swap madeleines for the ladyfingers if you like.

1 cup whipping cream
½ cup powdered sugar
8 oz. mascarpone cheese
1 tbsp. lemon zest
1 pkg. (3 oz.) soft ladyfingers
6 tbsp. limoncello or thawed frozen lemonade concentrate
6 oz. *each* blackberries, raspberries, and blueberries

1. In a large bowl, whip cream, sugar, mascarpone, and zest with a mixer until soft peaks barely form.

2. Lay half of the ladyfingers in a 2-qt. glass serving dish or an 8-in. square pan, separating them a bit if needed for fit. Brush

ladyfingers with half of the limoncello. Dollop and spread with half of cream mixture, then sprinkle with half of mixed berries. Repeat layers.

PER SERVING 342 CAL., 61% (209 CAL.) FROM FAT; 4.5 G PROTEIN; 23 G FAT (14 G SAT.); 30 G CHOL.

Buttery raspberry lemon cake

SERVES 15 | **TIME** 1½ hours, plus 1 hour to cool

If you find black or golden raspberries at a farmers' market, you can use them in this cake as well (black ones can be slightly tarter than red or golden). Yogurt and lemon curd add a subtle tang and citrus note to the batter. To make your own yogurt, see page 278.

1 cup butter, softened
1¼ cups granulated sugar
3 large eggs
¼ tsp. salt
1 tsp. vanilla extract
¼ cup plain low-fat yogurt
½ cup low-fat milk
¼ cup lemon curd*
2½ cups flour
¼ tsp. baking soda
½ tsp. baking powder
4¾ cups raspberries (about 18 oz.)
Powdered sugar

1. Preheat oven to 325°. Butter a 9- by 13-in. baking pan. In a large bowl with a mixer on medium speed, beat butter and granulated sugar until fluffy. Beat in eggs, salt, vanilla, yogurt, milk, and lemon curd until mostly blended.

2. Add flour, baking soda, and baking powder to bowl and beat until smooth. Spread half of batter in pan and scatter half of raspberries on top. Gently spread remaining batter over berries. Scatter remaining berries on top.

3. Bake until a toothpick inserted in center comes out clean, about 1 hour; if cake begins to brown too quickly, tent with foil. Let cool about 1 hour, then dust lightly with powdered sugar.

*Find with jams at grocery stores.

PER SERVING 316 CAL., 42% (133 CAL.) FROM FAT; 4.4 G PROTEIN; 15 G FAT (8.6 G SAT.); 43 G CARBO (2.8 G FIBER); 206 MG SODIUM; 78 MG CHOL.

Buttery raspberry
lemon cake

Blackberry chocolate
chunk ice cream

Blackberry chocolate chunk ice cream

MAKES 4½ cups | **TIME** 30 minutes, plus 4 hours to freeze

You can create variations of this marbled ice cream by folding in other ingredients, such as raspberries instead of blackberries and chopped nuts or granola instead of chocolate. To make your own vanilla ice cream, see page 278.

1½ pts. blackberries (about 9 oz.)
¼ cup sugar
1½ qts. vanilla ice cream, softened
½ cup roughly chopped dark chocolate

1. Mash berries with a fork in a microwave-safe bowl. Stir in sugar. Microwave, stirring every 20 seconds, until sugar has dissolved, 1 minute. Let mixture cool completely.

2. Beat ice cream in a stand mixer with the paddle attachment just until smooth, about 30 seconds.

3. Scoop ice cream into a freezer-safe straight-sided container, alternating with blackberry mixture and chocolate.

4. Fold ice cream to form a swirl, pulling up from the sides and bottom. Press plastic wrap onto surface; cover. Freeze until firm, about 4 hours.

PER ½-CUP SERVING 268 CAL., 43% (115 CAL.) FROM FAT; 4 G PROTEIN; 13 G FAT (6 G SAT.); 35 G CARBO (2.7 G FIBER); 71 MG SODIUM; 39 MG CHOL.

Blueberry sorbet

MAKES About 5 cups | **TIME** 1 hour, plus at least 1½ hours to chill and freeze

Blueberries and lavender share the stage in this bright-tasting sorbet. Look for dried lavender in the spice aisle of well-stocked markets or at cookware stores, or omit it for a blast of pure blueberry flavor.

¾ cup sugar
¼ tsp. dried culinary lavender (optional)
¼ tsp. salt
3 pts. fresh or frozen blueberries (6 cups)
3 tbsp. lemon juice

Blueberry sorbet

1. Bring sugar, 1 cup water, and lavender, if using, to a boil in a saucepan. Add salt and simmer 2 minutes. Transfer sugar syrup to a metal bowl and let cool to room temperature. Strain and discard lavender.

2. Purée sugar syrup, blueberries, and lemon juice in a blender. Strain and discard seeds and skins. Cover and chill sorbet mixture at least 30 minutes and up to overnight.

3. Freeze in an ice cream maker according to manufacturer's instructions. Transfer to a freezer-safe dish, cover, and freeze until hard, at least 1 hour and up to overnight.

PER ½-CUP SERVING 108 CAL., 3% (2.7 CAL.) FROM FAT; 0.6 G PROTEIN; 0.3 G FAT (0 G SAT.); 28 G CARBO (2 G FIBER); 64 MG SODIUM; 0 MG CHOL.

CHOCOLATE

Life would be far less sweet without chocolate. And like wine and olive oil, it is also one of the key elements of the *Sunset* kitchen.

Let's pick up the story of the cacao bean in the West in 1849, when an Italian immigrant named Domingo Ghirardelli came to California to prospect for gold. In 1852, he opted for treasure of a different kind, opening a chocolate factory in San Francisco. Around the same time, Etienne Guittard, a Frenchman and experienced chocolate maker, was on a similar path. He came looking for gold with chocolates in his pockets to trade for mining supplies. In San Francisco in 1868, he opened Guittard Chocolate Company. Today, Guittard's headquarters remain in the Bay Area, and while Ghirardelli chocolate has not been made in San Francisco for many years, the original factory, where you can still buy its namesake chocolate, is a beacon along the waterfront.

More than a century later, a new generation of chocolate makers, including Joseph Schmidt, John Scharffenberger and Robert Steinberg of Scharffen Berger, and Michael Recchiuti, sprang up in San Francisco, and Fran Bigelow opened in Seattle. Known for high-quality confections, and in the case of Scharffen Berger, cacao they sourced themselves, these were some of the pioneers who launched the craze for artisanal chocolate that continues today.

TYPES OF CHOCOLATE

As with wine, the world of chocolate is now one of varietal distinctions, origins, unique blends, and manufacturing methods. Also like wine, the best way to judge different types is to taste them. Here is a guide to what you'll find on most grocery store shelves. Keep in mind that chocolate absorbs odors and flavors readily, so wrap it well and store in a cool, dry place.

Unsweetened This is the hardened version of pure chocolate from the "liquor," which is the cocoa butter and cocoa solids created from grinding cacao beans. Some bakers believe using unsweetened chocolate allows them to better control the flavor balance and sweetness in final dishes.

Semisweet/bittersweet Both of these are often called "dark" chocolate and contain sugar and at least 35 percent by weight of chocolate liquor. The higher the percent indicated on the label the more "bitter" or chocolaty the taste. Because of its intense flavor, dark chocolate's popularity continues to grow.

Milk Chocolate liquor (at least 10 percent by weight) is mixed with cream or any kind of milk (at least 12 percent by weight) and sugar. Milk chocolate remains a staple in the lineup of many chocolatiers.

Cocoa powder Also called unsweetened cocoa, this is essentially pure chocolate minus part of the fat and crushed to a powder. It is used in many baked goods and as the "dust" on the outside of a truffle; it's also indispensable in American-style hot chocolate. Some cocoa powder is processed with alkali to tame the natural acidity of the powder.

White Believe it or not, it's not really chocolate. White chocolate is just cocoa butter mixed with cream or any kind of milk and sugar.

CHOCOLATE

Melting chocolate

Be gentle. Fill a saucepan with 2 to 3 in. of water. Put finely chopped chocolate in a heatproof bowl that will fit over the pan (the bottom of the bowl should not touch the water) and set bowl aside. Bring water to a boil, turn off heat, then set the bowl over the pan. Use a heatproof spatula or wooden spoon to stir the chocolate frequently and encourage even melting. Once the chocolate is melted, stir well and use immediately.

Mexican chocolate pots de crème

SERVES 6 | **TIME** 45 minutes, plus about 3½ hours to cool and chill

These small, creamy desserts come from reader Meg Matta, of Incline Village, Nevada. Spiced with cinnamon and cayenne, they have a flavor reminiscent of Mexican chocolate.

1 cup heavy whipping cream
1 cup whole milk
1 tsp. espresso powder
1 tsp. cinnamon
¼ tsp. cayenne
2 tbsp. coffee liqueur, such as Kahlúa
6 oz. high-quality bittersweet chocolate, finely chopped
6 large egg yolks
2 tbsp. superfine sugar

1. Preheat oven to 300°. In a small saucepan, bring cream, milk, espresso powder, and spices to a gentle simmer over medium-low heat; cook 10 minutes. Increase heat to medium and bring mixture to a boil, then remove from heat and stir in liqueur.

2. Put chocolate in a heatproof bowl and pour hot cream mixture over it. Let stand 1 minute, then stir until smooth.

3. Whisk together egg yolks and sugar in a separate bowl. Slowly drizzle yolk mixture into chocolate mixture, whisking constantly. Pour mixture through a fine-mesh sieve into a bowl and let cool at room temperature 15 minutes.

4. Meanwhile, bring about 4 cups water to a simmer in a kettle or small pot. Arrange a dish towel in the bottom of a 9- by 13-in. baking pan. Set 6 ramekins (4-oz. capacity each) on top of towel (this helps keep them in place), then fill each ramekin with custard. Pour simmering water into pan so that it comes half-way up sides of ramekins. Set pan in oven and bake pots de crème until the edges are set but their centers are still wobbly, about 25 minutes; do not overbake. Transfer ramekins to a cooling rack and let cool at room temperature for 30 minutes, then chill in refrigerator until fully set, about 3 hours.

PER SERVING 391 CAL., 71% (279 CAL.) FROM FAT; 6.9 G PROTEIN; 31 G FAT (17 G SAT.); 25 G CARBO (0.7 G FIBER); 42 MG SODIUM; 273 MG CHOL.

Malted milk ball ice cream pie

SERVES 12 to 14 | **TIME** 1 hour, plus 5 hours to freeze

A trifecta of semisweet chocolate, cocoa powder, and chocolate wafers meets crunchy malted milk balls in this swoon-worthy dessert.

Cookie Crust (recipe follows)
3½ cups malted milk balls, divided
1¾ qts. vanilla ice cream, softened
3 tbsp. unsweetened cocoa powder
1½ cups malted milk powder*
1 cup whipping cream, divided
6 oz. semisweet chocolate, chopped

1. Make crust. Arrange 3 cups milk balls in a tight layer over crust. Stir ice cream with cocoa powder and malted milk powder until smooth. Spoon into crust, set on a plate, and freeze 5 hours.

2. Heat ½ cup cream until simmering. Put chocolate in a small metal bowl, pour in cream, and let sit until chocolate is melted, about 2 minutes. Stir until smooth. Let cool completely.

3. Smooth chocolate ganache over top of pie and freeze until set, about 15 minutes.

4. Whip remaining ½ cup cream and swirl onto pie. Chop some milk balls and drop onto pie; add a few whole balls. Remove rim and serve immediately.

*Malted milk powder is made from milk, barley malt, and wheat; don't confuse it with Ovaltine, which has other ingredients added. Find it alongside chocolate milk powder in well-stocked grocery stores.

Make ahead Through step 3 up to 4 days, frozen, double-wrapped in plastic wrap; top just before serving.

PER SERVING 742 CAL., 48% (356 CAL.) FROM FAT; 13 G PROTEIN; 39 G FAT (23 G SAT.); 91 G CARBO (3.1 G FIBER); 414 MG SODIUM; 85 MG CHOL.

COOKIE CRUST

MAKES 1 crust | **TIME** 15 minutes

Preheat oven to 325°. In a food processor, grind 7 oz. **chocolate wafers** into fine crumbs. Drizzle in 6 tbsp. **melted butter** and whirl until crumbs start to come together. (If cookies are really buttery, start with 2 tbsp. butter and add only enough extra butter to make crumbs cling together.) Press crumb mixture firmly over bottom (not sides) of a 9-in. cheesecake pan with removable sides and bake until crust is set, about 10 minutes. Let cool completely.

Ice cream pie tips

1. Let the pie soften for 5 minutes at room temperature to make slicing easier.
2. If you have trouble freeing the pie from its pan, set it over a bowl of hot water for a couple of minutes, then slide a thin knife between the pan edge and the crust. It should pop right out.

AVOCADOS

AVOCADOS

Buttery flesh with delectable flavor and essential nutrients—is there anything better than avocados? We think not, and that's why we use them in soups, sandwiches, salads, tacos, and, naturally, guacamole. Despite tasting like a total indulgence, they are really good for you—rich in vitamins, including vitamins E and K, and monounsaturated fat.

A bit about their history: Avocados are native to Central America, but have been grown in California since the late 1800s (today, about 90 percent of the U.S. domestic crop is grown from San Luis Obispo south through San Diego). In the 1920s, an amateur horticulturist by the name of Rudolph Hass planted an avocado seedling of unknown origin in his grove in Southern California. The tree bore a dark, pebbly skinned fruit with unusually rich and tasty flesh. The Hass avocado now accounts for 80 percent of avocados sold commercially worldwide and is the avocado of choice in the West.

SEASONAL AVAILABILITY Hass avocados are available year-round. The green-skinned, mild-tasting Fuerte, another popular avocado grown in California, is harvested late fall through spring.

SELECTING AND STORING To tell if an avocado is ripe and ready to eat, hold it in your hand and give it a gentle squeeze: It should give just slightly to light pressure, about the same as a cube of chilled butter would. Avoid avocados that are mushy, moldy, or shriveled at the stem end. Even with a perfectly ripe avocado, you can't tell from the outside if there will be brown spots or bruises inside, but you can always cut away any damaged flesh. To buy avocados in advance, choose firmer fruit, then store them in a paper bag at room temperature until ripened, usually two to five days. Ripe fruit can be refrigerated for up to three days.

USING It is important to remove an avocado pit safely (see "Cutting an Avocado Safely," page 47). The skin of an avocado makes a wonderful container for eating an avocado right from its jacket. When you remove the flesh, make sure you include the tastiest part of the avocado—the thin layer of dark green just under the skin. You can cook the meat of the avocado (deep-fried slices are amazing), but we think avocados are perfect used raw and utterly natural.

Guacamole on the half-shell

SERVES 2 | **TIME** About 5 minutes

Eligio Hernández, of Newman, California, often ate this make-in-your-hand guacamole for a casual lunch or snack in Mexico, where he grew up. Its simple presentation also makes it a fun first course.

1 firm-ripe avocado (½ lb.)
2 tbsp. tomato salsa or ½ to 1 tsp. hot sauce
1 lime, rinsed and cut in half
4 to 6 warm corn tortillas (6 in.) or 2 to 3 cups
    (2 to 3 oz.) tortilla chips
Salt

1. Cut avocado in half lengthwise and remove pit (see "Cutting an Avocado Safely," page 47). Set each half, cut side up, on a salad plate. Spoon 1 tbsp. salsa into each cavity. Set lime halves and tortillas alongside.

2. To eat, squeeze lime halves over avocado and sprinkle with salt to taste. With a fork or a spoon, mash the avocado slightly with salsa in the peel, then spoon mixture onto tortillas.

PER SERVING 254 CAL., 50% (126 CAL.) FROM FAT; 4.6 G PROTEIN; 14 G FAT (2.2 G SAT.); 32 G CARBO (4.3 G FIBER); 194 MG SODIUM; 0 MG CHOL.

Avocado shrimp cocktail

SERVES 4 to 6 | **TIME** About 15 minutes

This Mexican-inspired starter is both a cocktail and an appetizer in one.

1 can (11½ oz.) Bloody Mary mix
⅓ cup tequila
3 tbsp. lime juice
⅓ cup finely chopped onion, rinsed and drained
⅓ cup chopped cilantro
2 to 3 tsp. minced jalapeño chile
2 firm-ripe avocados (1 to 1¼ lbs. total)
¾ lb. (about 30) peeled cooked shrimp, rinsed
Kosher salt
Lime wedges
Tortilla chips or saltine crackers*

Avocado shrimp cocktail

1. Stir together Bloody Mary mix, tequila, juice, onion, cilantro, and 2 tsp. chile in a medium bowl.

2. Pit and peel avocados (see "Cutting an Avocado Safely," page 47); cut into ½-in. cubes. Add avocados and shrimp to cocktail mixture. Mix gently and season to taste with salt and more chile. If you like, rub rims of margarita or martini glasses with a lime wedge and immediately dip into a dish filled with ¼ in. salt.

3. Spoon cocktail mixture into bowls or glasses. Garnish with lime wedges and serve with tortilla chips.

*In Mexico, saltine crackers are often served with seafood cocktails.

PER SERVING 196 CAL., 42% (83 CAL.) FROM FAT; 13 G PROTEIN; 9.2 G FAT (1.5 G SAT.); 8.1 G CARBO (1.3 G FIBER); 367 MG SODIUM; 111 MG CHOL.

Roasted tomatillo guacamole

Roasted tomatillo guacamole

MAKES 1½ cups | **TIME** 30 minutes

Take a tip from reader Flor Moreno, of Mountain View, California, and add more intense flavor to guacamole with pan-roasted jalapeños and tomatillos. You can also cook them on the grill rather than the stove if you prefer.

1 or 2 jalapeño chiles, halved and seeded
½ medium white onion
1 garlic clove
1 tomatillo, husk removed
1 avocado, cut into chunks (see "Cutting an Avocado Safely," page 47)
At least 1 tbsp. lime juice
⅓ cup loosely packed cilantro leaves, chopped
At least ½ tsp. salt

1. In a large, unoiled frying pan over medium heat, pan-roast the chiles, onion, garlic, and tomatillo on all sides, 20 to 25 minutes total.

2. Whirl the vegetables in a blender with ¼ cup water until blended but still chunky. Add avocado and lime juice; pulse until blended. Add cilantro and salt; pulse to combine, and season to taste with salt and lime juice.

PER TBSP. 16 CAL., 75% (12 CAL.) FROM FAT; 0.2 G PROTEIN; 1.3 G FAT (0.2 G SAT.); 1.2 G CARBO (0.3 G FIBER); 50 MG SODIUM; 0 MG CHOL.

Cowboy caviar

SERVES 10 to 12 as an appetizer or 6 as a salad
TIME About 30 minutes

Cowboy "caviar" (named for the beadlike appearance of the black-eyed peas) is often served in Texas as a good-luck dish on New Year's. Reader Leslee Mendel Coy, of Lake Forest, California, puts her own spin on it and suggests scooping it up with tortilla chips for an appetizer, or adding shredded cabbage to make a coleslaw, any day of the year.

2 tbsp. red wine vinegar
1½ to 2 tsp. hot sauce
1½ tsp. salad oil
1 garlic clove, minced
⅛ tsp. pepper
1 firm-ripe avocado (about 10 oz.)
1 can (15 oz.) black-eyed peas
1 can (11 oz.) corn kernels
⅔ cup thinly sliced green onions
⅔ cup chopped cilantro
½ lb. Roma tomatoes, coarsely chopped
Salt
1 bag (6 oz.) tortilla chips or 2 cups finely shredded cabbage

1. Mix vinegar, hot sauce, oil, garlic, and pepper in a large bowl. Pit and peel avocado (see "Cutting an Avocado Safely," page 47) and cut into ½-in. cubes. Add avocado to the vinegar mixture and mix gently to coat.

2. Drain and rinse peas and corn. Add peas, corn, onions, cilantro, and tomatoes to bowl; mix gently to coat. Season to taste with salt. Serve with chips as an appetizer or add cabbage and mix to make a salad.

PER APPETIZER 159 CAL., 42% (66 CAL.) FROM FAT; 3.9 G PROTEIN; 7.3 G FAT (1.3 G SAT.); 22 G CARBO (2 G FIBER); 272 MG SODIUM; 0 MG CHOL.

Cowboy caviar

Mango avocado shrimp salad

Mango avocado shrimp salad

SERVES 6 | **TIME** About 20 minutes

Mangoes and avocados are a popular combo for salads such as this one from reader Alicia Karl, of Newport Beach, California. It's a quick, no-cook entrée made with delicate pink shrimp and a three-ingredient dressing.

3 tbsp. lime juice
2 tbsp. grapeseed or vegetable oil
1 tbsp. sugar
2 large firm-ripe mangoes (2 lbs. total)
2 medium firm-ripe avocados (1 lb. total)
⅔ cup *each* thinly sliced green onions and chopped cilantro
1 tbsp. minced hot red or green chile or ½ tsp. red chile flakes
1 lb. (70 to 110 per lb.) peeled cooked shrimp

1. In a large bowl, whisk together juice, oil, and sugar until sugar dissolves.

2. Dice mangoes (see below) and avocados (see box at right) into ¾-in. cubes; add to bowl. Add green onions, cilantro, chile, and shrimp. Mix gently. Serve or cover and chill for up to 1 hour.

PER SERVING 288 CAL., 44% (126 CAL.) FROM FAT; 18 G PROTEIN; 14 G FAT (2.1 G SAT.); 26 G CARBO (2.6 G FIBER); 180 MG SODIUM; 148 MG CHOL.

Dicing mangoes

Place the mango on a cutting board and slice through the flesh along the sides of the center pit to remove the two "cheeks" of the mango. Place each cheek on a cutting board. With a paring knife, score a checkerboard pattern in the flesh without slicing through the skin. Using a spoon, scoop out the cubed flesh.

Cutting an avocado safely

1. Cut the avocado lengthwise around the pit with a sharp knife and twist the halves apart.

2. Place half containing pit on a cutting board (do not place it in your hand). Whack a chef's knife into pit and twist it out. To get the pit off the knife, slide it against the inner rim of a sink; do not try to pull it off with your hand.

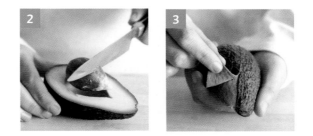

3. If you're mashing the avocado, scoop it out of its peel with a spoon. If you want perfect slices or a dice, turn over each half and score skin down center with a paring knife, then carefully pull off peel.

Black bean soup with avocado, orange, and cucumber

1. Heat oil in a large pot over medium heat. Add onion and garlic and cook until translucent, about 5 minutes. Add broth, beans, pimientos, seasonings, and hot sauce and bring to a boil. Reduce heat to low and simmer, uncovered, 10 minutes.

2. Mix avocado, lime juice, orange, and cucumber in a medium bowl. Divide soup among bowls; top with avocado mixture and a sprinkle of cheese.

PER 2-CUP SERVING 336 CAL., 45% (152 CAL.) FROM FAT; 9.7 G PROTEIN; 17 G FAT (3.4 G SAT.); 37 G CARBO (12 G FIBER); 1,350 MG SODIUM; 7.5 MG CHOL.

Avocado, red onion, and prosciutto sandwiches

SERVES 2 | **TIME** About 40 minutes

These open-faced tartines are garnished with quick-pickled onions that provide crunch and color. Thickly slice the avocado and fan out over the prosciutto for the best effect.

1 tbsp. sugar
¼ cup red wine vinegar
1 cup thinly sliced red onion
1 tbsp. mayonnaise
2 slices (4 to 4½ in. square) whole-wheat bread, toasted
4 slices (2 oz. total) prosciutto
1 firm-ripe avocado (½ lb.), thickly sliced (see "Cutting an Avocado Safely," page 47)
Salt and pepper

1. Bring 1 cup water and the sugar to a boil in a 1- to 2-qt. pan over high heat. Add vinegar and onion, and stir occasionally until boiling again. Remove from heat and let cool, about 30 minutes.

2. Meanwhile, spread mayonnaise on toast and set each slice, mayonnaise side up, on a plate. Arrange half the prosciutto, then half the avocado on each slice of toast.

3. Drain onions well and mound half on each open-face sandwich. Sprinkle with salt and pepper. Eat with a knife and fork.

Make ahead Through step 1 up to 1 day, covered and chilled.

PER SANDWICH 359 CAL., 60% (216 CAL.) FROM FAT; 14 G PROTEIN; 24 G FAT (4.1 G SAT.); 29 G CARBO (4.9 G FIBER); 729 MG SODIUM; 27 MG CHOL.

Black bean soup with avocado, orange, and cucumber

SERVES 4 | **TIME** 30 minutes

You can serve this soup chunky with a clear broth, or blend it to create a smooth purée. To make your own vegetable broth, see page 276.

2 tbsp. vegetable oil
1 cup chopped onion
2 garlic cloves, minced
3 cups vegetable broth
2 cans (15 oz. each) black beans, rinsed
2 jars (4 oz. each) pimientos, drained
1 tsp. *each* ground cumin and dried oregano
½ tsp. kosher salt
2 tsp. hot sauce, such as Tapatío
1 avocado, cubed (see "Cutting an Avocado Safely," page 47)
Juice of 1 lime
1 orange, peeled and chopped
½ English cucumber, chopped
¼ cup crumbled *cotija* cheese

Avocado, red onion, and prosciutto sandwiches

Chile and lime steak tortas

Golden State fish tacos with avocado and salted lemon salad

MAKES 12 to 14 tacos | **TIME** 1 to 1½ hours

People up and down the West Coast swear by their fish taco preparations, and we swear by this one: grilled halibut with a salty, lemony garnish spiked with chiles. To make your own yogurt, see page 278.

¼ tsp. *each* kosher salt and pepper
1½ tsp. ground coriander
Zest of 1 lemon
1½ lbs. boned, skinned halibut fillets (1 in. thick), cut into 1½-in. chunks
1 tbsp. olive oil
12 to 14 corn tortillas* (5 to 6 in.), warmed on grill
3 cups iceberg lettuce, cut into fine shreds
Avocado and Salted Lemon Salad (recipe follows)
Yogurt Sauce (recipe follows)

1. Heat grill to high (450° to 550°). Mix seasonings and zest in a small bowl. Put halibut on a rimmed baking sheet; coat with oil. Sprinkle with seasonings. Thread fish on 6 to 8 slender metal skewers. Oil cooking grate, using tongs and a wad of oiled paper towels.

2. Grill fish, covered, turning over once, until just cooked through, 3 to 4 minutes total. Fill tortillas with lettuce, fish, and salad. Serve with yogurt sauce.

*If tortillas are very thin, buy double and stack 2 per taco.

PER TACO WITH 1 TBSP. SAUCE 235 CAL., 54% (126 CAL.) FROM FAT; 9.3 G PROTEIN; 14 G FAT (2.3 G SAT.); 18 G CARBO (3.5 G FIBER); 190 MG SODIUM; 24 MG CHOL.

AVOCADO AND SALTED LEMON SALAD

Cut ½ **lemon** lengthwise, then slice crosswise paper thin, discarding seeds and ends. Cut slices in half again. In a bowl, mix lemon with ½ tsp. **kosher salt**. Let stand until wilted, 45 to 60 minutes. Rinse, drain, and return to bowl. Stir in 2 small chopped **avocados** (see page 47), 2 tbsp. diced **white onion**, 1 seeded and minced red **Fresno chile**, and 2 tsp. *each* **lemon juice** and **olive oil**.

YOGURT SAUCE

Mix 1 cup plain **whole-milk yogurt**, ½ tsp. **kosher salt**, and 2 tbsp. chopped **parsley**.

Chile and lime steak tortas

SERVES 8 | **TIME** 30 minutes, plus at least 30 minutes to marinate

Tortas are Mexican sandwiches and are often eaten as an alternative to tacos or burritos. We use flap meat, a thin steak that marinates and grills quickly, but skirt steak is a great alternative.

Juice of 1 lime
1½ tsp. ground dried ancho chiles
4 tsp. vegetable oil
½ tsp. kosher salt
1 lb. flap meat* or skirt steak, cut into 3- to 4-in.-wide strips if needed
8 small dinner rolls, split
1 cup shredded jack cheese
1 avocado, sliced thinly (see "Cutting an Avocado Safely," page 47)
2 cans (4 oz. each) sliced jalapeño chiles, drained
About ¼ cup Mexican *crema* or sour cream

1. Mix lime juice, chile powder, oil, and salt in a medium bowl. Add steak, turning to coat evenly with marinade. Chill at least 30 minutes and up to 3 hours.

2. Heat grill to high (450° to 550°). Cook steak, covered, turning over once, until grill marks appear and steak is slightly pink in the center, about 4 minutes. Transfer to a cutting board, tent with foil, and let rest 10 minutes, then slice thinly to fit in rolls.

3. Open rolls and sprinkle each one with about 2 tbsp. cheese. Grill rolls, cut sides up and covered, until crisp and cheese starts to melt, about 1 minute.

4. Fill rolls with steak, avocado, half the jalapeños, and a drizzle of *crema*. Serve with remaining jalapeños on the side.

*Find at most Latino markets.

PER SANDWICH 301 CAL., 54% (163 CAL.) FROM FAT; 18 G PROTEIN; 18 G FAT (6.5 G SAT.); 17 G CARBO (3.1 G FIBER); 481 MG SODIUM; 42 MG CHOL.

TOMATOES

TOMATOES

We all cook with tomatoes, but only recently have we really started *tasting* them. With the boom in heirloom varieties and vine-ripened options in the market, there are better-quality tomatoes and more ways than ever to use them.

Some of our favorite varieties are Early Girl, named for its early ripening; Beefsteak, a large, bright-red tomato with meaty flesh; Brandywine, a favorite for its near-purple color and sweet taste; Green Zebra, an intentionally green, citrusy tomato; Roma, the elongated classic for sauces and canning; Sun Gold, a flavorful, juicy yellow cherry tomato; and Sweet 100, the quintessential red cherry tomato with a balance of acidity and sweetness.

SEASONAL AVAILABILITY It's hard to beat a sun-warmed tomato from the garden, but since that's not an option for many of us, the next-best source is your summer farmers' market, where you'll find a large variety of locally grown and recently picked tomatoes. The good news is that grocers have caught on that customers are weary of pale, flavorless tomatoes, so vine-ripened tomatoes are available at many grocery stores too. Usually June through September is peak season, although different varieties come in at different times and some continue well into fall.

SELECTING AND STORING When choosing a tomato, look for fruit with unblemished skin. Lift it up and sniff it; even uncut, it should have a ripe aroma. The best way to tell if a tomato was ripened on the vine is to taste it, but that is not usually possible, so buying from a trusted vendor is key. Tomatoes will continue to ripen once picked. Store them out of the sun at room temperature in a single layer, stem side down, so they don't bruise. If you must refrigerate them, do so only briefly and bring them back to room temperature before cutting. Chilling for more than a few hours makes tomatoes mushy and forces aromas to become inactive, so a refrigerated tomato won't taste as good. But you can preserve your tomato season surplus in the freezer: Set ripe, unpeeled tomatoes in a single layer on a cookie sheet until frozen solid, then freeze them, double-bagged in plastic freezer bags.

USING Tomatoes are great raw in salads, salsas, and cocktails. Firm and meaty ones can be grilled, sautéed, and stewed. Early Girls make fabulous sauce (see page 65), while cherry tomatoes add bursts of sunshine to endless dishes. When thawed, frozen ripe tomatoes will have lost their firmness, but they're perfect for making fresh tomato sauce or adding to soups and stews all year long.

Caprese skillet eggs

SERVES 4 | **TIME** 25 minutes

Gardens overflow with fat tomatoes at the end of summer, bringing out the creativity in many home chefs. Reader Maryanne Welton, of Palo Alto, California, put her bounty to work in this one-pan breakfast that includes mozzarella and basil as well.

2 tbsp. olive oil
½ cup chopped onion
3 medium tomatoes, chopped
½ tsp. *each* **kosher salt and pepper**
4 large eggs
½ cup shredded fresh mozzarella cheese
¼ cup mixed chopped fresh basil, oregano, and chives
Toasted sliced *pane pugliese* **or ciabatta bread**

1. Heat oil in a medium frying pan over medium heat. Add onion and cook until translucent, about 3 minutes. Add tomatoes, salt, and pepper. Simmer, stirring occasionally, until the tomatoes have softened and released their juices, about 5 minutes.

2. Use a spoon to make 4 wells in the tomato mixture and crack an egg into each. Cover pan and cook until whites are firm and yolks are just starting to set, about 2 minutes. Sprinkle with cheese and cover again to melt cheese slightly, about 1 minute. Sprinkle with herbs and serve with toast.

PER SERVING 192 CAL., 67% (129 CAL.) FROM FAT; 10 G PROTEIN; 14 G FAT (4.3 G SAT.); 6.6 G CARBO (1.6 G FIBER); 262 MG SODIUM; 194 MG CHOL.

Garden pot pappardelle

SERVES 3 | **TIME** 45 minutes

Roma tomatoes would be a great choice for this hearty tomato sauce; their texture holds up well to roasting, which gives this dish its richness. Use your own homegrown tomatoes or ones from the farmers' market for the ultimate flavor.

1 lb. tomatoes, cut in half horizontally
3 unpeeled garlic cloves
1 jalapeño chile
8 oz. pasta, such as pappardelle
Kosher salt and pepper
¼ cup chopped fresh purple basil leaves
2 tbsp. chopped chives

Caprese skillet eggs

1. Preheat oven to 450°. Line a rimmed baking sheet with foil. Top with tomatoes, cut side up, garlic, and jalapeño. Roast until tomatoes soften and jalapeño is beginning to blacken, about 20 minutes.

2. Meanwhile, cook pasta as package directs. When roasted vegetables are cool enough to handle, finely chop jalapeño, mash and chop garlic, and chop tomatoes. Stir this mixture in a bowl and season with salt and pepper.

3. Drain pasta and toss with tomato sauce. Plate and top each portion with basil and chives.

PER SERVING 322 CAL., 10% (33 CAL.) FROM FAT; 12 G PROTEIN; 3.7 G FAT (0.9 G SAT.); 61 G CARBO (4.4 G FIBER); 24 MG SODIUM; 64 MG CHOL.

Smoky huevos rancheros with roasted tomato and three-chile salsa

Smoky huevos rancheros with roasted tomato and three-chile salsa

SERVES 4 (1 egg each) | **TIME** 25 minutes

The smokiness in this West-Mex breakfast comes from the roasted vegetables, pan-toasted chiles, and chipotle pepper in the topping. It's a deeply flavored salsa, and it would be hard to find a store-bought substitute that would taste as good. Fortunately, you can make the salsa ahead and chill it up to a week. Then the rest of the recipe comes together in a snap.

1 can (15 oz.) black beans, drained and rinsed
1 tsp. dried Mexican oregano
1 garlic clove, halved
4 corn tortillas
3/4 cup canola oil, divided
4 large eggs
Roasted Tomato and Three-Chile Salsa (recipe at right)
1 chopped tomato

1. In a small saucepan, simmer beans in 1/2 cup water with oregano and garlic about 10 minutes.

2. In a small frying pan over medium-high heat, fry tortillas in about 2/3 cup oil until crisp, 30 to 40 seconds per side; keep warm.

3. Fry eggs in remaining oil in a large nonstick frying pan over medium heat.

4. Drain beans. Set tortillas on plates and top with spoonfuls of beans, eggs, and plenty of salsa. Scatter tomato on top.

PER SERVING 618 CAL., 73% (450 CAL.) FROM FAT; 11 G PROTEIN; 51 G FAT (5 G SAT.); 29 G CARBO (5 G FIBER); 458 MG SODIUM; 212 MG CHOL.

ROASTED TOMATO AND THREE-CHILE SALSA

MAKES 2 1/2 cups | **TIME** 1 1/4 hours

2 medium firm-ripe tomatoes
1 medium onion, cut crosswise in 4 slices
5 unpeeled garlic cloves
10 dried cascabel chiles*
10 dried arbol chiles*, stems removed
2 tbsp. olive oil
1 canned chipotle chile in *adobo* sauce*
3 tbsp. lemon juice
About 1 1/2 tsp. kosher salt

1. Preheat broiler with oven rack 3 in. from heat. Line a large rimmed baking sheet with foil and put tomatoes, onion, and garlic in it. Broil the vegetables, turning as needed, until browned in spots all over, 15 to 20 minutes; transfer to a bowl as done. Let cool.

2. Meanwhile, wipe dried chiles clean with a damp cloth. Pull out and discard seeds and stems from cascabels (break chiles open a bit if needed). Turn on fan over stove. Heat olive oil in a large frying pan over medium-high heat, add cascabels and arbols, and cook, turning often with a slotted spoon, until slightly softened and darkened in spots, 1 to 2 minutes.

3. Reserve oil in pan. Transfer chiles to a small, deep bowl and pour 2 cups boiling water on top. Let stand until chiles are softened, about 20 minutes. Discard 1 cup liquid.

4. Whirl chiles and remaining liquid with chipotle in a food processor until very smooth. Cut tomatoes and onion into chunks. Peel garlic. Add vegetables to chile purée and pulse until nearly smooth.

5. Reheat oil in pan over medium-high heat. Add chile mixture and bring to a simmer, stirring. Cook, stirring, for about 3 minutes to blend flavors.

6. Pour salsa into a bowl and let cool. Stir in lemon juice and season to taste with salt.

*Find dried and canned chiles in the international foods aisle or at a Latino market.

Make ahead Up to 1 week, chilled airtight.

PER 1/4-CUP SERVING 43 CAL., 63% (27 CAL.) FROM FAT; 0.7 G PROTEIN; 3 G FAT (0.4 G SAT.); 4.3 G CARBO (1 G FIBER); 205 MG SODIUM; 0 MG CHOL.

Tomato and melon salad with scallops and pink peppercorns

1. Slice melons thinly and lay on a large shallow platter. Slice tomatoes crosswise and lay on platter with melons.

2. In a small bowl, whisk together juices, chiles, sugar, 1 tsp. salt, 3 tbsp. oil, the ginger, and ¾ tsp. peppercorns. Pour all but 2 tbsp. dressing over melons and tomatoes. Let marinate 10 minutes.

3. Meanwhile, heat a large (not nonstick) frying pan over high heat. Pat scallops dry and season with remaining salt and pink peppercorns. When pan is hot, pour in remaining 2 tbsp. olive oil. Place scallops one at a time in pan, spacing evenly, and cook until golden brown and crusty, 2 minutes. Turn scallops over and cook 1 minute.

4. Add warm scallops to platter, drizzle with the remaining dressing, and serve.

PER SERVING 265 CAL., 42% (112 CAL.) FROM FAT; 21 G PROTEIN; 13 G FAT (1.8 G SAT.); 18 G CARBO (2.1 G FIBER); 716 MG SODIUM; 37 MG CHOL.

Cherry tomato and asparagus salad

SERVES 4 to 6 | **TIME** 30 minutes

Breeze down the produce aisle to collect the ingredients for this crunchy, healthy salad created by reader Barb Mansinne, of Rohnert Park, California.

1 lb. asparagus, trimmed and halved
6 cups halved cherry, grape, and pear tomatoes in varied colors
½ cup crumbled gorgonzola cheese
1 ripe avocado, cut into cubes (see "Cutting an Avocado Safely," page 47)
1 cup sliced fresh basil leaves
¼ cup extra-virgin olive oil
2 tsp. lemon juice
2 tsp. Dijon mustard
½ tsp. *each* kosher salt and pepper

Boil asparagus in a large pot of salted water for 2 minutes; drain and rinse with cold water. Mix asparagus with remaining ingredients in a large bowl, stirring well to coat evenly with dressing.

PER SERVING 213 CAL., 72% (153 CAL.) FROM FAT; 5.9 G PROTEIN; 17 G FAT (4.1 G SAT.); 13 G CARBO (5.9 G FIBER); 347 MG SODIUM; 8.3 MG CHOL.

Tomato and melon salad with scallops and pink peppercorns

SERVES 6 | **TIME** 40 minutes

For the most visual impact, select a few different colors and sizes of tomatoes for this sophisticated salad. Serve it as a first course on special occasions.

1 lb. seedless watermelon, rind trimmed
1 lb. cantaloupe, seeded, rind trimmed
1 *each* medium yellow, red, and green vine-ripe tomatoes (about 2 lbs. total)
3 tbsp. *each* lemon and lime juice
1 or 2 serrano chiles, sliced paper-thin
1 tbsp. packed light brown sugar
2 tsp. kosher salt, divided
5 tbsp. extra-virgin olive oil, divided
2 tsp. finely shredded ginger
1½ tsp. pink peppercorns, crushed, divided
12 dry-packed sea scallops

*Cherry tomato and
asparagus salad*

Rosemary bacon,
lettuce, and
tomato salad

Rosemary bacon, lettuce, and tomato salad

SERVES 4 | **TIME** 30 minutes

Trusty head lettuce makes a welcome appearance in this riff on the classic wedge salad. Add in the elements of a BLT and who could resist? To make your own yogurt, see page 278.

8 strips applewood-smoked bacon, chopped
1 tbsp. chopped fresh rosemary
½ cup low-fat Greek yogurt
½ cup crumbled blue cheese
1 garlic clove, minced
½ tsp. kosher salt
¼ tsp. pepper
1 head iceberg lettuce (about 1¼ lbs.), cored and cut into
    16 wedges
1 avocado, chopped (see "Cutting an Avocado Safely," page 47)
1 cup (8 oz.) halved grape or cherry tomatoes

1. Cook bacon in a medium frying pan over medium heat until browned and crisp, about 10 minutes. Transfer to paper towels to drain and sprinkle with rosemary; set aside.

2. Mix yogurt, cheese, garlic, salt, pepper, and 2 tbsp. water in a medium bowl.

3. Divide lettuce wedges among 4 plates. Drizzle 3 tbsp. dressing over each portion. Top with avocado, tomatoes, and bacon.

PER SERVING 258 CAL., 64% (166 CAL.) FROM FAT; 13 G PROTEIN; 18 G FAT (6.4 G SAT.); 13 G CARBO (5.7 G FIBER); 798 MG SODIUM; 28 MG CHOL.

Heirloom tomato soup

SERVES 6 to 8 | **TIME** 30 minutes

Long summer days are great for growing deeply flavored heirloom tomatoes, which are the key to this stellar soup. Caterers Dana Ewart and Cameron Smith, who serve this at vineyard dinners in the up-and-coming Okanagan Valley wine region in Western Canada, add a touch of vinegar to balance the sweetness and acidity of the tomatoes.

Heirloom tomato soup

5 lbs. ripe heirloom tomatoes, cored and cut into ½-in. pieces
About 1 tsp. kosher salt
About ¼ cup extra-virgin olive oil
2 tbsp. unseasoned rice vinegar
10 to 12 fresh basil leaves, stacked, rolled, and thinly sliced

1. Purée tomatoes in batches in a blender, adding 1 tsp. salt, ¼ cup oil, and the vinegar to final batch.

2. Strain purée through a fine-mesh strainer into a large bowl or pitcher. Season to taste with salt if you like. Serve chilled or at room temperature, garnished with a drizzle of oil and a sprinkle of basil.

Make ahead Up to 2 days, chilled.

PER SERVING 107 CAL., 61% (65 CAL.) FROM FAT; 2.3 G PROTEIN; 7.5 G FAT (1.1 G SAT.); 10 G CARBO (3.1 G FIBER); 253 MG SODIUM; 0 MG CHOL.

Chicken puttanesca

1. Preheat oven to 450° with rack 5 in. from heat source. Heat oil in a large ovenproof frying pan over high heat.

2. Sprinkle chicken with salt and pepper. Brown chicken in hot oil on one side, about 4 minutes. Turn the chicken over and add chile flakes, garlic, tomatoes, oregano, and olives.

3. Transfer pan to oven and bake until chicken is cooked through, about 20 minutes. Lay cheese over chicken and bake just until melted and browned, 2 minutes.

PER SERVING 417 CAL., 49% (205 CAL.) FROM FAT; 40 G PROTEIN; 23 G FAT (6.6 G SAT.); 5.4 G CARBO (1.2 G FIBER); 815 MG SODIUM; 122 MG CHOL.

Open-face Caprese sandwiches

SERVES 4 | **TIME** 25 minutes

Who says they grill only beef in Texas? Reader Lisa Johnson, of Austin, came up with this ingenious way to use her barbecue: Melt mozzarella over tomatoes on grilled bread, then top with basil for a sandwich version of the famous Italian salad.

2 tbsp. olive oil, divided
1 tsp. minced garlic
8 slices (about ½ in. thick) crusty Italian bread
3 ripe medium tomatoes, sliced
1 lb. fresh mozzarella cheese, sliced thinly
16 medium fresh basil leaves
2 tbsp. balsamic vinegar
Sea salt and pepper

1. Heat grill to medium (350° to 450°). Combine 1 tbsp. oil and the garlic and brush onto 1 side of each bread slice.

2. Lay bread oiled side down on grill and cook until slightly toasted, about 2 minutes. Turn bread over, lay tomato slices on bread to fit, overlapping if needed, then lay cheese slices over tomatoes. Cover grill and cook until cheese starts to melt, about 4 minutes.

3. Transfer sandwiches to a platter. Put 2 basil leaves over each sandwich and drizzle with remaining 1 tbsp. oil and the vinegar. Sprinkle with salt and pepper.

PER SERVING 605 CAL., 55% (333 CAL.) FROM FAT; 30 G PROTEIN; 37 G FAT (19 G SAT.); 35 G CARBO (3.2 G FIBER); 820 MG SODIUM; 100 MG CHOL.

Chicken puttanesca

SERVES 4 | **TIME** 30 minutes

Reader Leigh Trivino, of Spokane, Washington, reinterpreted puttanesca by using the ingredients as a sauce for chicken instead of pasta. You can serve the dish on its own with a salad or put it over pasta or polenta. If you have large tomatoes on hand instead of cherry tomatoes, cut them into pieces so they cook quickly and release their juices into the sauce.

2 tbsp. olive oil
4 boned, skinned chicken breast halves (about 1½ lbs. total)
½ tsp. *each* **kosher salt and pepper**
¼ tsp. red chile flakes
1 tbsp. minced garlic
1 pt. cherry tomatoes, halved
1 tbsp. fresh oregano leaves
⅔ cup pitted kalamata olives
4 oz. fresh mozzarella cheese, sliced

Open-face Caprese sandwiches

Tomato, prosciutto,
and ricotta tart

Tomato, prosciutto, and ricotta tart

SERVES 8 as a first course | **TIME** 1 hour

You can make this tart with any ripe tomatoes, but a mix of big multicolor heirlooms and smaller varieties looks stunning. To create a crisp, flat surface, partially bake the puff pastry with a cooling rack on top before adding the other ingredients.

1 pkg. frozen puff pastry (1 or 2 sheets, 14 to 17 oz. total), thawed
6 oz. thinly sliced prosciutto
1⅓ cups ricotta cheese
½ tsp. *each* pepper and Meyer or regular lemon zest
½ tsp. kosher salt, divided
1¾ lbs. ripe tomatoes, larger ones sliced ¼ in. thick, tiny ones
    cut in half
4 tsp. extra-virgin olive oil
1 tbsp. chives thinly sliced on a diagonal
2 tbsp. tiny whole fresh basil or mint leaves; or use chopped leaves

1. Preheat oven to 400°. (If pastry is in 2 sheets, cut 1 sheet in thirds along fold lines. On a lightly floured board, overlap pieces slightly with second sheet—1 piece at a short side and 2 pieces end to end along a long side. Trim to fit, then press to join.) Roll pastry on floured board into a 12- by 16-in. rectangle. Lift pastry to a large baking sheet lined with parchment paper.

2. Cover pastry with another piece of parchment and a metal cooling rack turned upside down. Bake until pastry is golden all over, about 15 minutes.

3. Remove cooling rack and top sheet of parchment. Arrange prosciutto on pastry to cover. Bake until pastry is golden brown with no raw-looking spots in center, about 15 minutes; prosciutto will shrink. Gently press down any large air bubbles. Slide pastry on parchment to a rack and cool at least 10 minutes.

4. Combine ricotta, pepper, lemon zest, and ¼ tsp. salt in a bowl. Dollop small spoonfuls of ricotta evenly over pastry, leaving border clear, then smear ricotta a bit (it shouldn't cover completely).

5. Arrange tomatoes over ricotta. Sprinkle with remaining ¼ tsp. salt. Drizzle with oil and sprinkle with chives and basil. Cut into pieces.

PER SERVING 390 CAL., 58% (223 CAL.) FROM FAT; 16 G PROTEIN; 25 G FAT (8.6 G SAT.); 26 G CARBO (2.3 G FIBER); 980 MG SODIUM; 32 MG CHOL.

Pim's super-quick and fantastic tomato sauce

SERVES 2 to 4 (enough for 8 to 10 oz. pasta)
TIME 30 minutes

Pim Techamuanvivit of Northern California is a huge fan of the Early Girl tomato, especially when it's dry-farmed so that the roots have to dig deep for water. The plant drops the fruit it can't nurture and what stays on the vine becomes more concentrated. It's her top choice for this sauce, which you can use on pasta, homemade pizza, or cold from the fridge on toasted crusty bread.

About 2 lbs. Early Girl tomatoes
About ¼ cup olive oil
1 to 2 garlic cloves (optional), minced
Salt
2 tsp. balsamic or sherry vinegar (optional)
Red chile flakes (optional)
Handful of fresh basil leaves (optional)

1. Bring a large pot of water to a boil. Cut a cross on the bottom of each tomato. Remove pot from heat, plunge tomatoes into the hot water, and let sit for 1 to 2 minutes, until skins loosen at cross mark. Spoon tomatoes into a colander and rinse with cold water.

2. Skin and stem tomatoes; if really juicy, squeeze out some juice into sink. Crush pulp with your hands into a bowl, breaking it up into small chunks.

3. Pour oil into a large frying pan and heat over medium heat. Add garlic, if using, tomato pulp, and a big pinch of salt. Cook 1 to 2 minutes, until pulp breaks down and releases juices. Using a slotted spoon, put pulp back in bowl, leaving juice in pan.

4. Simmer juice until thick enough to leave a mark when you scrape bottom of pan, 2 to 3 minutes. If your tomatoes are not very tasty, add vinegar, a bit more salt, and chile flakes if you want a kick. Stir pulp and basil, if using, into sauce.

Make ahead Up to 1 week, chilled.

PER SERVING 157 CAL., 78% (122.5 CAL.) FROM FAT; 1.9 G PROTEIN; 14 G FAT (1.9 G SAT.); 8.1 G CARBO (2.5 G FIBER); 86 MG SODIUM; 0 MG CHOL.

Western bouillabaisse

SERVES 8 to 10 | **TOTAL TIME** About 5 hours

Making true bouillabaisse is a commitment, but the rewards are huge, as proven by this recipe from Northern California cookbook author Georgeanne Brennan. By using impeccably fresh, sustainable fish and shellfish from cold Pacific waters and keeping true to the authentic principles of this Provençal dish, she has created a version that belongs completely to the West. Using at least 3 kinds of shellfish gives the soup depth and character.

¼ cup extra-virgin olive oil
1 leek, white parts only, chopped and cleaned
   (see "Cleaning Leeks," page 94)
1 medium yellow onion, chopped
3 garlic cloves, chopped
Platter of Marinated Fish (recipe follows)
3 large, ripe red tomatoes, peeled and chopped,
   or 6 good-quality canned Roma tomatoes
4 cups **Fish Stock (recipe follows)**
1 cup white wine
1 bay leaf
3 sprigs thyme
¼ tsp. pepper
1 tsp. fine sea salt
½ lb. spot prawns or other West Coast shrimp,
   heads and tails intact, live if possible
3 cooked Alaskan snow crab legs, thawed if frozen and cut
   into 2-in. pieces, or ½ lb. cooked Dungeness crab,
   cracked (see pages 186 and 190)
1 lb. California mussels
1 lb. California squid (calamari), tubes and tentacles
   separated, tubes cut into ½-in. rings
Rouille and Toasts (recipe follows)

1. Heat oil in a large, wide pot over medium-high heat. Cook leek and onion until translucent, 2 minutes. Add garlic, then fennel slices from under fish on platter. Cook 2 minutes, then add tomatoes, stock, wine, bay leaf, thyme, pepper, and salt.

2. Remove fish from platter; set aside. Lift off fennel stalks and fronds and discard. Scrape marinade into broth. Bring to a boil, covered; then simmer, covered, until fennel slices are meltingly soft, 30 minutes. Meanwhile, bring 1 qt. water to a boil.

3. Bring broth to a rolling boil. Lay in the halibut and add enough boiling water to just cover fish. Cook until just opaque, 5 to 7 minutes; transfer to a platter and cover.

4. Add thinner fish fillets and spot prawns and cook just until opaque, 2 minutes; transfer to platter as done. Add crab and mussels and cook just until mussels open, 5 minutes. Transfer both to platter. Add squid and cook just until opaque, about 1 minute; transfer to platter. Bathe platter with a ladle of broth. Remove bay leaf and thyme.

5. Ladle about 1 cup broth each into big soup bowls (keep broth hot for a second serving, covered). Bring bowls, platter, rouille, and toasts to the table. Put a little of each seafood in every bowl and top with a dollop of rouille.

Make ahead Up to 5 days, fish added to remaining broth, chilled.

PER SERVING 737 CAL., 53% (391 CAL.) FROM FAT; 50 G PROTEIN; 45 G FAT (7.1 G SAT.); 34 G CARBO (3.4 G FIBER); 1,149 MG SODIUM; 296 MG CHOL.

MARINATED FISH

Use at least 4 types of fish for the best flavor and texture.

1 fennel bulb with stalks and fronds
1 lb. Pacific halibut fillets, cut into 1-in. chunks
½ lb. *each* of 4 Pacific fish fillets, such as petrale sole, Pacific cod,
   sablefish, and rockfish, in whole pieces
¼ tsp. saffron (threads or powder)
2 tbsp. pastis or Pernod
1 tsp. fennel seeds
½ tsp. fine sea salt
¼ cup extra-virgin olive oil

1. Slice fennel bulb thinly and lay on a platter along with its stalks and fronds. Lay fish on top in a single layer and sprinkle with remaining ingredients. Turn over several times to coat. Let stand at room temperature, lightly covered, 2 hours (chill if longer than 2 hours, and use within 4 hours).

2. Make fish stock, rouille, and toasts while the fish marinates.

FISH STOCK

MAKES About 9 cups

For this soup, it really is worth it to make your own fish stock.

2 tbsp. extra-virgin olive oil
1 large yellow onion, quartered
2 garlic cloves, crushed
2 medium carrots, each cut into 3 or 4 pieces
1 large leek, split lengthwise, cut into several pieces, and
    cleaned (see "Cleaning Leeks," page 94); white parts
    separated from green
2 lbs. non-oily fish heads (gills removed) and bones*
3 or 4 sprigs flat-leaf parsley
3 or 4 sprigs thyme
8 peppercorns
1½ cups dry white wine

1. Heat oil in a large pot over medium-high heat. Add onion, garlic, carrots, and leek whites and cook, stirring, until vegetables are limp, 2 to 3 minutes. Add fish heads and bones and cook, stirring, until flesh begins to turn opaque, about 3 minutes. Add leek greens, parsley, thyme, peppercorns, wine, and 6 to 8 cups water (just enough to cover). Bring to a boil, then reduce heat to low, cover, and simmer 30 minutes. Skim off any foam.

2. Strain through a fine-mesh strainer or a colander lined with cheesecloth. Set stock aside.

*Check with the fishmonger at your farmers' market or order ahead from a seafood shop.

Make ahead 1 day, covered and chilled; up to 3 months frozen.

ROUILLE AND TOASTS

Prepare while fish marinates and stock simmers.

6 dried cayenne or arbol chiles, seeded and chopped
7 garlic cloves, finely chopped
1¼ tsp. coarse sea salt
3 tbsp. dried bread crumbs
4 large egg yolks
3 to 4 tbsp. Fish Stock (recipe above)
1 to 1⅓ cups extra-virgin olive oil
1 baguette, cut into ¼-in.-thick slices

Western bouillabaisse

1. Crush chiles, garlic, and salt in a mortar to form a paste. (Alternatively, mince chiles and garlic together, sprinkle with salt, and mash with flat side of a chef's knife.) Scrape into a bowl. Stir in bread crumbs, then blend in yolks and stock.

2. Add oil drop by drop to chile mixture, beating on low speed with an electric mixer, until the mixture starts to thicken. Increase the pour of oil to a thin stream, beating constantly, until a mayonnaise-like mixture forms. Preheat oven to 225°.

3. Arrange baguette slices in a single layer on 2 baking sheets. Bake until dry but not golden, about 20 minutes, turning slices over once.

Make ahead Rouille, up to 4 days, chilled; baguette toasts, up to 3 days, stored airtight at room temperature.

Grilled halibut with
fennel, tomatoes, and
roasted garlic rouille

Grilled halibut with fennel, tomatoes, and roasted garlic rouille

SERVES 4 | **TIME** About 1¼ hours

The robust mix of halibut, tomatoes, and garlicky mayonnaise presents a fish dish that goes with both white and red wine. Try a light-bodied red, such as Sangiovese, or an aromatic Rhône-style white, such as Roussanne or Marsanne.

About 3 tbsp. olive oil
5 cups thinly sliced sweet onions (about 1½ lbs.)
3 cups thinly sliced fennel bulb (about ½ lb.; save green fronds for garnish if you like)
2 tbsp. minced garlic
½ cup dry white wine
1 tbsp. *each* orange zest and chopped fresh thyme leaves
½ tsp. saffron threads, crumbled
2 cups coarsely chopped firm-ripe tomatoes (about ¾ lb.)
Kosher salt and pepper
4 boned, skinned halibut fillets (1 in. thick, 5 to 6 oz. each), rinsed and dried
Roasted Garlic Rouille (recipe follows)

1. Heat 3 tbsp. oil in a large frying pan over medium heat. When hot, add onions, fennel, and garlic and cook, stirring occasionally, until very soft, about 15 minutes. Add wine, zest, thyme, and saffron; boil over medium-high heat, stirring often, until liquid has evaporated, about 3 minutes. Add tomatoes and salt and pepper to taste; reduce heat to low and cook, occasionally stirring gently, just until heated through, about 2 minutes.

2. Meanwhile, heat grill to medium-high (about 450°); oil grill well. Rub halibut all over with oil and sprinkle with salt and pepper. Lay halibut on cooking grate; close lid if using a gas grill. Cook, gently turning over once, just until fish is opaque but still moist in center of thickest part (cut to test), 6 to 10 minutes total.

3. Spoon vegetables onto plates and top with halibut; garnish with fennel fronds if you like. Serve rouille alongside.

PER SERVING (WITHOUT ROUILLE) 310 CAL., 38% (117 CAL.) FROM FAT; 21 G PROTEIN; 13 G FAT (1.7 G SAT.); 26 G CARBO (5.8 G FIBER); 100 MG SODIUM; 25 MG CHOL.

ROASTED GARLIC ROUILLE

MAKES 2¼ cups

1 garlic head
1 cup mayonnaise
1 cup drained jarred roasted red peppers
½ cup fresh bread crumbs
2 tbsp. lemon juice
1 tbsp. fresh thyme leaves
½ tsp. kosher salt
⅛ tsp. hot sauce
Pepper

1. Preheat oven to 375°. Cut top off garlic head to expose tops of cloves. Wrap head in foil; bake until soft when pressed, 40 to 45 minutes.

2. When cool enough to handle, squeeze cloves into a food processor. Add mayonnaise, red peppers, bread crumbs, lemon juice, thyme, salt, hot sauce, and lots of pepper. Whirl until smooth.

PER TBSP. 49 CAL., 90% (44 CAL.) FROM FAT; 0.2 G PROTEIN; 4.9 G FAT (0.7 G SAT.); 1.3 G CARBO (0.1 G FIBER); 62 MG SODIUM; 3.6 MG CHOL.

Garden Bloody Mary

SERVES 2 | **TIME** 5 minutes

Here's a great cocktail made with ingredients you can grow yourself or buy at the farmers' market.

2 ripe tomatoes, quartered
½ jalapeño chile
2 tbsp. chopped chives
6 medium fresh purple basil leaves, plus more for garnish
2 tbsp. lemon juice
½ tsp. *each* kosher salt and pepper
¼ cup vodka
Ice

Pulse tomatoes in a food processor until coarsely chopped. Add remaining ingredients except ice and whirl until smooth. Strain if you like. Pour into 2 ice-filled glasses and garnish with more basil leaves.

PER SERVING 113 CAL., 3% (3.9 CAL.) FROM FAT; 1.9 G PROTEIN; 0.4 G FAT (0.1 G SAT.); 9.2 G CARBO (2.6 G FIBER); 490 MG SODIUM; 0 MG CHOL.

OLIVE OIL

Olive oil has been produced in California since the late 1700s. In the last few decades, there has been a boom in artisanal olives grown in the state, which means that some of the best olive oil in the world is now made right here.

The first olive trees were brought to California by Spanish padres who planted them in the late 1700s at missions up and down the state. They believed the trees would thrive here because of the climate, which reminded them of the Mediterranean environment at home. It's an enduring legacy—a common variety in California today is the Mission olive, descended from those original trees.

In the 1980s, there was intense renewed interest in olive oil for its robust flavor and contribution to a healthy diet, and in response, groves were planted with many varieties, mostly imported from Italy and Spain. Today California produces 99 percent of the olive oil in the U.S., and to ensure quality, the California Olive Oil Council (COOC) was established in 1992. They train tasters to sip and sniff hundreds of local oils every year and approve the flawless ones as "Certified Extra Virgin" on the label. Any oil with the COOC seal, if properly stored, is reliably good.

HOW OLIVE OIL IS MADE

Olive oil is made by crushing the fruit of olive trees—pits and all—into a paste. Most producers use a giant tank mixer and a centrifuge to extract the oil from the paste. Extra-virgin oil is produced from the first pressing of olives; additional pressings, often with heat or chemicals, produce lesser-quality oils.

USING OLIVE OIL

Use extra-virgin olive oil for dressings, drizzling over dishes just before serving, and dipping with bread (a less expensive olive oil, not extra-virgin, is better for all-purpose cooking).

TYPES OF OLIVE OIL

The USDA has adopted these international standards for olive oil grades.

Extra-virgin The highest grade you can buy; the olives are pressed without using chemicals or adding heat, and they go through the press only once. To qualify as extra-virgin, the oil must also be free of specified taste "defects" and have less than 0.5 percent acidity.

Olio nuovo Italian for "new oil," this is an extra-virgin oil less than three months old. Intensely green, with a pungent, vibrant taste; it quickly loses its bite, so use it right away.

Virgin A lower grade than extra-virgin, lighter in flavor and higher in acidity.

Olive oil Virgin oil blended, in varying ratios, with refined oil, which comes from olives that have been pressed at least once. Heat or chemicals may be used to extract more oil from the paste. Neutral in flavor and cheap.

Light Refined oil with a small amount of virgin oil, if any; may also contain other vegetable oils. "Light" doesn't mean lower in calories, just a lighter taste.

Infused/flavored Oil in which fruit or herbs were steeped. It can also mean the olives were pressed with fruit or herbs, or that fruit or herb oils were added to the oil after pressing; both methods result in a more intense flavor than the steeping.

Finding and storing the good stuff

Taste it Try the oil before buying if you can (some stores allow sampling), not only to make sure it's fresh but also to get the style you like.

Buy fresh Choose bottles labeled with the harvest date—the oil should be consumed within 18 months.

Take care of it Heat and light break down olive oil, so find a cool, dark place to store it airtight (not next to the stove or in the refrigerator).

Braised spring vegetables

SERVES 4 | **TIME** 1 hour

Slowly cooking young vegetables with olive oil brings out their natural sweetness. If you can't find fava beans at your grocery store or farmers' market, you can omit them and double the amount of peas. Green garlic is very young, mild garlic, picked before the cloves have formed; it resembles a green onion. It's available in spring at farmers' markets, but if you can't find it, double the green onions.

2 lbs. fava beans in the pod, shelled (about 2 cups)
4 large artichokes
1 lemon
1 fennel bulb, fronds attached
5 green garlic stems
5 green onions
¼ cup olive oil
About ½ tsp. salt
1 lb. English peas in the pod, shelled (about 1 cup)
2 tbsp. extra-virgin olive oil

1. Bring a large pot of water to a boil. Add favas and cook 2 minutes. Drain and rinse with cold water. Peel beans: Pull the top off tough skin and pop bean out of skin. Set beans aside.

2. Trim artichokes (see "Trimming Artichokes," page 20), squeezing juice from lemon into the bowl of soaking water. Quarter artichokes lengthwise.

3. Trim fennel bulb of dark and medium green tops. Chop feathery fronds and reserve 2 tbsp. Discard remaining tops. Halve bulb lengthwise and cut into ¼-in.-thick wedges. Set aside.

4. Trim root ends and dry or tough dark green leaves from green garlic and green onions. Cut into 2-in. pieces (if the green garlic has a small bulb on the end, halve it lengthwise). Set aside.

5. Heat olive oil in a large pot over medium-high heat. Add fennel wedges and drained artichokes. Sprinkle with ½ tsp. salt and stir until sizzling. Add green garlic, green onions, and 1 cup water; cover, reduce heat to medium, and cook, stirring occasionally, until artichokes are tender, about 20 minutes.

6. Add peas and fava beans, cover, and cook 2 minutes. Stir in fennel fronds and remove from heat. Season to taste with salt.

7. Divide evenly among 4 shallow bowls and drizzle with extra-virgin olive oil.

PER 1-CUP SERVING 420 CAL., 47% (198 CAL.) FROM FAT; 15 G PROTEIN; 22 G FAT (3.1 G SAT.); 49 G CARBO (19 G FIBER); 515 MG SODIUM; 0 MG CHOL.

Tangerine olive oil cake

SERVES 16 | **TIME** 1¼ hours

Olive oil is traditional in Italian cakes, and a flavored oil intensifies the citrusy notes in this recipe. Try to find one where the olives and fruit were pressed together, rather than infused after pressing. Fruity white wine, such as Roussanne, adds a delicate floral note as well.

4 large eggs
2 cups sugar, divided
1½ cups Roussanne or any floral, fruity white wine,
    such as Viognier, divided
¾ cup tangerine olive oil or very fresh, fruity
    unflavored extra-virgin olive oil
1 tsp. vanilla extract
5 tsp. tangerine zest (from about 4 tangerines),
    plus 1 whole tangerine
2½ cups flour
½ tsp. salt
2¼ tsp. baking powder
Lightly sweetened softly whipped cream (optional)

1. Preheat oven to 350°. Oil and flour a 12-cup Bundt pan.

2. Beat eggs and 1½ cups sugar in a large bowl with a mixer on medium speed until thoroughly combined, about 30 seconds. Add 1 cup wine, the tangerine olive oil, vanilla, and tangerine zest. Beat on low until blended, about 30 seconds.

3. Whisk together flour, salt, and baking powder in another bowl. Add flour mixture to egg mixture and beat on low speed to incorporate. Increase speed to medium and beat 30 seconds, then scrape down side of bowl. Increase speed to medium-high; beat 30 seconds more to blend well and then pour into the prepared pan.

4. Bake cake until a wooden skewer inserted in the center comes out clean, about 30 minutes. Let cake cool on rack, 5 minutes. Carefully run a thin knife between cake and pan to loosen, then invert cake onto rack.

5. Peel whole tangerine with a vegetable peeler. Bring remaining ½ cup sugar, ½ cup wine, and the tangerine peel to a simmer in a small saucepan over medium heat; simmer until sugar has dissolved completely, about 5 minutes.

6. Poke deep holes in cake (about 50 holes spaced ½ in. apart) with a thin skewer. Remove peel from hot syrup and spoon syrup over the still-warm cake. Let cool completely and serve with whipped cream if you like.

PER SERVING 287 CAL., 37% (105 CAL.) FROM FAT; 3.7 G PROTEIN; 12 G FAT (1.9 G SAT.); 42 G CARBO (0.7 G FIBER); 161 MG SODIUM; 53 MG CHOL.

CHILES

CHILES

Necklaces of red and green peppers strung on wooden beams is an iconic Western image for good reason: Those chiles play a huge role in enlivening our salads, stews, salsas, other Mexican dishes, and Asian-inspired recipes.

Why are the chiles grown in New Mexico so good? Warm days, cool nights, and intense light create their unusually robust flavors. Picked green, chiles, such as Hatch, taste fresh and lively; if left on the plant to fully mature and turn red, they develop an earthy sweetness. Dried chiles, such as ancho, pasilla, and arbol, are complex and almost meaty, while chipotles, which are dried and smoked jalapeños, add a distinctive spiciness.

SEASONAL AVAILABILITY Fresh chiles are at their peak in late summer through early fall, although some grocery stores carry varieties such as Anaheim, jalapeño, and serrano all year long. Dried and canned chiles are available at well-stocked grocery stores and Latino markets. You can also buy ground dried chile powder (not to be confused with chili powder, which has other ingredients in it) and frozen roasted Southwest chiles online any time of year.

SELECTING AND STORING Look for firm, glossy fresh chiles with moist stems and no blemishes or gashes. Choose dried chiles that are supple and not brittle or dusty. To store fresh chiles, refrigerate them, unwashed, in a plastic bag up to five days. Store dried chiles in an airtight container at room temperature away from light, up to several months.

USING Chiles can be grilled, roasted, sautéed, or stir-fried, but they are also added raw to many recipes. The key is to manage the heat level, which comes from a compound called capsaicin that is concentrated in the ribs and seeds. The intensity of a chile is rated on a scale known as Scoville heat units and ranges from practically zero for bell peppers to 350,000 SHU for fiery habaneros. In general, smaller chiles tend to be hotter than larger ones, but the heat can vary wildly, even among chiles of the same type. The best policy is to start with fewer chiles in a dish and taste as you go; it's a lot easier to add heat than to remove it. Chiles can irritate your skin, so wear kitchen gloves or hold the pepper with a fork, don't touch your eyes, and wash your hands when you are finished handling them.

Shrimp jalapeño poppers

SERVES 8 | **TIME** 1 hour

To give these appetizers even more flair, we use Leyden, a Dutch cheese that's like gouda made with cumin seeds, a spice often used in Mexican dishes. If you can't find Leyden, use regular gouda and a few more toasted cumin seeds.

12 jalapeño chiles
¼ tsp. cumin seeds
8 oz. cream cheese, softened
8 oz. Leyden cheese, shredded
3 green onions, thinly sliced
1 cup cooked bay shrimp

1. Heat grill to medium (350° to 450°). Wearing kitchen gloves, halve chiles lengthwise. Scoop out seeds and ribs with a spoon.

2. In a small frying pan over medium heat, toast cumin seeds until fragrant, 1 minute. Transfer to a food processor, add cheeses, and whirl to blend. Put cheese mixture in a bowl and stir in onions and shrimp.

3. Spoon cheese filling into chiles. Lay a sheet of greased foil on cooking grate. Set chiles, filling side up, on greased foil. Cook, covered, until chiles are tender and cheese is melted and starting to brown, 15 minutes. Let cool slightly before serving.

PER 3-POPPER SERVING 217 CAL., 74% (161 CAL.) FROM FAT; 11 G PROTEIN; 18 G FAT (11 G SAT.); 3.7 G CARBO (0.7 G FIBER); 415 MG SODIUM; 84 MG CHOL.

Grilled corn poblano salad with chipotle vinaigrette

SERVES 6 to 8 | **TIME** 30 minutes

Not-too-fiery poblanos are especially good grilled. Chipotle, a smoked jalapeño, adds more heat. When cutting corn kernels from the cob, stand the cob in a bowl and slice down the cob's sides; the bowl corrals the flying kernels.

3 ears corn, shucked
1 poblano chile
3 tbsp. canola oil, divided
1 tbsp. lime juice
1 tsp. finely chopped canned chipotle chile

Shrimp jalapeño poppers

½ tsp. kosher salt
1 avocado, cut into chunks (see "Cutting an Avocado Safely," page 47)
¼ cup cilantro leaves
½ cup slivered sweet onion, rinsed and patted dry

1. Heat grill to high (450° to 550°). Rub corn and poblano with 1 tbsp. oil. Grill both, turning occasionally, until poblano is mostly blackened, 5 to 10 minutes, and some corn kernels have browned, 10 to 20 minutes. Let cool.

2. Cut corn kernels from cobs into a large bowl. Peel and seed poblano, cut into ½-in. pieces, and add to corn. In a small bowl, whisk remaining oil with lime juice, chipotle, and salt. Stir avocado, cilantro, and onion into corn mixture along with chipotle dressing.

PER ½-CUP SERVING 283 CAL., 35% (99 CAL.) FROM FAT; 5.7 G PROTEIN; 11 G FAT (1.2 G SAT.); 43 G CARBO (1.7 G FIBER); 171 MG SODIUM; 0 MG CHOL.

Spicy watermelon salad

Spicy watermelon salad

SERVES 8 | **TIME** 20 minutes

Icy melon really hits the spot on a hot day, but Matthew Lewis, chef-owner of the Where Ya At Matt food truck in Seattle, takes the idea a step further by adding chiles to play off the cool, sweet juice of the fruit.

¾ cup red wine vinegar
1 white onion, sliced into thin rings
2 qts. (2 lbs.) cubed watermelon
¼ cup lime juice
1 jalapeño chile, halved, seeded, and sliced
1 tbsp. _each_ chopped fresh basil and mint leaves
8 oz. feta or _cotija_ cheese, broken into chunks
½ tsp. kosher salt
1 tsp. pepper
¼ tsp. cayenne

1. Heat vinegar in a small saucepan over high heat until boiling. Add onion and cook, turning as needed, until the rings are pink and most of vinegar is absorbed, about 5 minutes. Spoon onion out of pan, let cool slightly, then roughly chop.

2. Mix remaining ingredients in a large bowl. Add onion and toss just to combine.

PER 1-CUP SERVING 134 CAL., 42% (56 CAL.) FROM FAT; 5.2 G PROTEIN; 6.3 G FAT (4.3 G SAT.); 15 G CARBO (1 G FIBER); 413 MG SODIUM; 25 MG CHOL.

Poblano and _nopales_ chimichangas

SERVES 8 | **TIME** 45 minutes

Stuffed and folded little burritos are known as chimichangas. They're traditionally deep-fried, but here we bake them instead for a flaky crust and a lot less fat.

2 tbsp. vegetable oil, divided
1 tbsp. unsalted butter, melted
1 poblano chile, halved, seeded, and sliced
½ cup sliced onion
1 cup cubed _nopales_*
½ tsp. kosher salt
1 cup shredded jack or pepper jack cheese
1 cup canned black beans, drained and rinsed
8 flour tortillas (8 in.), warmed slightly
Salsa and guacamole

1. Preheat oven to 400°. Mix 1 tbsp. oil with the butter, and brush some onto a baking sheet. Heat remaining oil in a large frying pan over medium heat. Add chile, onion, _nopales_, and salt; cook, stirring often, until vegetables soften and start to brown, about 5 minutes.

2. Put 2 tbsp. _each_ cheese and beans and about ¼ cup of the vegetable mixture onto center of a tortilla. Fold in sides and roll up like a burrito. Set chimichanga on greased baking sheet, seam side down. Fill remaining tortillas and space about 2 in. apart on pan. Brush remaining butter mixture over chimichangas.

3. Bake, turning halfway through, until browned and crisp, about 20 minutes. Cut chimichangas in half diagonally and serve with salsa and guacamole.

*_Nopales_ are cactus pads that taste a little like cooked green beans; find at Latino markets.

PER 2-PIECE SERVING 294 CAL., 39% (114 CAL.) FROM FAT; 9.7 G PROTEIN; 13 G FAT (4.9 G SAT.); 34 G CARBO (4 G FIBER); 477 MG SODIUM; 16 MG CHOL.

Poblano and nopales
chimichangas

Hanger steak sandwiches
with chile lime mayo

Hanger steak sandwiches with chile lime mayo

SERVES 4 | **TIME** 45 minutes

This recipe from reader Kris Schenck, of Meridian, Idaho, is a quick entrée for weeknight dinners.

⅓ cup *each* soy sauce and vegetable oil
4 garlic cloves, finely chopped, divided
1 tbsp. packed dark brown sugar
1 tbsp. plus 1 tsp. chili powder
2 tsp. ground cumin
1 tsp. cayenne
2 tbsp. lime juice, divided
1 lb. hanger steak
1 cup mayonnaise
1 tbsp. finely chopped cilantro
1 tsp. finely chopped green onion
1 jalapeño chile, seeded and finely chopped
1 large red bell pepper, stemmed, seeded, and quartered
12 oz. ciabatta bread (from a 1 lb. loaf), halved horizontally
1 cup lightly packed arugula
½ medium red onion, thinly sliced

1. Heat grill to medium (350° to 450°). In a baking dish, whisk together soy sauce, oil, three-quarters of garlic, the brown sugar, 1 tbsp. chili powder, the cumin, cayenne, and 1 tbsp. lime juice. Add steak and turn to coat with marinade. Set aside.

2. Combine mayonnaise, cilantro, green onion, jalapeño, and remaining chili powder, lime juice, and garlic in a bowl. Whisk to blend, then chill.

3. Oil cooking grate, using tongs and a wad of oiled paper towels. Lift steak from marinade. Grill steak and pepper with lid down, turning over as needed, until grill marks appear and steak is done the way you like, 7 to 10 minutes total for medium-rare. Transfer to a platter. Thinly slice pepper.

4. Spread insides of bread with half the mayonnaise and scatter arugula on bottom half. Thinly slice steak across the grain, then arrange over arugula, adding meat juices if you like. Top with pepper, red onion, and bread top. Cut into 4 sandwiches. Serve remaining mayonnaise on the side.

PER SANDWICH (USING HALF OF MAYO) 765 CAL., 46% (352 CAL.) FROM FAT; 42 G PROTEIN; 39 G FAT (8.3 G SAT.); 119 G CARBO (2.2 G FIBER); 1,086 MG SODIUM; 92 MG CHOL.

New Mexico green chile and Frito burgers

SERVES 4 | **TIME** 30 minutes

Chiles spice up these burgers three ways: grilled, in the pepper jack cheese, and in the chipotle mayo. If you have access to fresh Hatch chiles from New Mexico (see page 76), by all means use them, but feel free to substitute readily available Anaheims or use canned chiles.

1 lb. ground chuck
1 tsp. kosher salt
¼ tsp. pepper
2 tsp. vegetable oil, divided
2 fresh Hatch or Anaheim chiles (4 oz. total) or 1 can (7 oz.) Hatch* or regular green chiles, sliced
4 slices (4 oz. total) pepper jack cheese
4 kaiser rolls, split
2 cups Fritos
3 tbsp. mayonnaise
2 tsp. chipotle barbecue sauce

1. Heat grill to medium (350° to 450°). Mix meat, salt, and pepper in a large bowl until just combined (do not overmix). Divide into 4 portions and form into ½-in.-thick patties, making a slight depression with your thumb in the center of each to help them cook evenly. Brush with 1 tsp. oil.

2. Rub fresh chiles with remaining 1 tsp. oil. Grill over high heat, turning often, until blackened, about 4 minutes. Cover with a towel to steam, about 10 minutes. When cool, rub off skins, then stem, seed, and slice chiles into strips.

3. Grill burgers until cooked the way you like, about 7 minutes for medium. In the last few minutes, lay a cheese slice on each burger and lay split rolls on grill.

4. Arrange burgers on roll bottoms and top each with one-fourth of the chiles and Fritos. Mix mayonnaise and barbecue sauce and dollop about 2 tsp. onto each burger. Set tops of rolls in place.

*Find canned Hatch green chiles at some grocery stores and online.

PER BURGER 693 CAL., 51% (353 CAL.) FROM FAT; 34 G PROTEIN; 39 G FAT (13 G SAT.); 50 G CARBO (2.7 G FIBER); 1,263 MG SODIUM; 103 MG CHOL.

Chile cheesesteak with avocado

SERVES 4 | **TIME** About 20 minutes

We've given the Philly standard a Western makeover by substituting green chiles for sweet peppers. Use canned chiles for convenience or roast and peel Hatch or Anaheim chiles in season (see page 76).

1 lb. fat-trimmed skirt steak
1 tsp. olive oil
¼ cup tequila
1 tbsp. red wine vinegar
1 can (7 oz.) whole green chiles, drained, or 8 oz. Hatch*
    or Anaheim chiles, roasted and peeled
¼ lb. jack cheese, thinly sliced
1 firm-ripe avocado (10 to 12 oz.)
Salt and pepper

1. Rinse steak and pat dry. Cut into 4 equal pieces.

2. Heat oil in an 11- to 12-in. frying pan with ovenproof handle over high heat; tilt to coat pan bottom. Add steak and cook, turning over once, until browned on both sides but still rare in the center (cut to test), 6 to 7 minutes total. Remove from heat and add tequila and vinegar to pan. Light with a match (not under an exhaust fan or any flammable materials) and shake pan until flames subside.

3. Preheat broiler with oven rack 4 in. from heat. Lay chiles equally on steaks and top with cheese slices; broil just until cheese is melted, 1 to 2 minutes.

4. Meanwhile, pit and peel avocado (see "Cutting an Avocado Safely," page 47), then thickly slice.

5. Transfer steaks to plates. Spoon any pan juices around meat. Arrange avocado equally on portions. Season to taste with salt and pepper.

*Find canned Hatch green chiles at some grocery stores and online.

PER SERVING 425 CAL., 55% (234 CAL.) FROM FAT; 31 G PROTEIN; 26 G FAT (10 G SAT.); 7.2 G CARBO (1.6 G FIBER); 543 MG SODIUM; 87 MG CHOL.

Chicken tortilla soup

SERVES 4 | **TIME** 30 minutes

Reader Christine Datian, of Las Vegas, likes to use lots of spices in this soup recipe. Our version is medium-hot, but if you like it a little spicier, use the larger amount of serrano chile and a pinch more cayenne. To make your own chicken broth, see page 276.

1 qt. reduced-sodium chicken broth
1½ lbs. boned, skinned chicken thighs, cubed
½ white onion, chopped
1 can (14.5 oz.) diced tomatoes
½ to 1 serrano chile, halved and sliced
1 can (15 oz.) black beans, drained and rinsed
½ tsp. chili powder
½ tsp. cayenne
½ tsp. pepper
2 cups coarsely crushed corn tortilla chips, divided
½ cup crumbled *cotija* cheese
½ cup cilantro leaves
Lime wedges

1. Heat broth, covered, in a medium pot over high heat until boiling. Add chicken, onion, tomatoes, chile, beans, and spices. Reduce heat and simmer 10 minutes to blend flavors. Stir in 1 cup tortilla chips; ladle into bowls.

2. Serve soup with remaining 1 cup chips, the cheese, cilantro, and a squeeze of lime from the wedges.

PER 2-CUP SERVING 530 CAL., 30% (159 CAL.) FROM FAT; 49 G PROTEIN; 17 G FAT (4.9 G SAT.); 45 G CARBO (5.4 G FIBER); 1,459 MG SODIUM; 154 MG CHOL.

Chicken tortilla soup

Creamy pumpkin
seed and green
chile posole

Creamy pumpkin seed and green chile posole

SERVES 8 | **TIME** 2¼ hours

Posole is a celebratory soup often served in New Mexico around the holidays. Traditionally made with meat, this vegetarian version is fired up with fresh poblano and serrano chiles and toasted anchos. A puréed salsa made with roasted pumpkin seeds adds layered flavor and a chowderlike texture. To make your own vegetable broth, see page 276.

1 large yellow onion, cut into wedges
3 large poblano chiles
1 serrano chile
1½ lbs. tomatillos, husks removed, rinsed
4 unpeeled garlic cloves
2 dried ancho chiles, stemmed and seeded
About 1 cup salted, roasted pumpkin seeds (*pepitas*), divided
2 cans (29 oz. each) white hominy, rinsed and drained
5 to 6 cups vegetable broth
About 5 tsp. dried Mexican oregano, divided
1 tsp. ground cumin
1 large zucchini, cut into large dice
Accompaniments: corn tortillas, cilantro leaves, thinly sliced
    green onions, and crumbled *cotija* cheese

1. Preheat broiler with oven rack 3 in. from heat. Set yellow onion, poblanos, serrano, tomatillos, and garlic on a rimmed baking sheet. Broil, turning, until vegetables are browned to blackened all over, 15 to 30 minutes, moving them to a bowl as browned. Let cool.

2. In a large pot over medium heat, toast anchos until fragrant, pressing down with tongs and turning occasionally, about 3 minutes. Turn off heat.

3. Peel and seed poblanos and serrano. Peel garlic. Whirl serrano, garlic, onion, tomatillos and any juices, and ½ cup pumpkin seeds in a food processor until very smooth. Pour into pot with anchos. Coarsely chop poblanos and add to pot.

4. Stir in hominy, 5 cups broth, 2 tsp. oregano, and the cumin. Cover, bring to a boil over high heat, then reduce heat and simmer, stirring occasionally, until cumin flavor is mellow, about 45 minutes. Discard any large pieces of ancho.

5. Stir zucchini into posole and simmer just until tender, about 5 minutes. Add more broth if you like for a thinner soup.

6. Ladle posole into bowls and serve with remaining pumpkin seeds and oregano and other accompaniments to taste.

PER SERVING 299 CAL., 31% (93 CAL.) FROM FAT; 9.7 G PROTEIN; 10 G FAT (1.7 G SAT.); 45 G CARBO (9.7 G FIBER); 1,123 MG SODIUM; 0 MG CHOL.

Roasted chile-lime broccolini

SERVES 16 to 18 | **TIME** 40 minutes

There's no better method for cooking slender broccolini spears than roasting. With the ground chile powder used here, they turn out spectacularly toasty and robust. Created by photographer Shelly Strazis and cinematographer Gilbert Salas, of Long Beach, California, to go with Chile and Spice Grilled Turkey (see page 86) for Thanksgiving on the beach, it's a great recipe for casual dinners at home too.

4 lbs. broccolini
⅔ cup butter
½ tsp. *each* kosher salt and pepper
2 tbsp. ground dried ancho chiles
Zest of 6 Mexican limes or 2 large regular limes

1. Preheat oven to 425°. Trim leaves and sides of stalks from broccolini. Put broccolini on 2 large rimmed baking sheets (they will be very full).

2. Melt butter with salt and pepper in a small saucepan over medium heat. Stir in chile powder, remove from heat, and stir in zest. Drizzle butter over broccolini and turn until well coated.

3. Roast broccolini, switching pan positions and turning with tongs halfway through cooking, until tender-crisp, 15 to 18 minutes.

Make ahead Up to 1 day, chilled; reheat, tented with foil, in a 350° oven on 1 large rimmed baking sheet until hot, 30 minutes.

PER SERVING 89 CAL., 70% (62 CAL.) FROM FAT; 2.4 G PROTEIN; 7 G FAT (4.4 G SAT.); 5 G CARBO (1.1 G FIBER); 129 MG SODIUM; 18 MG CHOL.

Chile and spice grilled turkey with *mole* gravy

SERVES 16 to 18, with leftovers | **TIME** 3½ hours, plus overnight to brine

If you want to give your Thanksgiving menu amazing Western flavor, feature a grilled ancho–rubbed bird as the main event and Mexican *mole*–style gravy made with spices, chocolate, and more chiles. This recipe was originally created by photographer Shelly Strazis and cinematographer Gilbert Salas, of Long Beach, California, who cooked it for us on the beach as the ultimate West Coast holiday.

To make this, plan in advance. Brine the turkey one day ahead (see "Brining," opposite). The day of your feast, make the rub and let it infuse the turkey for a few hours before cooking.

Get your grill ready 4 hours before serving (to preheat and cook for 3½ hours). If you are using charcoal, have plenty of extra briquets on hand to feed it.

Start your gravy 3 hours before eating to have plenty of time to prep the ingredients and simmer the flavored broth.

To serve the bird, garnish the platter lavishly with mandarins, tangerines, or kumquats and their greens, or use unsprayed fresh bay leaves or lemon leaves.

Brine and turkey

1⅓ cups kosher salt
⅔ cup packed light brown sugar
6 large garlic cloves, crushed
4 cinnamon sticks (each 3½ in.)
6 dried ancho chiles, rinsed
1 turkey (16 to 18 lbs.)

Chile and spice rub

2 tbsp. ground dried ancho chiles
2 tbsp. dried Mexican oregano
¼ cup olive oil

1. Make brine: In a large pot, heat 1 qt. water with salt and sugar, stirring to dissolve. Remove from heat; add 5 qts. cold water, garlic, cinnamon, and chiles; and let cool to room temperature.

2. Remove leg truss from turkey; discard. Remove neck, tail, and giblets. Discard tail; save the rest, chilled, for *Mole* Gravy (recipe follows). Pull off and discard lumps of fat. Rinse bird inside and out. Pour brine over turkey (see "Brining," opposite). Chill, covered, 12 hours.

3. Prepare grill for indirect medium-low heat (about 325°). *For charcoal:* Light 40 briquets on firegrate. When coals are spotted with ash, about 20 minutes, bank evenly on opposite sides of firegrate and let burn to medium-low. Set a metal or foil drip pan (9 by 15 in. and 2½ in. deep) between coal mounds and fill with ½ in. warm water. To each mound of coals, add 5 briquets now and every 30 minutes while cooking. Oil cooking grate and set in place. *For gas:* Set a metal or foil drip pan on center burner and fill with ½ in. warm water. Turn other burners to high (leave center burner under drip pan off), close lid, and heat 10 minutes. Reduce heat for active burners to 325°. Oil cooking grate and set in place.

4. Remove turkey from brine, rinse, and pat dry. Discard brine. Tuck wing tips under turkey.

5. Make rub: Combine ground chiles and oregano. Rub turkey all over with oil, then sprinkle evenly inside and out with seasoning.

6. Set turkey, breast up, on cooking grate over drip pan. Grill, covered, until a meat thermometer inserted straight down through thickest part of breast to the bone registers 160°, 2 to 3 hours; as turkey cooks, use foil to tent any areas that start to get too dark.

7. Hold turkey with oven mitts and tip turkey so that cavity juices run into drip pan. Transfer turkey to a cutting board; save pan juices for gravy. Tent turkey with foil and let rest in a warm place 15 to 30 minutes while you make gravy.

8. Carve and serve with gravy.

PER ¼-LB. SERVING (WHITE AND DARK MEAT WITH SKIN) 253 CAL., 42% (107 CAL.) FROM FAT; 32 G PROTEIN; 12 G FAT (3.2 G SAT.); 2.5 G CARBO (0.5 G FIBER); 731 MG SODIUM; 93 MG CHOL.

MOLE GRAVY

MAKES 2 qts. | **TIME** 2½ hours

4 dried ancho chiles, stemmed, seeded, and rinsed
1 tbsp. olive oil
1 large onion, cut into thick slices
1 medium carrot, chopped
4 large garlic cloves
7 cups reduced-sodium chicken broth (to make your own broth, see page 276)
½ tsp. _each_ cinnamon and cayenne
½ cup chopped toasted almonds (see "Toasting Nuts," page 224)
¼ cup toasted sesame seeds
Neck, giblets, and pan juices from Chile and Spice Grilled Turkey (recipe opposite)
¼ cup flour
2 oz. bittersweet chocolate, chopped
1 tbsp. balsamic vinegar

1. Toast chiles in a 5- to 6-qt. pan over medium heat, pressing down with a wide spatula and turning once, until fragrant, 1 to 2 minutes. Transfer to a plate.

2. Add oil, onion, carrot, and garlic to pan; cook, stirring occasionally, until onion is golden, about 10 minutes. Add chiles, broth, cinnamon, cayenne, almonds, and sesame seeds. Enclose turkey neck and giblets (save liver for another use) in a piece of cheesecloth and tie securely with string. Add to broth. Heat mixture to boiling, then reduce heat and simmer, covered, to blend flavors, about 1 hour. Discard giblet packet.

3. Strain _mole_ broth into a heatproof bowl. Purée contents of strainer in a blender with 2 cups of the broth until very smooth. Add puréed mixture to bowl and set aside.

4. Strain turkey pan juices into a second heatproof bowl. Skim fat and pour ¼ cup of fat into a large saucepan; discard remaining fat. Measure 1 cup pan juices; save rest for another use.

5. Whisk flour into fat and cook over medium-high heat, whisking constantly, until it smells toasted, 2 minutes. Whisk in the 1 cup pan juices and about 1 cup reserved _mole_ broth. Add remaining broth and cook over medium-high heat, whisking often, until bubbling, about 12 minutes. Remove from heat and whisk in chocolate and vinegar. Pour into gravy boats.

PER ⅓ CUP 86 CAL., 66% (57 CAL.) FROM FAT; 3.1 G PROTEIN; 6.4 G FAT (1.2 G SAT.); 5 G CARBO (1.3 G FIBER); 143 MG SODIUM; 7.8 MG CHOL.

Chile and spice grilled turkey with mole _gravy_

Brining

Brining is the secret to a moist bird, so order your turkey in time to brine it the day before the feast (if you are using a frozen turkey, start thawing it in the refrigerator 4 days ahead). To brine the turkey, place the bird breast down in an oversize pot such as a boiling-water canner (make sure it fits in the fridge) and pour the brine over it. Weight the turkey down with a platter or plate and cover the pot with foil, plastic wrap, or a clean dish towel. Or use an ice chest as a makeshift cooler: Put the turkey in a turkey brining bag (available at grocery stores), place the bagged bird in the ice chest, pour brine over the turkey, and seal the bag tightly. Add ice to cover.

Braised grouper with ginger,
shiitake mushrooms, and chiles

Braised grouper with ginger, shiitake mushrooms, and chiles

SERVES 4 | **TIME** 30 minutes

Red jalapeños, which add color and subtle heat to this Asian-inspired dish, are simply green jalapeños that have been left to ripen on the plant. Any firm, white-fleshed fish other than grouper could be used. To make your own broth, see page 276.

4 grouper fillets (6 oz. each)
Salt and pepper
1 tbsp. vegetable oil
4 cups vegetable broth
2 heads baby bok choy, leaves separated
12 shiitake mushrooms, cleaned and stems removed
   (see page 204)
2 tbsp. soy sauce
2 tsp. minced ginger
2 tsp. *each* thinly sliced green onion and thinly sliced
   red jalapeño chile
2 tsp. toasted sesame oil (see "Sesame Oil 101," below)

1. Season fillets with salt and pepper. Heat a frying pan (not nonstick) over medium-high heat; add oil, then fillets. Cook until fillets start to brown on one side, about 2 minutes. Turn over fillets and reduce heat to medium. Add broth, bok choy leaves, mushrooms, soy sauce, and ginger. Cover and cook until fish is opaque in the center, about 3 minutes.

2. Divide fish, mushrooms, and bok choy among 4 deep, wide soup plates. Pour broth over fish and vegetables (you may have extra stock). Garnish with green onion and jalapeño and drizzle with sesame oil.

PER SERVING 246 CAL., 28% (68 CAL.) FROM FAT; 35 G PROTEIN; 7.6 G FAT (1.2 G SAT.); 7.2 G CARBO (1.2 G FIBER); 1,600 MG SODIUM; 63 MG CHOL.

Sesame oil 101

Look for dark amber–colored Asian sesame oil; it is extracted from toasted seeds and has a bold, nutty taste and full aroma. Don't use light-colored cold-pressed or plain sesame oil found in natural-food stores; it doesn't have the flavor power for Asian dishes.

Roasted chile cornbread

MAKES 24 pieces | **TIME** 1 hour, plus 20 minutes to cool

This rustic cornbread, pebbled with corn, green onions, and chopped green chiles, is a great accompaniment to grilled poultry. Or serve as part of a Thanksgiving dinner with Chile and Spiced Grilled Turkey (see page 86).

¾ lb. Anaheim chiles
2 cups flour
2 cups cornmeal, preferably stone-ground*
¼ cup sugar
5 tsp. baking powder
1½ tsp. salt
4 large eggs
2 cups buttermilk
½ cup butter, melted
1 cup thawed frozen petite corn
½ cup thinly sliced green onions

1. Preheat broiler with oven rack 4 in. from heat. Put chiles on a rimmed baking sheet and broil until blackened all over, turning as needed, about 15 minutes. Let chiles cool, then remove stems, seeds, and skins. Coarsely chop chiles and set aside. Preheat oven to 400°.

2. Mix flour, cornmeal, sugar, baking powder, and salt in a large bowl. In another bowl, beat together eggs, buttermilk, and butter to blend. Pour egg mixture into flour mixture. Add chiles, corn, and onions; stir just until blended. Spread in a buttered 9- by 13-in. baking dish.

3. Bake until a toothpick inserted in center comes out clean, 25 to 30 minutes. Let cool at least 20 minutes. Serve warm or cool, cut into pieces.

*Find at grocery stores or natural-food stores.

Make ahead Up to 1 day; wrap in foil and reheat in a 350° oven about 10 minutes.

PER PIECE 148 CAL., 32% (48 CAL.) FROM FAT; 4.1 G PROTEIN; 5.4 G FAT (2.9 G SAT.); 22 G CARBO (1.3 G FIBER); 312 MG SODIUM; 46 MG CHOL.

ONIONS

ONIONS

The first step in countless recipes is to sauté an onion. It's the underpinning of flavor you may not even know is there, but you'd miss if it weren't. Onions, in short, are essential to good cooking.

The onions we cook with the most are either dried (yellow, red, and white bulbs and shallots) or fresh (green onions, sweet onions, spring onions, and leeks). They are all alliums, members of the lily family, related by their pungent flavor and crisp texture, but varying from type to type. Many come from the West: Washington, Idaho, Eastern Oregon, and California are the top onion-producing areas in the country.

SEASONAL AVAILABILITY Onions are available year-round. The dried red, white, and yellow ones with papery skins store for months with subtle differences in flavor and shape due to where they are grown and when they are harvested. The fresh, sweet ones, like Maui (available in spring) and Walla Walla (available in late summer), have a shorter shelf life and usually a higher price. Spring onions really do come in spring and are young red or white onions that are pulled from the ground when the bulb is just beginning to form, as opposed to green onions, which are harvested before the bulb forms and are grown all year. Shallots, available year-round, are small, cloved onions with subtler flavor. Leeks resemble giant green onions with a mild white stem and are in season usually from late fall through spring.

SELECTING AND STORING When buying leeks and green onions, look for clean, white, and fresh bottoms and taut, crisp green tops. The same goes for spring onions, although their tops are sometimes floppy. With dried onions and shallots, choose firm, smooth skins without soft or dark spots; avoid those with green shoots. Place dry, unwrapped onions and shallots in a basket (to allow air circulation) and put in a cool, dark location for up to two months. Green onions, leeks, and spring onions should be stored, unwashed, in a plastic bag in the refrigerator for up to one week.

USING How *can't* you use an onion? Other than dessert, they are ubiquitous in recipes, adding flavor foundation here, sharp bite there, and, when slowly cooked, caramelized sweetness in between. Just a few possibilities: Use raw sweet onions in salads or as a garnish, grill spring onions and eat them whole, blend leeks into soups (to clean leeks, see page 94), and cook shallots with balsamic vinegar for unforgettable flavor.

Bacon, onion, and muenster tart

MAKES About 48 appetizers | **TIME** About 1 hour

Chef-owner Greg Higgins of Higgins Restaurant and Bar, in Portland, Oregon, was one of the first in the West to cultivate an extensive beer menu. He developed this version of the Alsatian specialty called *flammekueche*—a tart topped with onions and smoky bacon—to pair with some of the 150 or so brews on his list. Blanching the onions before baking mellows their bite and blanching the bacon removes any excess salt.

1 tsp. vegetable oil for pan
3 tbsp. cornmeal
1 lb. store-bought pizza dough
½ lb. meaty, thick-cut bacon, cut crosswise into ¼-in.-thick pieces
2 cups thinly sliced yellow onions
½ lb. Alsatian muenster, taleggio, or other washed-rind cheese, rind removed and cheese cut into ½-in. dice
½ tsp. *each* kosher salt and pepper

1. Preheat oven to 450°. Bring a medium pot of water to a boil. Pour oil into a 12- by 17-in. rimmed baking sheet and lightly oil with a paper towel. Sprinkle pan with cornmeal.

2. Stretch dough with hands or roll with a rolling pin on a lightly floured surface, shaping dough into a rectangle approximately the same size as the pan. Transfer dough to pan, stretching to fit. Fold over ½ in. of dough around edges to form a slightly raised rim for the tart. Prick dough all over with a fork.

3. Add bacon to boiling water and blanch 30 seconds. With a slotted spoon, transfer to paper towels to drain. Add onions to water and blanch 2 minutes, then drain in a colander; spread onions evenly over dough. Scatter cheese over onions, then bacon over cheese. Sprinkle with salt and pepper.

4. Bake tart until cheese is melted and beginning to brown and crust is crisp and well browned, 20 to 25 minutes. Lift out of pan with a spatula, cut into roughly 2-in. squares, and serve.

Make ahead Up to 2 days, wrapped in waxed paper at room temperature; to serve, unwrap and reheat 10 minutes at 200°.

PER APPETIZER 72 CAL., 56% (40 CAL.) FROM FAT; 2.3 G PROTEIN; 4.4 G FAT (1.9 G SAT.); 5.8 G CARBO (0.3 G FIBER); 143 MG SODIUM; 7.2 MG CHOL.

Bacon, onion, and muenster tart

VEGETARIAN VARIATION: MUSHROOM, ONION, AND MUENSTER TART

In step 1, skip boiling the water. In step 3, follow these instructions instead: Heat a large frying pan over high heat. When hot, add 2 tbsp. **olive oil** and swirl to coat. Add 1 lb. sliced **cremini mushrooms** and leaves from 7 to 8 sprigs **fresh thyme**; sprinkle with **kosher salt** and **pepper** to taste. Cook mushrooms, stirring, until they stop giving off liquid and start to brown. Add 2 cups chopped **yellow onions**, reduce heat to medium-high, and cook, stirring, until onions are softened, about 4 minutes. Scatter mushrooms and onions over tart dough, then sprinkle cheese evenly on top. Move on to step 4.

PER APPETIZER 37 CAL., 24% (9 CAL.) FROM FAT; 1 G PROTEIN; 1 G FAT (0.2 G SAT.); 6.2 G CARBO (0.4 G FIBER); 69 MG SODIUM; 0 MG CHOL.

Spinach, leek, and potato soup

SERVES 4 | **TIME** 30 minutes

You could call this lightened-up vichyssoise because it's made without the cream of the French classic and with spinach to give it extra color and nutrients. To make your own vegetable or chicken broth, see page 276.

2 tbsp. butter
2 leeks (1 lb. total), white parts only, thinly sliced and cleaned (see below)
About ½ tsp. salt
4 cups vegetable or chicken broth
1 Yukon Gold potato (12 oz.), peeled and chopped
1 lb. spinach, roots and stems discarded
Pepper
About 1 cup croutons

1. Melt butter in a large saucepan over medium-high heat. Add leeks and ½ tsp. salt and cook, stirring often, until soft, about 5 minutes. Add broth and potato. Bring to a boil, covered; reduce heat and simmer until potato is tender when pierced, 10 to 15 minutes. Add spinach and cook until wilted, about 1 minute.

2. Purée in a blender, in batches if necessary, holding lid down with a towel. Pour back into saucepan and thin with more broth if you like; reheat until hot. Season to taste with salt and pepper. Divide soup among 4 bowls and top each with about ¼ cup croutons.

PER 1½-CUP SERVING 198 CAL., 30% (60 CAL.) FROM FAT; 5.5 G PROTEIN; 6.7 G FAT (3.7 G SAT.); 30 G CARBO (3.9 G FIBER); 2,001 MG SODIUM; 16 MG CHOL.

Cleaning leeks

Because these members of the onion family are grown in sandy soil, there's often dirt between their layers that requires extra care to remove. Cut off the coarse green tops and root ends and slice leeks crosswise. Immerse in a large bowl of water and agitate to release dirt; transfer leeks to a colander using your hands, leaving dirt behind. Rinse leeks again in fresh water to be sure all dirt is removed.

Camp pizza with caramelized onions, sausage, and fontina

SERVES 4 to 6 | **TIME** 45 minutes

Just the thing you crave after a long hike, this pizza was inspired by one that Alan Rousseau, a guide with Seattle-based Mountain Madness mountaineering company, makes for his trekkers. If you are making this on the trail, bring the olive oil in its bottle, and pack the other ingredients in separate sealed containers (you'll also need a large frying pan and large cutting board). Or just fire up the grill in your backyard and have a hometown pizza cookout. Yellow or red onions work equally well.

About 3 tbsp. olive oil, divided
1 baked 10- to 11-in. pizza crust, such as Boboli
2 onions, halved lengthwise, then thinly sliced
8 oz. bulk Italian sausage
¼ tsp. *each* salt and pepper
1 tbsp. fresh thyme leaves or 2 tsp. dried
About ½ cup store-bought or homemade pizza sauce
1½ cups (6 oz.) coarsely shredded fontina cheese
2 tbsp. grated parmesan cheese
1 tbsp. fresh oregano leaves

1. Heat grill to medium (about 350°) or set up a camp stove and use medium heat. Heat a large, heavy frying pan, then oil pan bottom and sides. Toast pizza crust (cheesy side down, if there is one), pressing down on edges, until crunchy and golden on bottom, 4 to 5 minutes. Transfer to a cutting board. If using charcoal, stoke fire with 12 to 15 more briquets.

2. Add 2 tbsp. oil to pan, then add the onions, sausage, salt and pepper, and thyme. Cook, stirring often, until onions are soft and medium golden brown, 8 to 12 minutes. Remove pan from heat. Scoop onion mixture into a bowl and wipe out pan.

3. Brush pan with remaining oil. Fit pizza crust into pan with toasted side up. Spoon on pizza sauce and two-thirds of onion mixture, followed by cheeses, remaining onion mixture, and oregano. Return pan to heat. Cook, covered with lid or foil, until cheese begins to melt (check underside to be sure it doesn't burn), 3 to 5 minutes. Transfer pizza to board. Tent with foil to melt cheeses completely, then slice.

PER SERVING 482 CAL., 49% (237 CAL.) FROM FAT; 21 G PROTEIN; 26 G FAT (9.2 G SAT.); 40 G CARBO (2.7 G FIBER); 1,023 MG SODIUM; 62 MG CHOL.

Camp pizza with
caramelized
onions, sausage,
and fontina

Grilled spring onions and rib-eye

Grilled spring onions and rib-eye

SERVES 2 | **TIME** 30 minutes, plus at least 1 hour to marinate

Spring onions are young, underdeveloped onions that are harvested with their tops attached. They are sweeter and more tender than large onions and are perfect for grilling whole and serving alongside marinated steak. Find them at Latino markets, farmers' markets, and some grocery stores. Don't confuse spring onions with green onions, which are a separate variety.

2 bunches spring onions, halved lengthwise
1 rib-eye steak (about 1 lb.)
¼ cup *each* **olive oil and red wine vinegar**
1 garlic clove, minced
2 tbsp. chopped flat-leaf parsley
1 tsp. kosher salt
½ tsp. pepper

1. Lay onions and steak in a 9- by 13-in. baking dish. Mix the remaining ingredients in a small bowl and pour over onions and steak, turning ingredients to coat. Chill at least 1 hour and up to overnight.

2. Heat grill to high (450° to 550°). Grill steak, covered, turning over once and moving it from flame as needed to prevent charring, until done the way you like, about 8 minutes for medium-rare. In the last few minutes, add onions to grill, laying them perpendicular to the grate. Cook, turning as needed, until onions start to soften and grill marks appear.

PER SERVING 608 CAL., 60% (364 CAL.) FROM FAT; 51 G PROTEIN; 41 G FAT (12 G SAT.); 8.9 G CARBO (3.1 G FIBER); 601 MG SODIUM; 199 MG CHOL.

Tomato, sweet onion, and parsley salad

SERVES 8 | **TIME** 10 minutes

We learned a great trick for this salad from chef Christopher Hartfield, best known for stints at Bandoleone and Serafina in the Seattle area, who shared the recipe with us: Soak the onions in water to smooth out their rough raw flavor.

Tomato, sweet onion, and parsley salad

2 medium sweet onions, such as Walla Walla or Maui,
    cut into ¼-in.-thick wedges
2 lbs. grape or small cherry tomatoes, cut in half
1 can (14.5 oz.) hearts of palm, drained and cut into thin
    disks (optional)
¾ cup chopped flat-leaf parsley
¼ cup lime juice
½ tsp. *each* **kosher salt and pepper**

Put onions in a bowl of cold water and soak for 5 minutes; drain. Toss onions with remaining ingredients in a large bowl.

Make ahead Up to 1 day.

PER SERVING 54 CAL., 2% (0.9 CAL.) FROM FAT; 2.4 G PROTEIN; 0.1 G FAT (0 G SAT.); 12 G CARBO (2.5 G FIBER); 143 MG SODIUM; 0 MG CHOL.

Green onion mashed potatoes

Green onion mashed potatoes

SERVES 12 | **TIME** 30 minutes

Here's a duo the Irish made famous: green onions and potatoes. We've put a health-conscious twist on them with two low-calorie tricks: broth instead of whipping cream and neufchâtel cheese for creaminess with one-fourth the fat of butter.

2 lbs. russet potatoes, unpeeled and cut into chunks
½ pkg. (4 oz.) neufchâtel (light cream cheese)
⅔ cup reduced-sodium chicken broth
2 tsp. kosher salt
⅔ cup chopped green onions

1. Cover potatoes with water in a large pot and boil until tender when pierced, about 20 minutes. Drain and return to pot.

2. Mix potatoes with a hand mixer just to break up. Add cheese, broth, salt, and green onions and mix just until blended.

PER SERVING (ABOUT ½ CUP) 87 CAL., 23% (20 CAL.) FROM FAT; 2.8 G PROTEIN; 2.2 G FAT (1.2 G SAT.); 14 G CARBO (1.2 G FIBER); 379 MG SODIUM; 7 MG CHOL.

Pan-roasted fish on mushroom leek ragout

SERVES 4 | **TIME** 35 minutes

A mound of sautéed mushrooms and leeks makes a great bed for fish. To make your own chicken broth, see page 276.

2 slices (2 oz. total) bacon, chopped
1 lb. portabella mushroom caps, gills trimmed out, rinsed and sliced
2 leeks (1 lb. total), white parts only, thinly sliced and cleaned (see "Cleaning Leeks," page 94)
¼ cup *each* finely diced carrot and finely diced celery
½ cup *each* low-sodium chicken broth and dry white wine
1½ tsp. minced fresh thyme leaves or ½ tsp. dried
Salt and pepper
½ oz. dried porcini or shiitake mushrooms
4 pieces (1 in. thick; 5 oz. each) boned, skinned tender, white-fleshed fish, such as sturgeon or black cod, rinsed and dried
1½ tbsp. olive oil

1. Cook bacon in a large frying pan over medium-high heat, stirring often, until browned and crisp, 6 to 7 minutes. Add portabellas and stir often until golden brown, about 5 minutes; pour into a bowl. Add leeks, carrot, and celery to pan; reduce heat to medium and stir often until vegetables are soft, 8 to 10 minutes.

2. Return portabellas to pan and add chicken broth, wine, and thyme; simmer, stirring often, until liquid is almost evaporated, about 10 minutes. Season to taste with salt and pepper.

3. Meanwhile, preheat oven to 450°. In a spice or coffee grinder, grind dried mushrooms to a fine powder; pour into a wide, shallow bowl. Sprinkle both sides of fish with salt and pepper, then coat with the ground mushrooms.

4. Pour olive oil into another large, ovenproof frying pan over medium-high heat. Add fish and cook until browned on the bottom, 3 to 4 minutes. Turn pieces and transfer pan to oven. Bake just until fish is opaque in center of thickest part, about 8 minutes.

5. Divide ragout among four plates and top with fish.

PER SERVING 349 CAL., 49% (171 CAL.) FROM FAT; 29 G PROTEIN; 19 G FAT (5.1 G SAT.); 15 G CARBO (3.2 G FIBER); 213 MG SODIUM; 95 MG CHOL.

Pan-roasted fish on mushroom leek ragout

Red onion confit
with merlot and
balsamic vinegar

Caramelized
shallots and
walnuts

Red onion confit with merlot and balsamic vinegar

SERVES 10 to 12 (makes about 4½ cups)
TIME About 45 minutes

Sweet red torpedo or regular red onions are the basis of this lushly flavored side dish, which is almost a savory jam or warm relish. It's ideal for the holidays, especially with roast beef or prime rib for Christmas dinner. You can make it up to 3 days ahead, covered airtight and chilled until ready to use; reheat in a microwave-safe dish in the microwave for about 4 minutes, stirring halfway through.

6 tbsp. butter
3 tbsp. olive oil
3 lbs. red onions, thinly sliced
About 2 cups Merlot or other dry red wine
6 tbsp. sugar
¼ cup balsamic vinegar (see below)
Salt

1. Melt butter with olive oil in a 5- to 6-qt. pan over medium-high heat. Add onions and stir often until soft and liquid has evaporated, 8 to 10 minutes.

2. Add 2 cups wine and the sugar; stir occasionally until liquid has evaporated and onions are sweet to taste and very tender, about 30 minutes. Add balsamic vinegar and salt to taste; stir often until flavors are blended, about 5 minutes. Serve warm.

PER SERVING 155 CAL., 54% (84 CAL.) FROM FAT; 2 G PROTEIN; 9.3 G FAT (4 G SAT.); 18 G CARBO (1.8 G FIBER); 73 MG SODIUM; 16 MG CHOL.

Balsamic vinegar 101

There is a wide range of quality of balsamic vinegar, and for recipes such as the one above, you need to use thick, syrupy, true balsamic vinegar, so check the label. Authentic Italian balsamic vinegar comes from Modena and Reggio Emilia and the label will say *aceto balsamico tradizionale*; it tends to be expensive. You can find affordable variations in well-stocked grocery stores; Elsa and Fini are good brands. Avoid mass-produced balsamic vinegars that list caramel and sugar on their labels.

Caramelized shallots and walnuts

SERVES 8 | **TIME** 45 minutes

In the same vein as the Red Onion Confit (at left), this relish-like dish from chef Paul Canales, formerly of Oliveto in Oakland, California, is simultaneously sweet and savory, is served warm, and is especially good with beef. Vin santo is a late-harvest Italian wine sold at liquor stores; if you prefer, substitute madeira, marsala, port, or any other sweet wine.

¼ cup butter
2 lbs. shallots
½ tsp. salt
1 cup walnut halves
1 cup vin santo
5 thyme sprigs

1. Melt butter in a large frying pan over medium-high heat. Add shallots and sprinkle with salt. Cook, stirring occasionally, until shallots are well browned all over, about 20 minutes.

2. Add walnuts, vin santo, and thyme. Bring to a boil, then reduce heat to low, cover, and simmer until shallots are tender, about 5 minutes.

3. Uncover, turn heat to medium-high, and cook until liquid is almost completely evaporated. Serve warm.

PER SERVING 234 CAL., 58% (135 CAL.) FROM FAT; 4.8 G PROTEIN; 15 G FAT (4.4 G SAT.); 23 G CARBO (1.6 G FIBER); 220 MG SODIUM; 16 MG CHOL.

DRIED BEANS

DRIED BEANS

They look so humble, yet they have sustained native cultures in America and ancient cultures in the Mediterranean for eons. A pot of slowly cooked beans adds sustenance and rich flavor to modern meals as well, and beans are really good for you, providing lots of protein in a low-fat, nutrient-rich package.

An exciting culinary development of late has been the reemergence of almost-extinct heirloom bean varieties, where farmers in New Mexico, California, and other states are keeping these "lost" beans alive. While they can cost more per pound than supermarket white, red, and black beans, they are still a bargain ounce for ounce (dried beans swell when cooked and just a handful can stretch to feed several people). A few of the dried beans we love include cannellini, chickpeas (garbanzos), meaty black beans and kidney beans, and heirlooms such as creamy tepary, Anasazi, and Rio Zape.

SEASONAL AVAILABILITY Bean plants grow from early summer through early fall and, in season, you can buy fresh shell beans in the pod at farmers' markets. Available all year, dried beans are shell beans that are grown until their pods become brittle or shatter; they are then removed from their pods, dried, and stored. And another year-round, handy, and practical choice for your pantry is canned beans.

SELECTING AND STORING Avoid shriveled or dusty dried beans. Because older dried beans can take longer to cook and the quality can deteriorate over time, buy dried beans from a trusted brand, from a market that sells in bulk and has a lot of turnover, or from the farmer directly. When stored airtight in a cool place, dried beans can keep for up to a year. To store fresh shell beans, remove them from their pods and refrigerate in a plastic bag for up to 14 days. Canned beans are a time-saver that we turn to without worrying about a sacrifice in flavor, but check the can's use-by date.

USING Before dried beans are added to recipes, they are usually rehydrated and softened by soaking them overnight in cool water or quick-soaking them in boiling water. The length of cooking time for dried beans depends on their variety and age, so follow the recipe, but taste as you go.

Ancho-marinated steak with warm black bean salad

SERVES 6 | **TIME** About 1¼ hours, plus at least 4 hours to marinate

Super beefy skirt steak and black beans are a Western team that's hard to beat. With lots of black pepper, smoke from the grill, and roasted and dried chiles to flavor this rendition, we recommend a spicy Syrah for both the marinade and to drink.

½ cup Syrah or other dry red wine
½ cup red wine vinegar, divided
About 6 tbsp. olive oil, divided
2 tbsp. minced garlic, divided
1 tbsp. plus 1 tsp. pepper
2 tsp. kosher salt, divided
2 tsp. ground cumin, divided
2 tbsp. chopped fresh oregano leaves
1 tbsp. ground dried ancho chiles or chili powder
1 skirt steak (about 1½ lbs.)
2 fresh poblano chiles
1 large sweet onion, chopped
3 cans black beans (15 oz. each), drained and rinsed
1 large red pepper, stemmed, seeded, and cut into ½-in. chunks
1½ cups cherry tomatoes, halved
3 green onions including green tops, sliced on the diagonal, divided
¼ cup chopped cilantro
1 firm-ripe avocado, diced (see "Cutting an Avocado Safely," page 47)

1. Combine wine, ¼ cup *each* vinegar and oil, 1 tbsp. *each* garlic and pepper, 1 tsp. *each* salt and cumin, the oregano, and ground chiles in a large resealable plastic food bag. If steak is in one long piece, cut in half crosswise; rinse, add to bag, seal, and turn to coat. Chill at least 4 hours and up to 1 day.

2. Preheat broiler with oven rack 4 in. from heat. Halve, stem, and seed the poblanos. Lay skin side up on a baking sheet and broil until well charred, 6 to 7 minutes. Let stand 10 minutes, then peel and coarsely chop.

3. Heat grill to high (450° to 550°). In a large frying pan over medium-high heat, sauté onion and the remaining 1 tbsp. garlic in 2 tbsp. oil until soft, about 5 minutes. Stir in beans and the

Ancho-marinated steak with warm black bean salad

remaining ¼ cup vinegar and 1 tsp. *each* pepper, salt, and cumin; turn heat to low.

4. Oil cooking grate well. Lift steak from marinade (discard marinade) and grill, turning over once, until browned on both sides but still pink in the center (cut to test), 7 to 10 minutes total. Transfer to a board and let rest at least 5 minutes.

5. Meanwhile, add poblanos, red pepper, tomatoes, 2 green onions, and cilantro to bean mixture, and stir occasionally until warm. Stir in avocado just before serving. Slice steak on the diagonal across the grain and serve on warm bean salad. Garnish with the remaining green onions.

PER SERVING 354 CAL., 36% (127 CAL.) FROM FAT; 25 G PROTEIN; 14 G FAT (3.5 G SAT.); 28 G CARBO (7.8 G FIBER); 541 MG SODIUM; 39 MG CHOL.

Garlicky white bean dip

Garlicky white bean dip

MAKES 2¼ cups | **TIME** About 10 minutes

White beans, such as cannellini or navy, are the basis of this dip, which can be paired with other Mediterranean-style appetizers, such as olives and roasted red peppers for an easy tapas party. Serve the dip with fresh vegetables or pita bread.

1 or 2 garlic cloves
2 cans (15 oz. each) white beans, drained and rinsed
¼ cup extra-virgin olive oil
½ tsp. lemon zest
1 tbsp. lemon juice
1 tbsp. very finely chopped fresh oregano leaves
Salt and pepper

Whirl garlic in a food processor until finely chopped. Scrape down the inside of the bowl and add beans, oil, zest, and juice. Whirl until smooth and blended. Transfer dip to a small bowl. Stir in oregano, then season to taste with salt and pepper.

PER TBSP. 27 CAL., 52% (14 CAL.) FROM FAT; 0.9 G PROTEIN; 1.6 G FAT (0.2 G SAT.); 2.3 G CARBO (0.7 G FIBER); 38 MG SODIUM; 0 MG CHOL.

White bean gratin

SERVES 10 to 12 | **TIME** 4 hours

Homey as they are, dried beans can be elegantly presented, as this crusty gratin proves. To make your own chicken broth, see page 276.

3 cups dried cannellini beans
About 2 cups reduced-sodium chicken broth
1 onion, sliced into thin half-moons
2 oz. piece slab bacon or 2 oz. thick-cut regular bacon
4 garlic cloves, crushed, plus 1 tsp. finely chopped garlic
2 large sage sprigs plus 2 tsp. finely chopped fresh sage
2 bay leaves
1 tsp. pepper, divided
1 tbsp. kosher salt
6 tbsp. extra-virgin olive oil, divided
2 tsp. finely chopped fresh rosemary
1 tbsp. lemon zest
1 cup *panko* (Japanese-style bread crumbs)

1. Put beans in a large pot and cover with 1 in. cold water. Bring to a boil; turn off heat and let sit, covered, 1 hour. Drain and return to pot. Add 2 cups chicken broth, 7 cups water, the onion, bacon, crushed garlic, sage sprigs, bay leaves, and ½ tsp. pepper. Simmer, uncovered, until beans are just tender, about 1 hour.

2. Preheat oven to 375°. Add salt and cook beans until soft but not falling apart, 20 to 30 minutes. Discard bacon, sage sprigs, and bay leaves. Drain beans into a colander set over a bowl; reserve liquid. Pour beans back into pot.

3. Blend 2 cups beans, ½ cup bean liquid, and ¼ cup oil in a blender until smooth. Stir purée into beans along with chopped garlic and sage, rosemary, and remaining ½ tsp. pepper. Pour beans into a 3-qt. gratin dish and add enough bean liquid to just cover beans (if you have liquid left, save for soup; if you don't have enough, use more broth).

4. Bake until top is starting to set, 25 minutes. Mix together zest, *panko*, and remaining 2 tbsp. oil in a bowl. Sprinkle over beans and bake until bubbly and browned and liquid has thickened, 30 minutes.

PER SERVING 261 CAL., 28% (73 CAL.) FROM FAT; 13 G PROTEIN; 8.5 G FAT (1.6 G SAT.); 33 G CARBO (8.4 G FIBER); 432 MG SODIUM; 5.2 MG CHOL.

White bean gratin

Squash and chickpea fritters with winter greens and hazelnut salad

Squash and chickpea fritters with winter greens and hazelnut salad

SERVES 4 | **TIME** 30 minutes

Here's a vegetarian main dish that sums up autumn on one plate. The patties are not hard to make, and if you pair them with a salad of crispy greens, it's plenty for a main course. You can find blanched hazelnuts in the nut section of most grocery stores, or skin them yourself after toasting.

⅓ cup blanched hazelnuts
8 oz. cubed butternut squash
2 slices whole-wheat bread
1 can (about 14.5 oz.) chickpeas (garbanzos), drained
1 large egg
2 tbsp. flour
1 tsp. chopped fresh sage leaves
½ tsp. *each* kosher salt and pepper
¼ tsp. red chile flakes
6 tbsp. olive oil, divided
4 cups mixed winter greens, such as radicchio and escarole
1 tbsp. lemon juice

1. Toast hazelnuts, then skin if needed (see "Toasting Nuts," page 224).

2. Put squash in a microwave-safe container with ¼ cup water and cover with plastic wrap. Cook on high until squash is tender when pierced, about 3 minutes. Drain.

3. Pulse bread in a food processor until fine crumbs form. Add squash and chickpeas and pulse until slightly chunky. Add egg, flour, sage, salt, pepper, and chile flakes, and pulse just until blended.

4. Heat 3 tbsp. oil in a large frying pan over high heat. Drop ¼-cup portions of squash mixture into oil, making a few fritters at a time, and cook, turning over once, until golden brown, about 3 minutes on each side. Transfer to a platter.

5. Toss greens with remaining 3 tbsp. oil, the lemon juice, and hazelnuts. Serve squash fritters with salad.

PER SERVING 435 CAL., 63% (273 CAL.) FROM FAT; 11 G PROTEIN; 31 G FAT (3.8 G SAT.); 35 G CARBO (9.7 G FIBER); 454 MG SODIUM; 54 MG CHOL.

Bean and fennel ragout

SERVES 4 | **TIME** 2¼ hours, plus 4 hours to soak

The ingredients in this stew are minimal because the depth of flavor really comes from the beans. Use the heirloom varieties suggested here, other Southwestern beans, or regular pintos (find a good selection at *nativeseeds.org* or *ranchogordo.com*).

½ lb. (1¼ cups) dried tepary, Anasazi, or Rio Zape beans, cleaned of debris and rinsed
1 fennel bulb, trimmed, fronds reserved
2 tbsp. olive oil, divided
1 large carrot, diced
1 medium onion, chopped
1½ tsp. kosher salt
2½ tsp. chopped fresh thyme, divided

1. Soak beans in 1 qt. water in a medium bowl overnight or boil 2 minutes in 1 qt. water in a medium pot, then remove from heat and let stand, covered, 4 hours.

2. Halve fennel lengthwise, then thinly slice lengthwise, discarding core. In a medium saucepan, cook fennel with 1 tbsp. oil over medium heat until edges brown, 7 to 10 minutes. Pour into a bowl and chill.

3. Add remaining 1 tbsp. oil, the carrot, and onion to pan; cook until starting to brown, about 8 minutes. Add beans and their liquid, cover, and bring to a boil. Reduce heat and simmer until tender, 1½ to 1¾ hours, stirring occasionally and adding a little more water if beans start to look dry. Stir in salt, 2 tsp. thyme, and the fennel slices; return to a simmer and cook about 10 minutes more.

4. Chop enough fennel fronds to make 1 tbsp. and stir into beans with remaining ½ tsp. thyme.

PER SERVING 302 CAL., 23% (68 CAL.) FROM FAT; 14 G PROTEIN; 7.7 G FAT (1.1 G SAT.); 46 G CARBO (12 G FIBER); 785 MG SODIUM; 0 MG CHOL.

Shrimp and white bean salad with harissa dressing

Put arugula, beans, celery, parsley, and shrimp in a large bowl. Mix remaining ingredients in a small bowl and serve on the side to dress the salad.

*Find in the international foods aisle.

PER 1½-CUP SERVING 315 CAL., 37% (115 CAL.) FROM FAT; 25 G PROTEIN; 13 G FAT (2 G SAT.); 25 G CARBO (7 G FIBER); 677 MG SODIUM; 147 MG CHOL.

Quick chickpea and summer vegetable stew

SERVES 4 to 6 | **TIME** 30 minutes

Canned beans are a fast, inexpensive source of protein. Pair them with a passel of fresh summer vegetables for a nutritious one-pan meal. To make your own broth, see page 276.

2 tbsp. olive oil
1 small onion, chopped
2 small carrots, cut into coins
1 qt. reduced-sodium chicken broth
1 can (about 14.5 oz.) chickpeas (garbanzos), drained
    and rinsed
2 small zucchini, cut into coins
1 small yellow squash, cut into coins
1 cup fresh or frozen corn kernels
1 tsp. kosher salt
¼ tsp. pepper
1 cup cherry tomatoes, halved
6 oz. thin asparagus, trimmed and cut into 2-in. pieces
¼ cup thinly sliced fresh basil leaves

1. Heat oil in a medium pot over medium heat. Add onion and cook until translucent but not browned, about 7 minutes. Add carrots and cook until slightly softened, 3 to 4 minutes.

2. Stir in broth, chickpeas, squashes, corn, salt, and pepper and bring to a boil. Reduce heat and simmer 2 minutes, then stir in tomatoes and asparagus and cook until squashes are tender but not mushy, about 3 minutes more. Ladle into bowls and garnish with fresh basil.

PER SERVING 190 CAL., 28% (53 CAL.) FROM FAT; 8.4 G PROTEIN; 5.8 G FAT (0.8 G SAT.); 29 G CARBO (5.9 G FIBER); 853 MG SODIUM; 0 MG CHOL.

Shrimp and white bean salad with *harissa* dressing

SERVES 4 to 6 | **TIME** 10 minutes

Harissa is a North African paste made from hot chile peppers, spices, herbs, and oil. The heat varies by brand, so taste the dressing as you make it to adjust the quantity of *harissa* accordingly. If you like your food spicy, use it generously.

3 cups arugula
2 cans (15 oz. each) cannellini beans, rinsed and drained
1 celery stalk, sliced thinly diagonally
⅓ cup flat-leaf parsley leaves
1 lb. (26 to 30 per lb.) peeled cooked shrimp
3 to 4 tbsp. *harissa**
¼ cup lemon juice
⅓ cup extra-virgin olive oil
1 large garlic clove, minced
½ tsp. kosher salt

Quick chickpea and summer vegetable stew

*Whiskey and triple pork
black bean chili*

Whiskey and triple pork black bean chili

SERVES 4 to 6 | **TIME** 2½ hours

Why make the same old thing when you can cook up a chili rich and smoky with bacon and Spanish chorizo, mellowed by whiskey, and fired up with chipotles? To make your own broth, see page 276; to make your own crème fraîche, see page 279.

1 lb. pork shoulder (butt), cut into 1- to 1½-in. chunks
Vegetable oil (if pork is lean)
5 slices (½ lb. total) thick-cut applewood-smoked bacon, chopped
1 large onion, chopped
2 celery stalks, sliced
1½ cups dried black beans, cleaned of debris and rinsed
2 chopped canned chipotle chiles
1½ tsp. ground cumin
1 qt. reduced-sodium chicken broth
¾ cup whiskey, such as Jack Daniel's, divided
4 oz. Spanish smoked chorizo, quartered lengthwise and thinly sliced crosswise
½ cup coarsely chopped flat-leaf parsley
Crème fraîche or shredded jack cheese
Chopped chives

1. Brown pork in a large pot over medium-high heat, turning occasionally, about 10 minutes, adding a little oil if pork is very lean. Transfer pork to a plate. Add bacon to pot and cook, stirring often, until browned but still soft, about 5 minutes. Spoon out fat and return 2 tbsp. to pot. Add onion and celery and cook, stirring often, until onion is translucent, about 5 minutes.

2. Return pork to pot and add beans, chipotles, cumin, broth, and ½ cup whiskey. Cover and bring to a boil over high heat, then reduce heat and simmer until beans and pork are tender, about 1¼ hours.

3. Stir in chorizo and remaining ¼ cup whiskey. Simmer, covered, until flavors are blended, about 10 minutes more. Stir in parsley.

4. Ladle chili into bowls and top with crème fraîche and chives.

PER SERVING 579 CAL., 49% (284 CAL.) FROM FAT; 35 G PROTEIN; 32 G FAT (11 G SAT.); 32 G CARBO (11 G FIBER); 973 MG SODIUM; 105 MG CHOL.

Sausage and bean dutch-oven stew

SERVES 6 | **TIME** 1 hour

Here's a real-deal Western cookout made over an open fire in a cast-iron pot. The design of a dutch oven lets you heat it from above (by placing coals on the lid) and below (by placing the pot over coals). Because this recipe uses only the bottom-cooking method, you could also prepare it on the stovetop at home: Bring the ingredients to a boil over high heat, then reduce heat to medium, cover, and cook and stir as directed until done. Packaged, precooked sausages are usually found in the deli section. If you use uncooked sausages from the butcher, slice and fry them for a few minutes before adding the other ingredients to the pot.

2 cans (about 14.5 oz. size) *each* cannellini beans and chickpeas (garbanzos), drained and rinsed
⅓ cup olive oil
1 tbsp. chopped fresh rosemary
½ *each* red and yellow bell peppers, sliced
1 poblano chile, sliced
4 medium garlic cloves, chopped
1½ lbs. cooked Italian sausages, such as Saag's or Aidells, cut into 1-in. chunks
¼ cup fresh oregano leaves

1. Prepare fire: If you have a campfire going, move any large pieces of still-burning wood to the side and level out your hot coals to fit the size of the dutch oven. If using charcoal, burn 50 charcoal briquets till they're mostly gray, 10 to 15 minutes, and spread into an even layer the size of the dutch oven.

2. Mix ingredients except for oregano with ¾ cup water in a 4- to 6-qt. cast-iron dutch oven. Cover and set the dutch oven on top of the prepared coals.

3. Cook, stirring every 10 to 15 minutes, until peppers soften and sausages swell, 30 to 45 minutes. If the stew gets dry, add water. To decrease heat: Scrape away some fuel. To increase heat or to cook longer than 45 minutes: Every 30 minutes, add 6 to 10 briquets or more wood embers from the still-burning wood you moved to the side. Serve with oregano sprinkled on top.

PER SERVING 490 CAL., 44% (215 CAL.) FROM FAT; 32 G PROTEIN; 24 G FAT (4.5 G SAT.); 37 G CARBO (12 G FIBER); 804 MG SODIUM; 87 MG CHOL.

BREAD

Every culture has its bread. Native Americans had fry bread (still made in the Southwest), and the newcomers had sourdough. Gold Rush miners were called "sourdoughs" because they relied so heavily on this form of bread baking in the gold fields.

Sourdough is made when a portion of the dough—the "starter"—is allowed to ferment, adding its distinctive tang to the loaf. The starter is continually "fed" (with flour and liquid) and used over and over to start new batches of bread. It's a technique with a very long history, used as far back as ancient Egypt. In modern times, it's associated with the West because, as the story goes, a French immigrant named Isidore Boudin borrowed some sourdough starter from one of the miners to open his bakery in San Francisco in 1849. Boudin Bakery is still in operation, and its bakers have kept that starter alive for more than a century and a half, using some of it in every loaf they make.

LOCAL FLAVOR

As with other products that came West (chocolate, coffee, and beer), once this style of bread was established in San Francisco and also in the gold fields of Alaska, it took on local flavors—becoming, in San Francisco at least, distinctively sour. The bacterial strain that's responsible for sourdough's tangy tastiness was identified in the San Francisco Bay Area and named *Lactobacillus sanfranciscensis* in honor of San Francisco.

Scientists have since discovered that any bread made with a "sour" dough (a fermented starter, as opposed to one made with instant yeast) is full of *L. sanfranciscensis*—whether it's made in San Francisco, France, or Norway. However, there's still a local component to the bread. Over time, unique strains of *Lactobacillus* (and yeast) can emerge in a single bakery's environment and affect how the bread rises and the way it smells and tastes.

Speaking of bakers, the story of bread in the West cannot be told without mentioning Steve Sullivan, who, with his wife, Susie, established Acme Bread Company in Berkeley, California, in the 1980s. The French-style sourdough starter with wild yeast they created for their levain bread inspired an artisanal revolution that continues today, with talented bread makers, such as Chad Robertson of Tartine Bakery in San Francisco, pushing forward the story of bread in the West.

PIZZA

Sourdough is not the only bread made or consumed in the West. Inherited from the immigrants who came here, our bread-baking traditions also include flatbread, such as focaccia and tortillas; other kinds of yeast loaves; and no-yeast quick breads.

Then there's pizza. Italians settled here and brought their pizza-making skills with them. In the 1980s, chefs Alice Waters in Berkeley, Ed LaDou in San Francisco, and Wolfgang Puck in Los Angeles went native with the concept, creating what came to be known as "California-style pizza"—pies often cooked in a wood-fired oven and topped with unusual combinations such as goat cheese and duck sausage; smoked salmon, capers, and crème fraîche; or barbecued chicken. Pizza madness continues throughout the West today, from pizza trucks with portable ovens to cafes dedicated to one kind of pizza to restaurants that serve several styles. An easy and distinctively Western way with pizza is to grill it on a barbecue— a great method for achieving a crisp crust and the charred flavor of a wood-fired pizza without a special oven. See "Grilling Pizza" on page 116 to get started.

Brunch flatbread with eggs, bacon, and frisée

Grilling pizza

Use your grill to re-create the crisp char of a pizza baked in a wood-fired oven. Here's how:

1. Heat grill to medium (about 350°). For each pizza, pat out the dough on an oiled sheet of parchment paper with oiled hands.

2. Flip the dough onto the grill and peel off parchment. Cook, covered, until dough has puffed and grill marks appear underneath, about 3 minutes.

3. Transfer dough, grilled side up, to a baking sheet. Add toppings. Return pizza to grill and cook, covered, until crisp and evenly browned underneath, 4 to 6 minutes.

Brunch flatbread with eggs, bacon, and frisée

SERVES 6 to 8 | **TIME** About 1½ hours, plus about 45 minutes to rise

Flatbread are one of the easiest yeast doughs to make, but if you're pressed for time, use 1 pound of frozen bread dough. Thaw at room temperature, then divide and shape as directed in step 3. Purchased dough browns quickly, so reduce baking time by 5 minutes.

1 pkg. (2¼ tsp.) active dry yeast
About 1 tsp. salt
About ¼ cup olive oil, divided
About 3½ cups all-purpose flour
8 oz. thick-cut bacon, chopped
About ¼ cup yellow cornmeal
1⅓ cups shredded parmesan or manchego cheese
12 large eggs
Pepper
1 tbsp. red wine vinegar
3 oz. (about 2 cups) *each* baby spinach and frisée, rinsed
     and crisped

1. Sprinkle yeast over 1½ cups warm (110°) water in a large bowl. Let stand until yeast is softened, about 5 minutes. Stir in 1 tsp. salt and 1 tbsp. olive oil. Gradually stir in 3½ cups flour until a soft dough is formed. *If kneading by hand:* Scrape dough onto a lightly floured board. Knead until smooth, springy, and no longer sticky, 15 to 20 minutes; add flour as required to prevent sticking. *If using a dough hook:* Beat on high speed until dough no longer feels sticky and pulls cleanly from bowl, 5 to 7 minutes. If it is still sticky, beat in more flour, 1 tbsp. at a time. Place dough in an oiled bowl; turn over to coat top. Let rise, covered, in a warm place until double, 35 to 45 minutes.

2. Meanwhile, cook bacon in a frying pan over medium-high heat until browned and crisp, about 5 minutes. Transfer to paper towels to drain. Reserve 1 tbsp. bacon drippings to dress greens if you like.

3. Scrape dough onto a lightly floured board and press gently to expel air. Divide dough into four pieces; cover and let rest 10 minutes. Roll or gently stretch one piece at a time into a 13- by 7-in. oval about 1/16 in. thick. Place on an oiled and cornmeal-dusted 12- by 15-in. rimless baking sheet; stretch dough to reshape.

4. Preheat oven to 450°. Brush each oval with about 1/2 tbsp. olive oil; sprinkle each with about 1/3 cup cheese. Arrange a quarter of the bacon evenly over each. Bake flatbread two at a time for 10 minutes. Remove from oven and crack 3 eggs onto each oval (for firm-cooked eggs, crack eggs onto flatbread 5 minutes into baking). Sprinkle lightly with salt and pepper. Return flatbreads to oven, switching pan positions, and bake until crust is well browned, 5 to 8 minutes.

5. Meanwhile, mix 1 tbsp. olive oil or reserved bacon drippings and the vinegar in a large bowl. Add spinach and frisée and mix to coat.

6. Slide each flatbread onto a cutting board or plate. Mound greens equally on top. Cut each oval in half lengthwise, then crosswise into eight slices. Season to taste with salt and pepper.

Make ahead Dough, through step 1, up to 8 hours, punched down, covered, and chilled; remove from refrigerator at least 2 hours before serving and let stand at room temperature 45 minutes before proceeding with step 2.

PER SERVING 547 CAL., 44% (243 CAL.) FROM FAT; 25 G PROTEIN; 27 G FAT (8.5 G SAT.); 49 G CARBO (2.7 G FIBER); 849 MG SODIUM; 339 MG CHOL.

Beer rye bread

MAKES 2 loaves (12 slices per loaf) | **TIME** About 3½ hours

Adding ale to a simple yeast dough produces a mild-tasting loaf with a tender crumb. We like Abbey ale from New Belgium Brewing in Colorado.

2 tbsp. active dry yeast
1 bottle (12 oz.) Belgian-style ale or other dark, fruity ale
2 tbsp. light brown sugar
¼ cup butter, melted
1½ tbsp. caraway seeds
¼ cup molasses (not blackstrap)
1 tbsp. kosher salt, divided
2 cups *each* all-purpose, whole-wheat, and rye flour
1 large egg

Beer rye bread

1. Combine yeast with 1/2 cup warm water in a mixing bowl. Let stand 5 minutes. Stir in beer, sugar, butter, caraway seeds, molasses, 2 tsp. salt, and 1 cup of each flour. Beat well, then gradually add remaining 1 cup of each flour until dough is stiff and no longer sticky.

2. Turn dough out on a lightly floured work surface and knead until smooth and elastic. Put dough in a lightly oiled bowl, turning once to grease the top and bottom. Let rise, covered, in a warm place until double, 1 to 1½ hours.

3. Punch down dough, divide in half, and shape the halves into balls. Put balls on a large baking sheet, cover, and let rise until almost double, 45 to 60 minutes. Beat egg with 1 tbsp. water and brush on loaves; sprinkle each loaf with 1/2 tsp. salt.

4. Meanwhile, preheat oven to 375°. Bake until crusts are well browned and loaves make a hollow sound when tapped, 35 to 40 minutes. Transfer loaves to rack and let cool.

PER SLICE 144 CAL., 17% (24 CAL.) FROM FAT; 4.1 G PROTEIN; 2.7 G FAT (1.3 G SAT.); 27 G CARBO (3.2 G FIBER); 271 MG SODIUM; 14 MG CHOL.

APPLES

APPLES

Washington put apples on the map. Today the state produces half the nation's crop, so much of the thanks goes to those farmers for the crisp, robust range of apples we have to choose from every year.

Different apple varieties are suited to different uses, so know what you plan to do with an apple—eat it out of hand, put it into pie, bake it whole, or slice it into a salad—before you buy it. We like to buy organic, because studies have shown that conventionally grown apples are likely to have pesticide residue, even after you wash and peel them. Fiber-rich apples have also been shown in studies to be a healthy addition to a daily diet, so the saying "an apple a day keeps the doctor away" just might be true.

SEASONAL AVAILABILITY You can find apples in the produce section all year, but most have been in long-term cold storage or imported from the Southern Hemisphere. To truly experience an apple, enjoy it in season; few outings can match picking and eating apples right off the tree on a blustery autumn day—even the air smells like pie. Washington apples are harvested generally from August into November; Oregon has some that come in as early as July; and Gravensteins, found almost exclusively in California, have a short, early appearance from about mid-August to mid-September.

SELECTING AND STORING Choose an apple that is brightly colored for its variety, with smooth, bruise-free skin. Apples continue to ripen on the counter, so you can keep them at room temperature for a few days, but to store them for one week or longer, chill in a plastic bag in the coldest part of the refrigerator. The adage "one bad apple spoils the whole bunch" is true, so separate out any damaged apples.

USING Here are a few of the varieties we use over and over in the *Sunset* test kitchen: sweet, rich-flavored Braeburn for cakes or savory stews because it holds up well in cooking; Pink Lady for baking whole, with its strawberry and lemon notes; crisp, mild Gala in salads because when cut it doesn't turn brown as fast as other apples; tart, firm Granny Smith for pies, crisps, and even sorbet; and crunchy, juicy Fuji, a cross between two American apples that was bred in Japan, to eat out of hand.

Apple-pecan breakfast buns

SERVES 12 | **TIME** About 1 hour

Reader Betty Jean Nichols celebrates Oregon's apple season with these sticky buns filled with thin slices of fruit.

2 cups all-purpose flour
¼ cup granulated sugar
1 tbsp. baking powder
¾ tsp. salt
2 tsp. lemon zest
¼ cup butter, chilled, plus ½ cup
¾ cup milk
2 tbsp. light corn syrup
¾ cup firmly packed brown sugar
1½ tsp. cinnamon
¼ tsp. nutmeg
1 cup pecan halves
2 Granny Smith apples (about 12 oz. total)
⅓ cup raisins

1. Preheat oven to 375°. In a large bowl, whisk together flour, sugar, baking powder, salt, and zest. Cut the ¼ cup chilled butter into ¼-in. pieces. With a pastry blender or your fingers, cut or rub butter into flour mixture until it resembles coarse meal. Pour in milk all at once; stir just until combined. Cover with plastic wrap and chill until cool, 10 to 15 minutes.

2. Meanwhile, in a 1½- to 2-qt. pan over medium-low heat, melt remaining ½ cup butter. Stir in corn syrup, brown sugar, cinnamon, and nutmeg. Pour syrup mixture into the bottom of an 8- by 8-in. baking pan. Sprinkle pecans evenly over syrup. Peel and core apples and slice as thinly as possible.

3. Turn dough onto a lightly floured surface. Knead about 15 times, adding just enough flour to keep dough from sticking. With a floured rolling pin, roll dough into a 12-in. square.

4. Distribute apple slices and raisins over dough, leaving a 1-in. border along top edge. Working from the bottom, roll up dough, squeezing as you go; pinch edge to seal. Cut roll crosswise into 9 slices. Lay slices flat over syrup and pecans in pan.

Apple-pecan breakfast buns

5. Bake until rolls are golden brown, about 30 minutes. Invert a platter over pan and, holding both tightly together, invert again. Lift off pan and let rolls cool about 15 minutes. Serve warm.

PER SERVING 354 CAL., 46% (162 CAL.) FROM FAT; 3.7 G PROTEIN; 18 G FAT (8 G SAT.); 46 G CARBO (1.8 G FIBER); 402 MG SODIUM; 33 MG CHOL.

Buttermilk pumpkin waffles with apples and apple cider syrup

MAKES 16 waffles | **TIME** 1½ hours

When apples are in season, nothing beats the waffles they make at Garland's Oak Creek Lodge in Sedona, Arizona. The waffles' spices will remind you of a cross between pumpkin and apple pies. To keep waffles warm and crisp as you make them, put directly on a rack in a 200° oven for up to 40 minutes.

Apple topping and syrup
9 tbsp. butter, divided
2 tbsp. honey
7 tsp. lemon juice, divided
1 tsp. cinnamon, divided
6 tart cooking apples, such as Pippin or Granny Smith, peeled, cored, and sliced ¼ in. thick
¾ cup sugar
1½ tbsp. cornstarch
1½ cups unfiltered apple cider or juice

Waffles
2 cups flour
1 tbsp. baking powder
½ tsp. *each* baking soda and salt
5 tbsp. sugar
1 tsp. *each* ground ginger, nutmeg, and cinnamon
2 large eggs, separated
¼ cup vegetable oil
2 cups buttermilk
¾ cup canned pumpkin
Cooking-oil spray

1. Make apple topping and syrup: Melt 6 tbsp. butter in a 12-in. nonstick frying pan over medium heat. Add honey, 2 tsp. lemon juice, ¼ tsp. cinnamon, and apples. Cook, stirring occasionally, until apples are lightly glazed and have softened slightly, about 10 minutes.

2. Meanwhile, whisk together ¾ tsp. cinnamon, the sugar, and cornstarch in a medium saucepan. Add apple cider and 5 tsp. lemon juice and whisk to combine. Bring to a boil over medium heat and cook, stirring often, 2 minutes. Remove from heat and whisk in 3 tbsp. butter.

3. Make waffles: In a medium bowl, whisk together flour, baking powder, baking soda, salt, sugar, ginger, nutmeg, and cinnamon. In another medium bowl, whisk egg yolks until pale yellow; whisk in oil, buttermilk, and pumpkin.

4. In the bowl of a stand mixer fitted with the balloon whisk, beat egg whites until soft peaks form. Add egg yolk mixture to flour mixture, stirring to combine. Gently fold in egg whites just until blended.

5. Preheat oven to 200°. Preheat a waffle iron and coat it with cooking-oil spray. Pour 1 cup batter (or amount directed by waffle-iron maker) onto hot iron, spreading with a spatula, and cook until nicely browned, about 5 minutes. Transfer waffle directly to oven rack. Repeat with remaining batter. Meanwhile, reheat apples and syrup.

6. Break waffles into sections, divide among 8 plates, and top with apples and syrup. Serve remaining syrup on the side.

PER 2 WAFFLES WITH ¼ CUP SYRUP 552 CAL., 38% (207 CAL.) FROM FAT; 7.4 G PROTEIN; 23 G FAT (9.8 G SAT.); 82 G CARBO (3.1 G FIBER); 623 MG SODIUM; 90 MG CHOL.

Waffles 101

You've made the batter and the topping; you're hungry for breakfast and so is everyone else. You can't wait any more so you lift up the waffle iron lid to take a peek and...disaster. Making waffles requires patience, so follow these steps and your waffles will come out perfect every time:

1. To prevent sticking, oil even nonstick waffle irons (with oil or melted butter) after heating.

2. Wait until the iron is very hot, then pour batter into the center of each square—about ½ cup per 4-in. square. Pour the batter from a glass measuring cup—rather than ladling from a bowl—to prevent dripping.

3. Cook until the iron stops steaming before you lift the lid or you risk a split waffle. Belgian waffles can take up to 9 minutes, traditional ones 2 to 5 minutes. Gently nudge edges of waffle from iron with the tines of a fork if they are stubborn.

*Buttermilk pumpkin
waffles with apples
and apple cider syrup*

Warm buckwheat salad
with roasted shallots,
apples, and frisée

Radicchio and apples
in pine nut vinaigrette

Radicchio and apples in pine nut vinaigrette

SERVES 6 | **TIME** 30 minutes

Apples make a triple play in this sophisticated dish from Clarklewis restaurant in Portland, Oregon: in the hard cider and the cider vinegar in the sweet-tart vinaigrette plus sliced into the salad. The recipe calls for Pinova, a hybrid apple also called Piñata or Orange Pippin, but easy-to-find Galas and Honeycrisps are great as well.

½ cup hard apple cider*
1½ tsp. honey
1 shallot, minced
2 tbsp. apple cider vinegar
About ½ tsp. salt
½ cup toasted pine nuts (see "Toasting Nuts," page 224), divided
¼ cup extra-virgin olive oil
1 head radicchio, halved, cored, and cut into ¼-in. strips
2 Pinova, Gala, Honeycrisp, or other crisp apples, quartered, cored, and thinly sliced
6 slices prosciutto
¼ cup shaved parmesan
Pepper

1. Put cider and honey in a small pan over medium-high heat. Cook until reduced to about 1 tbsp. syrup, 10 to 15 minutes.

2. Put shallot, vinegar, and ½ tsp. salt in a medium bowl and let sit 5 to 10 minutes. Meanwhile, put ¼ cup pine nuts into a mortar and use a pestle to work into a rough paste. Set aside. Stir cider syrup into the shallot-vinegar mixture, then whisk in olive oil. Stir in pine-nut paste to create a creamy dressing and season to taste with salt.

3. Put radicchio in a large bowl. Drizzle with half of the dressing and toss thoroughly. Toss in apples, adding more dressing if necessary to coat the salad. Divide salad among 6 plates. Top each salad with prosciutto, parmesan, and remaining ¼ cup pine nuts, dividing evenly, and season to taste with pepper.

*Find alongside beer in grocery stores.

PER SERVING 239 CAL., 28% (68 CAL.) FROM FAT; 6.9 G PROTEIN; 18 G FAT (3.5 G SAT.); 17 G CARBO (2.2 G FIBER); 386 MG SODIUM; 9.9 MG CHOL.

Warm buckwheat salad with roasted shallots, apples, and frisée

SERVES 3 as a main course or 6 as a side | **TIME** 50 minutes

Kasha is roasted buckwheat that's been hulled and crushed. Its nutty, smoky flavor pairs well with sweet apples and mildly bitter frisée. Find it in the international aisle or swap in spelt or wheat berries for the buckwheat.

1 cup coarsely cracked buckwheat groats (kasha)
5 large shallots, quartered
2 tart-sweet apples, such as Gala, cored and cut into ½-in. wedges
1 tsp. *each* kosher salt and pepper, divided
5 tbsp. olive oil, divided
3 tbsp. sherry vinegar
1 tbsp. Dijon mustard
1 tsp. honey
1 cup frisée lettuce pieces
½ cup chopped flat-leaf parsley

1. Bring 2 cups water to a boil in a medium pot. Add buckwheat, cover, and reduce heat to low. Cook until water is absorbed, about 10 minutes. Set aside.

2. Preheat oven to 425°. Toss shallots and apples with ½ tsp. *each* salt and pepper and 1 tbsp. oil, spread on a baking sheet, and roast, stirring occasionally, until apples are golden and barely tender and shallots are lightly caramelized, 12 to 15 minutes.

3. Whisk together the remaining 4 tbsp. oil, remaining ½ tsp. *each* salt and pepper, the vinegar, mustard, and honey in a large bowl. Add reserved buckwheat, warm apples and shallots, frisée, and parsley and toss gently.

PER 1-CUP SERVING 257 CAL., 41% (106 CAL.) FROM FAT; 4.2 G PROTEIN; 12 G FAT (1.6 G SAT.); 37 G CARBO (4 G FIBER); 324 MG SODIUM; 0 MG CHOL.

Parsnip and apple soup

SERVES 4 | **TIME** 30 minutes

Cider and Fuji apples round out the earthy tones of parsnips in this soup from reader Louise Galen, of West Hollywood, California. It's easy to prepare, but special enough for your Thanksgiving menu or for other fall celebrations. To make your own chicken broth, see page 276; to make your own crème fraîche, see page 279.

½ cup apple cider
½ cup half-and-half
3 cups reduced-sodium chicken broth
5 large parsnips (1 lb.), peeled and roughly chopped
2 leeks, white parts only, roughly chopped (see "Cleaning Leeks," page 94)
2 shallots, quartered
3 Fuji apples (1½ lbs.), peeled, cored, and roughly chopped
½ tsp. kosher salt
¼ tsp. white pepper
About ¼ cup crème fraîche
Chopped chives

1. Pour cider, half-and-half, and broth into a medium saucepan. Cover and bring to a boil over high heat. Add the vegetables and apples and cook, covered, until tender, about 15 minutes.

2. Purée soup with salt and pepper until very smooth, using a hand blender (or regular blender, working in batches). Serve with a swirl of crème fraîche and chopped chives.

PER SERVING 320 CAL., 30% (97 CAL.) FROM FAT; 8 G PROTEIN; 11 G FAT (6.2 G SAT.); 51 G CARBO (7.5 G FIBER); 605 MG SODIUM; 43 MG CHOL.

Cider pork roast with apple-thyme gravy

SERVES 6 to 8 | **TIME** 5 to 7½ hours

Here's the quintessential dish for an autumn Sunday dinner: seared pork roast that's placed in the slow-cooker with cider and Calvados (apple brandy) while you go out and hike the hills or rake the leaves. Top it with sautéed apples in gravy and add mashed potatoes and a green salad.

1 boneless pork shoulder roast (about 3½ lbs.), tied (ask a butcher to do this)
1½ tsp. kosher salt, divided
2 tbsp. olive oil
1½ cups apple cider
⅓ cup Calvados or other apple brandy
1 tbsp. plus 1 tsp. finely chopped fresh thyme leaves, plus sprigs for garnish
1 tsp. pepper
4 Gala apples, peeled, cored, and sliced, divided
3 tbsp. butter, divided
1 tbsp. flour

1. Sprinkle pork with ½ tsp. salt, then brown in oil in a large frying pan over medium-high heat, turning as needed, 10 minutes. Transfer pork and pan juices to a 5- to 6-qt. slow-cooker. Add remaining 1 tsp. salt, the cider, Calvados, 1 tbsp. thyme, the pepper, and 1 sliced apple. Cover and cook until meat is very tender, about 4 hours on high or 7 hours on low.

2. Meanwhile, about 20 minutes before pork is done, heat 2 tbsp. butter in a large frying pan over medium heat. Add remaining 3 apples and cook, stirring frequently, until tender and light golden, about 10 minutes. Transfer to a bowl; tent with foil.

3. Transfer roast from slow-cooker to a platter and tent with foil. Strain slow-cooker juices and skim fat; set aside. Melt remaining 1 tbsp. butter in frying pan. Add flour; cook, whisking often, until golden and bubbling. Slowly whisk in juices and 1 tsp. thyme; cook until slightly thickened, 6 to 8 minutes. Transfer to a gravy boat.

4. Slice pork, scatter with reserved apples, and drizzle with gravy. Garnish with thyme sprigs and serve gravy on the side.

PER SERVING 442 CAL., 36% (159 CAL.) FROM FAT; 37 G PROTEIN; 18 G FAT (7.2 G SAT.); 17 G CARBO (2.2 G FIBER); 445 MG SODIUM; 131 MG CHOL.

Cider pork roast with apple-thyme gravy

Hazelnut-crusted halibut
with apple salsa

Hazelnut-crusted halibut with apple salsa

SERVES 4 | **TIME** 40 minutes

We were intrigued by the idea of apples in a mustardy salsa when we got this recipe from reader Jamie Burrell, of Carnation, Washington. Turns out it's a terrific garnish to nut-crusted, quickly roasted fish.

Hazelnut crust

¾ cup toasted, skinned hazelnuts (see "Toasting Nuts," page 224)
⅛ tsp. dry mustard
½ tsp. kosher salt
¼ tsp. cayenne
1 tbsp. lemon zest
1 tsp. fresh thyme leaves

Fish and salsa

4 Pacific halibut fillets (about 6 oz. each)
3 tbsp. melted unsalted butter
3 tbsp. roasted hazelnut oil
2 tbsp. minced shallots
1¾ cups chopped apple, such as Fuji
2 tbsp. lemon juice
2 tsp. Dijon mustard
½ tsp. chopped fresh thyme leaves, plus leaves for garnish
¼ tsp. *each* kosher salt and pepper
Pinch of cayenne

1. Preheat oven to 425°. Make crust: Whirl ingredients in a food processor until nuts are finely chopped.

2. Make fish: Brush halibut with butter, pat crust mixture all over fish, and set on a greased baking sheet. Cook just until fish is opaque in center, 10 to 15 minutes.

3. Make salsa: Heat oil in a medium frying pan over medium-low heat, add shallots and apple, and cook until slightly softened, about 2 minutes; remove from heat. In a small bowl, whisk together lemon juice and remaining ingredients; stir into apple mixture. Serve halibut with apple salsa and sprinkle with a little more thyme.

PER SERVING 495 CAL., 63% (312 CAL.) FROM FAT; 35 G PROTEIN; 35 G FAT (7.9 G SAT.); 14 G CARBO (3.8 G FIBER); 456 MG SODIUM; 106 MG CHOL.

Raw spiced applesauce

Raw spiced applesauce

SERVES 4 | **TIME** 15 minutes

This quick dish can be served for breakfast, as a snack, or as a light dessert. To make your own yogurt, see page 278.

4 Red Delicious apples (about 1¼ lbs.), left unpeeled, cored, and cut into small chunks
½ tsp. orange zest
2 tbsp. fresh orange juice
¼ tsp. ground cardamom
⅛ tsp. cinnamon
Pinch kosher salt
¼ cup *each* plain low-fat Greek yogurt and chopped toasted pecans

Combine all ingredients except yogurt and pecans in a food processor and whirl until smooth (bits of peel will be visible), 3 to 5 minutes, scraping down sides of bowl if necessary. Divide among 4 bowls and top each with a dollop of yogurt and pecans.

PER ½-CUP SERVING 129 CAL., 38% (49 CAL.) FROM FAT; 2.2 G PROTEIN; 5.4 G FAT (0.7 G SAT.); 21 G CARBO (3.9 G FIBER); 35 MG SODIUM; 0.9 MG CHOL.

Mini caramel apples

MAKES 16 to 20 | **TIME** 30 minutes

This clever trick (it involves a melon baller) makes for an unexpected twist on a classic treat. You can use wooden skewers rather than twigs as handles if you like.

¾ cup light corn syrup
1 cup sugar
½ cup unsalted butter
About 1¼ cups heavy whipping cream, divided
½ cup chopped toasted pecans (see "Toasting Nuts," page 224)
½ cup mini chocolate chips
½ cup decorative mini orange candies
2 large red apples
About 20 slender but sturdy twigs, about 4 in. long each

1. Heat together corn syrup, sugar, butter, and ¾ cup plus 2 tbsp. cream in a 3-qt. saucepan over medium-high heat until mixture reaches 275° on a candy thermometer*, about 15 minutes, stirring often with the thermometer or a wooden spoon once it starts to brown. While caramel boils, prepare the remaining ingredients (you'll need to have everything ready before beginning step 3).

2. Grease a baking sheet and set aside. Put pecans, chocolate chips, and candies on individual plates and set aside. Using a 1-in. melon baller, cut apples into balls (you should get 8 to 10 from each apple). Push thickest end of a twig into each apple ball through skin side to center. Set on paper towels to absorb moisture.

3. Remove caramel from heat when at 275° and pour in remaining cream, stirring until very smooth (it will come together after about 1 minute) and being careful of any splattering caramel.

4. Dip apple balls into the caramel, making sure the caramel comes over edges of skin and letting excess drip off. Dip bottom of each ball into either nuts, chocolate chips, or candies, then set on the baking sheet to cool.

*You will need an accurate candy thermometer. Check it by immersing in boiling water; it should read 212°. If it's a few degrees too high or low, cook the caramel to a corresponding few degrees more or less. If it's way off, get a new thermometer.

Make ahead Up to 3 hours, chilled; serve at room temperature.

PER MINI APPLE 214 CAL., 51% (109 CAL.) FROM FAT; 0.8 G PROTEIN; 12 G FAT (6.6 G SAT.); 28 G CARBO (1 G FIBER); 26 MG SODIUM; 26 MG CHOL.

Apple of my iced tea

SERVES 2 | **TIME** 10 minutes, plus 1 hour to steep

Blend apple cider with iced tea for this brisk drink from reader Lucy Leahy, of Oakland, California. She makes it with easy-to-grow anise hyssop, an herb with a minty licorice flavor. You can use regular mint leaves, and it will be just as refreshing.

1 cup sugar
¼ cup fresh anise hyssop or mint leaves
½ cup hard apple cider*
½ cup brewed black tea, cooled
Apple wedges for garnish

1. Put sugar and 1 cup water in a microwave-safe bowl. Microwave until very warm, then stir to dissolve sugar. Add anise hyssop, cover bowl, and set aside about 1 hour. Strain syrup.

2. Fill 2 glasses with ice and add 2 tbsp. syrup to each. Pour in cider and tea. Garnish each with an apple wedge. Chill remaining syrup to use another time.

*Find alongside beer in grocery stores.

PER SERVING 121 CAL., 0% FROM FAT; 0 G PROTEIN; 0 G FAT; 28 G CARBO (0 G FIBER); 0.3 MG SODIUM; 0 MG CHOL.

Apple of my
iced tea

Apple pumpkin galette

Apple pumpkin galette

SERVES 8 to 10 | **TIME** 2 hours, plus at least 2 hours to cool

Basically an open-face pie, this is a great dessert for pie-phobes to make because the crust is so easy to handle.

Half-recipe Easiest Pie Dough (recipe follows)
1½ lbs. peeled, sliced baking pumpkin or kabocha squash
3 large Granny Smith apples (about 1½ lbs.), peeled,
   cored, and sliced
1 tsp. cinnamon
¼ tsp. *each* ground nutmeg, ground cloves, and salt
3 tbsp. flour
⅓ cup brown sugar
1½ cups granulated sugar
2 tbsp. bourbon or whiskey
2 tbsp. coarse decorating or turbinado sugar

1. Set dough on a lightly floured surface and roll into a large round about ⅛ in. thick. Transfer to a parchment-lined baking sheet and chill until ready to fill.

2. Preheat oven to 375° with a rack set on bottom rung. Lay pumpkin slices on a greased baking sheet. Roast, turning over once, until tender when pierced, about 10 minutes.

3. Mix apples, spices, salt, flour, both sugars, and bourbon until evenly coated. Add pumpkin and toss just to combine.

4. Pour apple filling into center of dough, leaving a 1½-in. border. Fold edges over fruit, allowing dough to pleat as you go. Dip a pastry brush in water and brush folded edges of dough. Sprinkle edges with coarse sugar.

5. Bake galette until browned and bubbling, about 1¼ hours. Let cool before cutting.

PER SERVING 371 CAL., 23% (85 CAL.) FROM FAT; 3.2 G PROTEIN; 9.6 G FAT (5.9 G SAT.); 70 G CARBO (2 G FIBER); 174 MG SODIUM; 24 MG CHOL.

EASIEST PIE DOUGH

MAKES 2 (9-in.) crusts | **TIME** 10 minutes, plus 30 minutes to chill

Whirl together 3 cups **flour**, 1 tbsp. **sugar**, and 1½ tsp. **kosher salt** in a food processor. Add 1 cup cold, cubed **unsalted butter** and pulse into pea-size pieces. Drizzle ⅔ cup very cold water over crumbs and pulse just until moistened. Turn dough out onto a work surface and gather into a ball, turning to combine any dry crumbs. Divide dough in half, form each piece into a disk, wrap in plastic wrap, and chill at least 30 minutes.

Apple-crisp baked apples

SERVES 6 | **TIME** 1 hour, 15 minutes

Pink Lady or Jazz (a popular hybrid) apples tend to retain their color and shape well during baking, so they are our top pick for this recipe. You can substitute golden raisins for the walnuts.

⅓ cup walnuts, chopped medium fine
⅓ cup pecans, chopped medium fine
¼ tbsp. firmly packed dark brown sugar
¼ tsp. salt
¼ tsp. *each* cinnamon and ground cardamom
¼ cup rolled oats
4 tbsp. cold butter, cut into small cubes
6 medium Pink Lady, Jazz, or other firm baking apple
1½ cups apple cider
Vanilla ice cream (optional)

1. Preheat oven to 350°. In a medium bowl, combine walnuts, pecans, sugar, salt, cinnamon, cardamom, and oats. Add butter cubes and toss to combine.

2. Peel the top third of each apple and, using a melon baller, scoop out the stem and enough of the core so that the walls of the apple are about ½ in. thick. Take care, however, not to break through the bottom of the apple, or the filling will leak out when baking. Make the hole a bit wider at the top.

3. Stuff each apple generously using a small spoon or your fingers; mound extra filling on top.

4. Put the filled apples in a 2-qt. baking dish. Pour cider into the pan around the apples, cover the dish with foil, and bake 45 minutes. Remove foil and bake, basting every 15 minutes, for an additional 30 to 45 minutes, until apples are easily pierced with a sharp knife (they may split open a bit at the bottom). Serve apples drizzled with the sauce from the pan and a scoop of vanilla ice cream alongside if you like.

PER SERVING 273 CAL., 53% (144 CAL.) FROM FAT; 2.3 G PROTEIN; 16 G FAT (5.6 G SAT.); 33 G CARBO (3.9 G FIBER); 176 MG SODIUM; 21 MG CHOL.

CHEESE

CHEESE

Of all the handcrafted foods that have experienced a revival in the past few decades, cheese may be the most exciting. And many of the best artisanal cheeses in the country are made in the West from the milk of the cows, the sheep, and the goats that graze here.

In addition to which animal produced the milk, cheeses have different flavors and nuances from the milk's season. For instance, cheeses made from springtime milk can have floral and herbal characteristics from the animals' diet of new grasses, while cheeses made from winter milk from animals eating grains and hay might have an earthy quality. Aging also affects the flavor and texture: Fresh cheeses are reminiscent of fresh, rich milk and are either spreadable or just firm enough to slice; with less moisture, firm to hard cheeses can taste mellow to robust and have a sliceable or crumbly texture.

SEASONAL AVAILABILITY The cheesemaking process is a way of preserving fresh milk for long periods, so cheeses are generally available year-round.

SELECTING AND STORING To explore the world of cheese, shop where you can taste and ask questions, which means locating an informed vendor who hands out samples, such as specialty-foods stores, cheese shops, or farmers' markets. How to store a cheese depends on the way it's made. Fresh, delicate cheeses, like ricotta, chèvre, and mascarpone, are quite perishable; store in the refrigerator and use within a few days or by the date on the package. Soft-ripened cheeses, such as teleme and brie, develop rinds that influence flavors as they ripen; store whole in the original packaging or if cut, rewrap in plastic and chill up to a week. Semi-firm to firm cheeses, such as cheddar and gouda, are aged longer. Once cut, wrap pieces in parchment so they can breathe, then cover with plastic wrap or place in an airtight container and chill up to a month; trim any surface mold before eating. Nutty-tasting hard cheeses, such as dry jack and parmesan, should be treated the same way. Strong blue cheeses should be double-wrapped to prevent aromas from seeping out.

USING In these recipes, we showcase cheese as an essential ingredient, not as a garnish. Another way to showcase it is to assemble a cheese plate (see page 142), letting the cheeses come to room temperature before serving so their flavors are fully developed and their textures just right. However, grating cheese is easier to do when the cheese is cold, so leave it in the fridge until the last minute.

Cheesy pepper kale chips

MAKES 6 cups | **TIME** 35 minutes

The secret to crispiness in kale chips is to avoid crowding the leaves on the baking sheets and to keep a watchful eye so they don't scorch. They can be made ahead and stored airtight up to 1 week.

7 to 8 oz. Lacinato kale (often sold as "dinosaur kale" and "Tuscan kale")
1½ tbsp. olive oil
¼ to ½ tsp. coarse sea salt, such as *sel gris*
½ tsp. coarsely ground pepper
3 tbsp. grated parmesan cheese

1. Preheat oven to 300°. Rinse kale and thoroughly blot dry with a kitchen towel. Tear leaves from ribs; discard ribs. Tear leaves into 4-in. pieces. Pour oil into a large bowl; add kale, salt, and pepper, and toss to coat evenly.

2. Arrange leaves in a single layer on 2 rimmed baking sheets. Bake, switching pan positions after 13 minutes. Sprinkle with cheese and bake until leaves are crisp but not browned, 5 to 7 minutes more.

PER ⅓ CUP 18 CAL., 67% (12 CAL.) FROM FAT; 0.3 G PROTEIN; 1.4 G FAT (0.3 G SAT.); 0.9 G CARBO (0.1 G FIBER); 48 MG SODIUM; 0.7 MG CHOL.

Blue cheese and pear tart

SERVES 8 | **TIME** 30 minutes

This tart, from reader Nahed Hamdi, of University Place, Washington, can be cut into small squares for an appetizer or sliced into large wedges and served with a green salad for a light meal. Gorgonzola dolce is sweeter and creamier than aged Gorgonzola cheese, so check the label to be sure that is the kind you buy.

1 sheet thawed frozen puff pastry (8.6 oz.)
1 large egg
⅔ cup gorgonzola dolce cheese
½ small onion, sliced
1 tbsp. olive oil
1 ripe pear, thinly sliced
2 tbsp. fresh thyme leaves

Blue cheese and pear tart

1. Preheat oven to 425° with a rack set on bottom rung. Lay dough flat on a rimmed baking sheet lined with parchment paper. Poke holes all over the dough with a fork, leaving the outer inch untouched. Bake until dough starts to puff, about 10 minutes.

2. Whisk together egg and cheese until smooth and spread over dough, using a spoon to move mixture toward the corners. Cook onion in oil in a frying pan over medium-high heat until softened. Scatter onion and pear over cheese.

3. Bake until pastry is golden brown and egg has set, about 15 minutes. Sprinkle with thyme and cut into squares.

PER 2-PIECE SERVING 192 CAL., 62% (119 CAL.) FROM FAT; 5.2 G PROTEIN; 13 G FAT (4.7 G SAT.); 13 G CARBO (1.6 G FIBER); 285 MG SODIUM; 35 MG CHOL.

Asparagus and teleme tart

SERVES 4 to 6 | **TIME** 45 minutes

Melty, gooey teleme is the Western version of Italian taleggio. You can use mozzarella or muenster instead if you can't find teleme. You can also make this in a 9-inch round tart pan if you don't have a rectangular one; in that case, don't roll out the dough, just use it straight from the package (we especially like Pillsbury pie dough) and cut the asparagus stalks to fit.

1 sheet refrigerated pie dough for a 9-in. pie shell
8 oz. teleme cheese, whole-milk mozzarella (not fresh or water-packed), or muenster cheese, thinly sliced
1 lb. asparagus, trimmed and cut into 3½-in. pieces
½ tsp. olive oil
Pepper

1. Preheat oven to 425°. Unroll pie dough and fold in half. Roll into a 6- by 16½-in. rectangle. Fit into a 4- by 14-in. rectangular tart pan, press against sides, and roll over the top with a rolling pin; save scraps for another use.

2. Prick bottom of crust with a fork and bake until golden, 10 to 15 minutes.

3. Line tart bottom with cheese. In a medium bowl, toss asparagus with oil to coat. Arrange spears crosswise over cheese, tightly packed, alternating the direction of tip and stem pieces and cutting to fit as necessary (reserve extras for another use). Bake until cheese melts, about 15 minutes. Sprinkle generously with pepper.

PER SERVING 276 CAL., 62% (170 CAL.) FROM FAT; 12 G PROTEIN; 19 G FAT (11 G SAT.); 19 G CARBO (1 G FIBER); 331 MG SODIUM; 17 MG CHOL.

Celery soup with apples and blue cheese

SERVES 4 | **TIME** 30 minutes

Ever wonder what to do with that celery in your produce drawer? Reader Rita King, of Scottsdale, Arizona, whirled hers into this cozy soup. Apples and cheese provide a crunchy counterpoint to each bowlful. To make your own chicken or vegetable broth, see page 276.

1 head celery (1½ lbs.)
½ small onion, chopped
1 qt. reduced-sodium chicken or vegetable broth
2 tbsp. butter
1 Granny Smith apple, peeled and finely chopped
½ cup half-and-half
¼ tsp. *each* salt and pepper
¼ cup chopped flat-leaf parsley
¼ cup crumbled blue cheese

1. Cut celery stalks into 1-in. chunks. Put celery, onion, and broth into a large pot. Cover and boil until tender, 20 to 25 minutes.

2. Meanwhile, melt butter in a small frying pan over medium heat. Cook apple, stirring occasionally, until caramelized, about 10 minutes. Set aside.

3. Whirl celery mixture in a blender in batches until very smooth, about 2 minutes per batch. Stir in half-and-half and season with salt and pepper. Ladle soup into bowls; sprinkle with parsley, reserved apple, and cheese.

PER SERVING 204 CAL., 57% (116 CAL.) FROM FAT; 9 G PROTEIN; 13 G FAT (7.7 G SAT.); 14 G CARBO (2.8 G FIBER); 515 MG SODIUM; 37 MG CHOL.

*Celery soup with apples
and blue cheese*

Fig and ricotta
cheese flatbread

Fig and ricotta cheese flatbread

SERVES 12 as an appetizer or 6 as a main course
TIME About 1½ hours, plus 35 to 45 minutes to rise

Serve this savory-sweet pizza with California wine, such as a Pinot Noir from the North Coast, to complete the experience.

1 pkg. (2¼ tsp.) active dry yeast
About 1 tsp. salt, divided
2 tbsp. olive oil, divided
About 3½ cups all-purpose flour
3 red onions (about 1¾ lb. total), halved and thinly sliced
About 2 tbsp. good-quality balsamic vinegar
    (see "Balsamic Vinegar 101," page 101)
About ¼ tsp. pepper
About ¼ cup yellow cornmeal
About 2 cups (15-oz. carton) ricotta cheese (see "Ricotta 101,"
    below right)
1 lb. firm-ripe figs, stems trimmed and halved lengthwise
½ cup chopped walnuts
½ cup crumbled blue cheese (about 3 oz.; optional)
4½ cups arugula leaves (about 2 oz.)

1. Put 1½ cups warm (110°) water in a large bowl and sprinkle yeast over it. Let stand until softened, about 5 minutes.

2. Stir in ½ tsp. salt and 1 tbsp. olive oil. Gradually mix in 3½ cups flour until a soft dough forms. *If using a mixer:* Beat with a dough hook on high speed until dough no longer feels sticky and pulls cleanly from sides of bowl, 5 to 7 minutes. If dough is still sticky, beat in more flour, 1 tbsp. at a time. *If kneading by hand:* Scrape dough onto a lightly floured board. Knead until smooth, springy, and no longer sticky, 15 to 20 minutes; add flour as needed to prevent sticking. Place dough in an oiled bowl and turn to coat. Cover and let rise in a warm place until doubled, 35 to 45 minutes.

3. Meanwhile, in a 10- to 12-in. frying pan over medium-high heat, stir onions in remaining 1 tbsp. olive oil until very soft, 25 to 30 minutes. If onions start to burn or stick, reduce heat and stir in 1 tbsp. water. Add 2 tbsp. balsamic vinegar, ¼ tsp. pepper, and ½ tsp. salt and stir until liquid is evaporated, 1 to 2 minutes longer.

4. Preheat oven to 450°. Scrape dough onto a lightly floured board; press gently to expel air. Divide into 4 equal pieces. Place pieces on floured board and cover with plastic wrap; let rest 10 minutes. Roll or stretch one piece at a time into a 13- by 7-in. oval about 1⁄16 in. thick. Place each oval on a cornmeal-dusted 12- by 15-in. rimless baking sheet; stretch dough, if needed, to reshape.

5. Arrange about ½ cup onions evenly over each oval. Drop ricotta in ½-tbsp. portions over onions (about 12 on each oval); arrange figs, cut side up, around cheese. Sprinkle about 2 tbsp. walnuts and 2 tbsp. blue cheese, if using, evenly over each oval.

6. Bake until crust is well browned on top and bottom, 15 to 20 minutes. If baking two sheets in one oven, switch positions halfway through baking. Slide each flatbread onto a cutting board or plate. Sprinkle arugula leaves equally on top; cut each oval in half lengthwise, then crosswise into eight slices. Season to taste with salt, pepper, and a drizzle of balsamic vinegar.

Make ahead Through step 2 up to 1 day, punched down, bowl covered with plastic wrap, and chilled; let stand at room temperature about 1 hour before shaping in step 4.

PER APPETIZER 347 CAL., 34% (117 CAL.) FROM FAT; 12 G PROTEIN; 13 G FAT (4.9 G SAT.); 47 G CARBO (3.9 G FIBER); 333 MG SODIUM; 23 MG CHOL.

Ricotta 101

Ricotta is a fresh cheese originally from Italy that is now produced all over America. It gets its name from how the cheese is made: Whey, the liquid that separates from the curds, is reheated to form *ricotta* (literally "recooked" in Italian). In Italy, it's made from the milk of cows, sheep, goats, and domestic water buffalo; in the U.S., it is mainly made from cow's milk, though a handful of producers make ricotta from sheep's or goat's milk. Freshly made ricotta, often sold draining in its own basket, is worth seeking out at specialty grocers or cheese shops for its lush, subtle taste and billowy texture.

Assembling a cheese plate

Whether offered as an hors d'oeuvre, a first course, or a last course, there is no wrong way to compose a cheese plate. There's just a golden rule: Keep it simple.

You can feature a range of cheeses, such as one soft, one firm, one blue-veined, and one aged; a variety of milks, such as one cheese each made from cow's milk, goat's milk, and sheep's milk; or several varieties of one style of cheese, such as blue cheese, Roquefort, and gorgonzola. Or you can serve a single cheese with its ideal companion, such as fresh ricotta with a grating of orange zest and honey, or aged parmesan or dry jack with Medjool dates.

Below are some cheese suggestions; a good cheese vendor can provide you with alternatives if these are not available in your area.

Soft and creamy cheeses, such as Cowgirl Creamery's Mt. Tam, Redwood Hill Farm's Camellia, and Marin French Cheese Company's Rouge et Noir Le Petit Déjeuner, paired with crusty bread and black-olive tapenade.

A range of goat's-milk cheeses, from fresh, mild, and creamy to hard and crumbly, such as Laura Chenel's Chèvre and Achadinha Cheese Company's Capricious, paired with candied orange peel, caper berries, and baguette slices.

Bold and bright strong-tasting cheeses, such as Nicasio Valley Cheese's Nicasio Square, Point Reyes Farmstead Cheese Company's Original Blue, and Bellwether Farms' Pepato (with peppercorns through-out), paired with panforte, the Italian-style dried fruit and nut cake.

Spring vegetable macaroni 'n' cheese

SERVES 4 to 6 | **TIME** About 1 hour

This untraditional mac 'n' cheese recipe uses tangy goat cheese instead of the usual cheddar.

12 oz. asparagus, trimmed and cut into ½-in. pieces
2 leeks, cleaned (see "Cleaning Leeks," page 94)
4½ tbsp. butter, divided
1½ tsp. salt, divided
12 oz. orecchiette pasta
¾ cup frozen petite peas
2 slices sourdough bread
3 tbsp. flour
2 tsp. fresh thyme leaves
3 cups milk
2 tsp. lemon zest
1 tbsp. Dijon mustard
½ tsp. pepper
6 oz. fresh goat cheese
1½ cups shredded romano cheese, divided

1. Preheat oven to 400°. Stir asparagus, leeks, 1 tbsp. butter, and ½ tsp. salt in a medium pan over medium-high heat. Cook until asparagus is just tender, about 7 minutes, then remove from pan and set aside. Bring a large pot of water to a boil.

2. Cook pasta as package directs; stir in peas at the end. Drain and return to pot. Meanwhile, tear bread into chunks and put in a food processor with ½ tbsp. butter. Whirl until crumbs form.

3. Melt remaining 3 tbsp. butter in the medium pan over medium-high heat. Add the flour and thyme; stir until smooth and bubbling, about 30 seconds. Slowly whisk in milk and stir until boiling and thickened, 5 to 8 minutes. Add zest, mustard, pepper, and remaining 1 tsp. salt. Remove from heat and add goat cheese and 1 cup romano; stir until smooth. Pour sauce over pasta and peas. Add asparagus mixture and stir well. Scrape the mixture into a 2½-qt. baking dish and spread until level. Sprinkle evenly with remaining ½ cup romano and the bread crumbs. Bake until sauce is bubbling and bread crumbs are browned, 15 to 20 minutes.

PER SERVING 655 CAL., 41% (270 CAL.) FROM FAT; 30 G PROTEIN; 30 G FAT (19 G SAT.); 66 G CARBO (3.4 G FIBER); 1,353 MG SODIUM; 92 MG CHOL.

Spring vegetable macaroni 'n' cheese

Molten cheese log

Molten cheese log

SERVES 8 to 10 | **TIME** 15 minutes

What happens when you take all of the ingredients that go into the classic cheese log and put them in a fondue pot? You get molten cheese log, of course. Serve with Ritz crackers to complete the nostalgia.

4 oz. cream cheese
8 oz. sharp cheddar cheese, shredded
4 oz. Monterey jack cheese, shredded
1 tbsp. flour
½ tsp. cayenne
¾ cup heavy cream
½ cup chopped toasted pecans (see "Toasting Nuts," page 224)
1 green onion, chopped
Ritz crackers

Blend cheeses, flour, cayenne, and cream in a food processor until smooth. Put in a small fondue pot or slow-cooker to melt, about 20 minutes. Sprinkle with nuts and onion and serve with crackers.

PER SERVING 282 CAL., 83% (234 CAL.) FROM FAT; 9 G PROTEIN; 26 G FAT (15 G SAT.); 2.6 G CARBO (0.6 G FIBER); 250 MG SODIUM; 72 MG CHOL.

Chicken cheesesteaks

SERVES 4 | **TIME** 20 minutes

Reader Dianne Krahenbuhl, of Santa Barbara, California, elevated the standard chicken sandwich with a kick of cayenne and shredded jack cheese. If you want even more flavor, spread the rolls with a mixture of Dijon mustard and chili paste.

¼ cup olive oil
2 boned, skinned chicken breast halves (1 lb. total), sliced
1 cup *each* sliced mushrooms, onion, and green bell pepper
½ tsp. *each* smoked paprika, garlic powder, salt, and cayenne
2 tsp. butter
4 submarine or French bread rolls, split
4 romaine lettuce leaves
1 cup shredded jack cheese

Chicken cheesesteaks

1. Preheat oven to 350°. Heat oil in a large frying pan over high heat. Add chicken, mushrooms, onion, bell pepper, and seasonings and cook until chicken is browned and no longer pink inside, 6 minutes.

2. Spread ½ tsp. butter inside each roll and toast rolls, opened up, in oven on a baking sheet for about 4 minutes. Lay 1 lettuce leaf in each roll. Sprinkle ¼ cup cheese over lettuce, then divide chicken mixture among rolls.

PER SERVING 653 CAL., 45% (296 CAL.) FROM FAT; 50 G PROTEIN; 33 G FAT (11 G SAT.); 38 G CARBO (3.3 G FIBER); 864 MG SODIUM; 127 MG CHOL.

Lemon ricotta risotto with asparagus, peas, and prosciutto

SERVES 6 | **TIME** 1½ hours

A great way to pay homage to springtime is to put the best seasonal produce in risotto. To make your own broth, see page 276.

2 oz. thinly sliced prosciutto
1 lb. asparagus, trimmed
1 tsp. plus 1 tbsp. olive oil
Salt and pepper
8 cups reduced-sodium chicken broth
1 large yellow onion, coarsely chopped
2 cups Carnaroli or Arborio rice (see "Choosing the Right Rice," page 231)
½ cup dry white wine
¼ cup finely chopped fresh mint
½ cup whole-milk ricotta, such as Bellwether Farms
1 cup fresh or frozen peas
⅓ cup lemon juice (from 1 to 2 large lemons)
3 tbsp. unsalted butter
3 oz. finely shredded dry jack cheese, such as Spring Hill or Vella, or parmesan, plus 1 oz. shaved, using a vegetable peeler

1. Preheat oven to 400°. Set a rack in a rimmed baking sheet and lay prosciutto slices on rack.

2. Arrange asparagus in a single layer on another rimmed baking sheet. Drizzle with 1 tsp. oil. Sprinkle with salt and pepper; toss to coat. Bake prosciutto and asparagus until prosciutto is crisp and very light brown around the edges, about 8 minutes, and asparagus is a little darker and tender when pricked with the tip of a knife, 12 to 15 minutes. Remove both from oven and let cool. When cool enough to handle, break prosciutto into small shards and cut asparagus into 1-in. pieces.

3. Pour broth into a medium saucepan and bring to a simmer over medium heat.

4. Heat remaining oil in a large pot over medium-high heat. Add onion and cook, stirring occasionally, until soft but not brown, about 5 minutes. Add rice and cook, stirring constantly, until edges turn bright white, 5 minutes. Add wine; bring to a boil and cook until almost evaporated, about 2 minutes.

5. Add ½ cup of broth to rice and cook, stirring, until almost completely absorbed by rice. Continue adding broth ½ cup at a time, stirring until each addition is absorbed before adding the next, until rice is just tender to the bite, 15 to 30 minutes (you will have broth left over).

6. Add mint, ricotta, peas (if using fresh), and lemon juice; stir until most of juice is absorbed. Add butter and shredded cheese and stir until well mixed. Stir in peas (if frozen), asparagus, and pepper to taste. Divide risotto among bowls or plates. Top with prosciutto crisps and sprinkle with shaved cheese.

PER SERVING 405 CAL., 43% (174 CAL.) FROM FAT; 23 G PROTEIN; 20 G FAT (10 G SAT.); 34 G CARBO (3 G FIBER); 755 MG SODIUM; 77 MG CHOL.

White cheddar sage popovers

MAKES 12 | **TIME** 45 minutes, plus 1 hour for batter to rest

Use popover pans to get the airiest results. Muffin pans work too, but leave every other cup unfilled so heat circulates around popovers for even browning.

2 cups milk
4 large eggs
1¾ cups flour
1 tsp. kosher salt
½ tsp. pepper
1 tbsp. chopped fresh sage
1 cup finely shredded sharp white cheddar cheese, divided
¼ cup butter

1. Whisk together milk and eggs, then whisk in flour, salt, pepper, and sage. Stir in ½ cup cheese. Let stand 1 hour.

2. Preheat oven to 450° at least 30 minutes before baking. Divide butter among 12 popover cups. Put pans in oven 2 minutes to melt butter. Set a rimmed baking sheet on rack beneath to catch any dripping butter as popovers rise. Stir batter and ladle into cups. Bake 10 minutes. Without opening oven, reduce heat to 375° and bake until popovers are puffed and golden, about 15 minutes more. Top each with a large pinch of remaining cheese and return to oven to melt cheese, 5 minutes.

3. Free popovers from pan by running a thin metal spatula around edge; lift from bottom.

PER POPOVER 166 CAL., 40% (67 CAL.) FROM FAT; 8 G PROTEIN; 7.5 G FAT (4.1 G SAT.); 16 G CARBO (0.9 G FIBER); 268 MG SODIUM; 86 MG CHOL.

*Lemon ricotta risotto
with asparagus, peas,
and prosciutto*

Spiced apple carrot cake with
goat cheese frosting

Spiced apple carrot cake with goat cheese frosting

SERVES 10 | **TIME** 2½ hours (includes cooling and chilling time)

We were intrigued when reader Rachel Dornhelm, of Oakland, California, substituted tangy goat cheese for cream cheese in a carrot cake frosting. Turns out the sweetened cheese is the ideal complement to the richly spiced cake.

2 cups flour
1½ cups granulated sugar
2¼ tsp. baking soda
1½ tsp. *each* **baking powder and cinnamon**
¼ tsp. *each* **ground cloves and nutmeg**
2 tsp. unsweetened cocoa powder
⅛ tsp. pepper
¼ tsp. salt
1 cup vegetable oil
4 large eggs plus 1 egg yolk, lightly beaten
1½ cups packed coarsely grated carrots (about 3 medium)
1½ cups packed coarsely grated tart apples, such as Granny Smith (about 2 medium)
1 cup coarsely chopped walnuts, plus more for frosting garnish
10 oz. mild fresh goat cheese, at room temperature
8 oz. cream cheese, at room temperature
2 tbsp. unsalted butter, at room temperature
1 tsp. vanilla extract
2 cups powdered sugar

1. Preheat oven to 350°. Grease three 9-in. round cake pans and set aside. In a large bowl, combine flour, granulated sugar, baking soda, baking powder, spices, cocoa, pepper, and salt. Whisk to combine, then stir in oil and eggs. Stir in carrots, apples, and 1 cup walnuts.

2. Divide batter among pans and bake until cakes pull away from pan sides and a cake tester inserted in each center comes out clean, 25 minutes. Transfer pans to cooling racks and let cool 10 minutes. Turn cakes out onto racks and let cool completely.

3. Beat goat cheese, cream cheese, butter, and vanilla until smooth and fluffy, about 3 minutes. Gradually add powdered sugar and mix until combined.

4. Arrange first layer on a large plate or platter. Spread some frosting over it, then top with second layer. Frost second layer and top with the third. Generously frost top and sides of cake with remaining frosting. Chill cake at least 1 hour. Before serving, press remaining walnuts lightly into sides of cake.

PER SERVING 830 CAL., 54% (450 CAL.) FROM FAT; 15 G PROTEIN; 50 G FAT (15 G SAT.); 85 G CARBO (3.1 G FIBER); 628 MG SODIUM; 150 MG CHOL.

Cheese and chocolate bruschetta

SERVES 8 | **TIME** 20 minutes

For a big party, a dessert bruschetta is a fun way to finish that doesn't require any plates to eat. We love the combo of the rich, creamy cheese, slightly bitter chocolate, and sweet-tart fruit.

¼ lb. firm brie cheese, at room temperature
16 baguette slices, brushed with olive oil and grilled
16 cherries, halved and pitted
16 large bittersweet chocolate curls* (from a 3-oz. bar)

Slice cheese to fit baguette toasts and put 1 slice on each toast. Top each with 2 cherry halves and a chocolate curl.

*To make chocolate curls, microwave chocolate bar with smooth side up in 5-second increments until slightly softened, about 20 seconds total. Pull a vegetable peeler across the bar.

PER 2-TOAST SERVING 182 CAL., 35% (63 CAL.) FROM FAT; 7.6 G PROTEIN; 7 G FAT (4 G SAT.); 25 G CARBO (1.8 G FIBER); 302 MG SODIUM; 14 MG CHOL.

WINE

The defining moment for American wine was in 1976, when a California Cabernet and Chardonnay trumped the French competition at a legendary tasting in Paris. Generations of winemakers have built on this success, establishing a remarkable level of quality and innovation.

From the Napa Valley to Nampa, Idaho, great wines are made all over today. And everywhere these wines are made, creative local chefs are fostering a food scene to equal the excitement of what's going on in the glass. Here's a snapshot of the most popular regional varietals and a few of their best food matches, plus two recipes destined for wines that are growing in popularity right now.

CABERNET SAUVIGNON
The king of reds, Cabernet is a big-structured, dark-fruited wine. Some Cabs are made to be drunk right away; others need years to mellow. Pair with well-marbled beef and grilled red meat, duck, pot roast, mushrooms, spice rubs, sauces with lots of black pepper, and marinades with soy sauce.

MERLOT
This is the most popular red wine in the United States. It is no lightweight: It can be deeply concentrated, with firm, Cab-rivaling tannins. Pair with beef tenderloin, lamb, salmon, tuna, black olives, and meats with fruit sauces.

PINOT NOIR
A light-bodied, low-tannin red, Pinot Noir can have an earthy Old World style or a riper, more fruit-forward, New World style. Some winemakers in Oregon's Willamette Valley and the cooler parts of California make a hybrid that's lean and earthy yet still has generous fruit. Pair with boldly flavored poultry and duck, lamb, salmon, tuna, ham, lentils, Asian and eastern Mediterranean dishes, and cheeses.

ZINFANDEL
The quintessential American wine, Zinfandel is mostly grown in warm places; the grapes are allowed to get very ripe, producing jammy flavors and high alcohol levels. Zins from cooler places are slightly leaner. Pair with ribs, hamburgers, grilled leg of lamb, and Moroccan spices.

CHARDONNAY
California winemakers have traditionally made Chardonnay in a rich, buttery style by fermenting and aging it in oak barrels. Some winemakers are using stainless steel tanks for a leaner, crisper style. Pair with halibut, turkey, veal, risotto, pasta, cream and butter sauces, and dishes with tropical fruit flavors.

SAUVIGNON BLANC
A lean, crisp Sauvignon Blanc is extremely flexible with food. The majority are fermented in stainless steel to retain the fresh fruit character and natural acidity. Some are fermented in oak for a slightly rounder style and may be labeled Fumé Blanc. Pair with cheese (especially goat), asparagus, zucchini, peas, artichokes, oysters, sole, salads with mild vinaigrettes, and pesto.

SPARKLING WINE
Made primarily from Chardonnay and Pinot Noir grapes, good-quality sparklers get their bubbles from the traditional Champagne method of a second fermentation in the bottle. The acidity of a bubbly makes it an excellent choice with food, not just for drinking on special occasions. Pair with caviar, cheeses, fish and shellfish, Asian dishes, and salty foods like potato chips.

WINE

Safely storing wine

1. Keep wine where the temperature is fairly constant. A cool place is best, but what you really want to avoid is large temperature swings.

2. Store wine out of bright sunlight, which deteriorates it.

3. Keep it fairly still. Don't store wine on top of a refrigerator, for instance, because vibration deteriorates wine.

4. Place the bottle on its side or upside down so the wine is in contact with the cork. This prevents the cork from drying and shrinking, which can cause air to get in and oxidize the wine too fast. If you buy a case, set it on its side or turn it so the bottles are upside down.

Slow-braised red chile beef

SERVES 6 | **TIME** About 5 hours

A Malbec from eastern Washington can rival one from Argentina. The earth and spice of this wine make it a beautiful pairing with the warmth of the dried chiles and cumin in this recipe.

4 to 5 cups reduced-sodium beef broth, divided
12 dried California or New Mexico chiles (about 3 oz.), stemmed, seeded, and rinsed
1 large onion, cut into chunks
4 large garlic cloves
1 tbsp. ground cumin
1 tsp. dried oregano
1 boned, tied beef chuck roast (3½ to 4 lbs.), rinsed and patted dry
Kosher salt and pepper
2 tbsp. olive oil

1. Bring 3 cups beef broth to a boil. Put chiles in a blender and pour boiling broth over them. Let stand, stirring occasionally, until chiles are soft, about 10 minutes. Add onion, garlic, cumin, and oregano and whirl until very smooth.

2. Meanwhile, preheat oven to 325°. Sprinkle beef all over with salt and pepper. Pour oil into a large, heavy pot (not extremely wide) over medium-high heat. When hot, add roast and cook, turning as needed, to brown all over, about 10 minutes total. Pour chile mixture over meat and add enough beef broth to come a third to half of the way up the roast. Bring to a boil, cover pot, and transfer to oven.

3. Bake until beef is very tender when pierced, about 3½ hours, turning once. Transfer roast to a board. When cool enough to handle, remove string and pull meat into bite-size chunks, discarding excess fat.

4. Meanwhile, skim fat from chile sauce in pot. Boil sauce over high heat, stirring often, until reduced to about 4 cups. Season to taste with salt and pepper. Return beef to sauce and simmer until heated through.

PER SERVING 383 CAL., 33% (127 CAL.) FROM FAT; 53 G PROTEIN; 14 G FAT (4.2 G SAT.); 13 G CARBO (4.8 G FIBER); 499 MG SODIUM; 96 MG CHOL.

Pissaladière

SERVES 8 to 10 as an appetizer | **TIME** 1¾ hours

Winemakers in the West are producing ever-better rosés. Pair this Provençal-inspired tart with a crisp, minerally one, ideally from Grenache or Mourvèdre grapes. If you're anchovy-averse, go for the tuna and pepper version that follows.

4 medium onions (about 2 lbs. total), thinly sliced lengthwise
1½ tbsp. olive oil
1 tbsp. chopped fresh thyme leaves, plus whole leaves for garnish
½ tsp. *each* kosher salt and pepper
1 sheet good-quality frozen puff pastry*, such as Dufour
    (one 14-oz. pkg.), thawed
4 to 5 oz. good-quality anchovies, drained and blotted
    with paper towels
About ½ cup pitted Niçoise olives

1. Cook onions in oil in a large nonstick frying pan over medium heat, stirring often, until soft, 8 to 10 minutes. Reduce heat to low and cook, stirring occasionally, until onions are very limp and deep golden brown, about 45 minutes longer. Stir in chopped thyme, salt, and pepper and let cool.

2. Preheat oven to 400°. Cover a large baking sheet with parchment paper and spread puff pastry over it. Bake until puffed and golden brown, 18 to 20 minutes.

3. Spread onion mixture over pastry, leaving a thin border (toppings will deflate pastry).

4. Arrange anchovies in a grid of squares over onions and set an olive in the middle of each square. Bake until pastry is well browned, 10 to 15 minutes longer. Sprinkle with whole thyme leaves.

5. Slide tart onto a board and cut into squares. Serve warm or at room temperature.

*Puff-pastry packages vary. Pepperidge Farm's 17.3-oz. package contains 2 sheets; if using, spread the sheets on separate baking sheets and parbake 12 to 15 minutes, then divide toppings between the two and bake 10 to 12 minutes longer.

PER SERVING 258 CAL., 53% (138 CAL.) FROM FAT; 7.5 G PROTEIN; 15 G FAT (3.5 G SAT.); 22 G CARBO (2.2 G FIBER); 795 MG SODIUM; 11 MG CHOL.

VARIATION: TUNA AND ROASTED RED PEPPER PISSALADIÈRE

Follow directions for Pissaladière through step 3. Instead of anchovies, arrange **roasted red peppers** (1½ 8-oz. jars, drained and cut into strips) in a grid of squares over onions, add 2 pitted **Niçoise olives** to each square, and sprinkle with drained **capers** (2 tbsp. total). Bake as directed. Flake a little good-quality canned **tuna in olive oil** into each square (4 oz. total).

PER SERVING 261 CAL., 52% (136 CAL.) FROM FAT; 7 G PROTEIN; 15 G FAT (3.4 G SAT.); 24 G CARBO (2.5 G FIBER); 541 MG SODIUM; 3.1 MG CHOL.

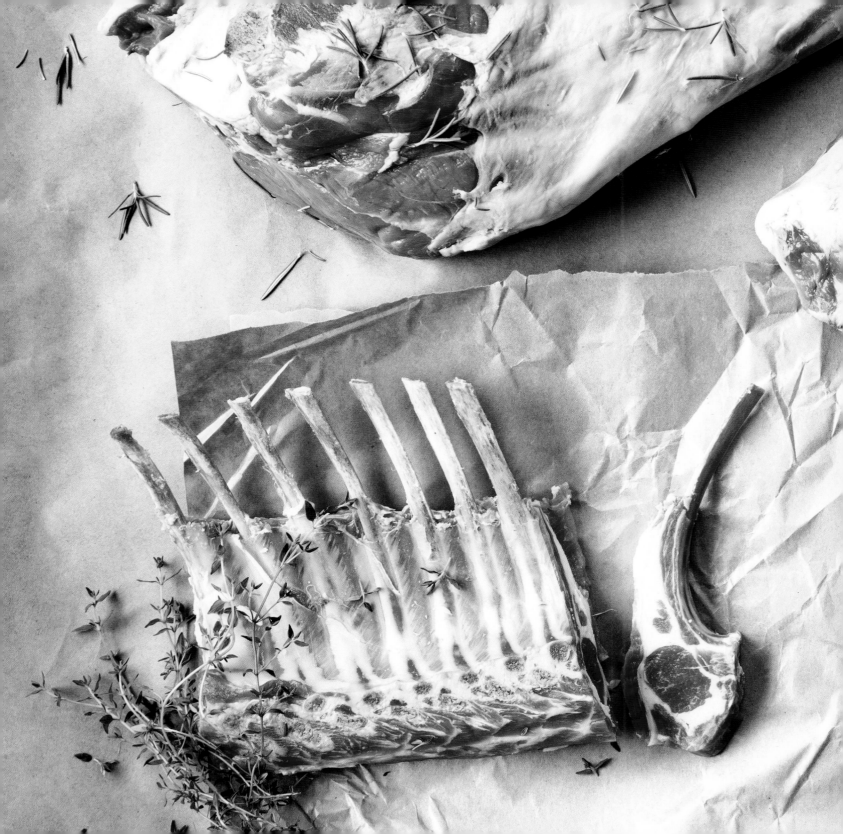

LAMB

LAMB

When it comes to meat, one of the most delicious options is mild-flavored local lamb. Ranches from California to Colorado and Idaho are raising animals sustainably while increasing the visibility of this underappreciated meat.

And local lamb means freshness: American lamb meat arrives at the butcher's counter within days of processing and will have traveled, according to one study, an average of at least 10,000 fewer miles than lamb imported from other countries. Lamb is naturally lean and is a good source of protein, niacin, zinc, and iron.

SEASONAL AVAILABILITY Traditionally, lamb was a seasonal treat, served as a sign of renewal and rebirth—which is why very young or "spring lamb" is often featured on Easter menus. Lamb is technically defined as meat from a sheep less than one year old (meat from older sheep is considered mutton) and is found in the marketplace all year long.

SELECTING AND STORING If the meat is labeled "natural," it has been minimally processed without artificial ingredients, but that label is confusing because technically all fresh meat could be considered "natural." A "certified organic" sticker means the lamb was raised according to strict USDA standards, without hormones or antibiotics and on organic feed and pasture. A "grass-fed"

label is the rancher's indication that the lamb grazed on at least a partial diet of grasses; if it says "100% grass-fed," the lamb was not finished for market on any grain products or corn. Because there are differences in flavor, it's worthwhile to try the different types of lamb to decide which you prefer. While you might splurge on a rack of lamb to roast for a special dinner, there are less expensive cuts to use, such as leg, shoulder, shanks, and ground lamb. Refrigerate lamb as soon as possible, and use large cuts such as chops, loin, and roasts within three to five days and ground lamb within a day. If the meat is well wrapped and frozen, it keeps up to three months in the freezer.

USING We find that lamb is just as versatile as beef—we love it grilled, roasted, seared, stewed, and rolled into meatballs—and it goes well with a range of savory seasonings from the Middle East, the Mediterranean, and India. Ground lamb is a great alternative to ground beef and makes fantastic burgers. For moist, juicy results, cook lamb just until it is barely pink in the center.

Spiced lamb chops with rosemary crumbs

SERVES 10 | **TIME** 30 minutes, plus at least 1 hour to marinate

Small rib chops are ideal for cocktail parties because you can eat them one-handed.

2 frenched racks of lamb (about 2½ lbs. total), cut between the bones into chops
3 tbsp. olive oil
1 large garlic clove, minced
½ tsp. *each* **ground cumin and coriander**
1 tsp. kosher salt, divided
1 tsp. chopped fresh rosemary, divided
½ cup plain or garlic croutons
1 tsp. lemon zest

1. Put lamb in a large bowl. Add oil, garlic, spices, ½ tsp. *each* salt and rosemary; toss to coat evenly. Chill, covered, at least 1 hour and up to 1 day ahead.

2. In a food processor, pulse croutons, zest, and remaining ½ tsp. *each* salt and rosemary into coarse crumbs.

3. Heat grill to high (450° to 550°). Grill lamb, turning over once, 6 to 8 minutes for medium-rare. Sprinkle with crumb mixture.

PER CHOP 146 CAL., 54% (79 CAL.) FROM FAT; 15 G PROTEIN; 8.8 G FAT (2.2 G SAT.); 1.3 G CARBO (0.2 G FIBER); 203 MG SODIUM; 45 MG CHOL.

Lamb blade chops with olive parsley salad

SERVES 4 | **TIME** 40 minutes

A simple, Mediterranean-style salsa tops these grilled chops. Look for preserved lemons at well-stocked grocery stores or make your own (see page 279). Serve this dish with roasted or grilled potatoes if you like.

4 lamb blade chops (½ to ¾ in. thick; about 2 lbs.)
½ tsp. *each* **kosher salt and pepper**
6 tbsp. extra-virgin olive oil, divided
1 tsp. lemon zest
2 garlic cloves, finely minced

Lamb blade chops with olive parsley salad

¾ cup pitted briny green olives, very coarsely chopped
1 cup flat-leaf parsley, very coarsely chopped
4 tsp. minced preserved lemon

1. Heat grill to medium-high (450°). Trim any hard fat from the outside of each lamb chop and season on both sides with salt and pepper. In a small bowl, mix 2 tbsp. oil, the zest, and garlic; slather mixture on both sides of chops.

2. In another small bowl, stir together olives, parsley, preserved lemon, and remaining 4 tbsp. oil.

3. Grill chops 4 minutes, then turn over and grill 2 to 3 minutes more for medium-rare. Transfer to a plate, tent with foil, and let rest 5 minutes. Serve each chop topped with a spoonful of olive parsley salad.

PER SERVING 656 CAL., 73% (480 CAL.) FROM FAT; 40 G PROTEIN; 53 G FAT (15 G SAT.); 2.9 G CARBO (0.8 G FIBER); 697 MG SODIUM; 157 MG CHOL.

Moroccan spiced lamb meatballs

SERVES 6 | **TIME** 1¼ hours

For authentic flavor, chef Dan Petrie, owner of Mise en Place, a San Francisco–based cooking-party business, seasons these appetizers with *ras el hanout*, a Moroccan spice mix available at well-stocked grocery or gourmet stores. He also advises using a razor-sharp grater, such as a Microplane, to speedily shred the ginger and garlic; if you don't have one, mince those seasonings into a paste. To make your own yogurt, see page 278.

Dipping sauce
1½ cups (14 oz.) low-fat Greek yogurt
Zest of 1 lemon
1 tbsp. *each* finely chopped fresh mint leaves and extra-virgin olive oil
½ tsp. *each* kosher salt and finely grated or minced garlic

Meatballs
2 tbsp. finely grated or minced fresh ginger
1 tbsp. finely grated or minced garlic
1 tbsp. *ras el hanout*
1 tsp. *each* salt and pepper
1½ lbs. ground lamb
½ lb. ground beef chuck
1 tbsp. olive oil or canola oil
Mint sprigs

1. Make dipping sauce: In a small bowl, stir yogurt with zest, mint, oil, salt, and garlic. Cover and chill until ready to serve.

2. Make meatballs: In a large bowl, combine ginger, garlic, *ras el hanout*, salt, and pepper. Add lamb and beef and gently mix just until seasonings are distributed.

3. Roll meat gently in your palms to form 1½-in. balls; set on a rimmed baking sheet.

4. Preheat oven to 200°. Line another rimmed baking sheet with paper towels and put it and a heatproof serving bowl in the oven to keep warm. Heat a 12-in. frying pan over medium heat. Add oil and swirl to coat. Brown meatballs in 2 batches on all sides, 10 to 12 minutes for medium-rare. Transfer meatballs to the paper towel–lined pan.

5. Transfer meatballs to the warm serving bowl, garnish with mint sprigs, and serve with yogurt dipping sauce.

Make ahead Through step 2 up to 1 day, wrapped and chilled (their texture will be a little softer than if just made).

PER SERVING 383 CAL., 61% (234 CAL.) FROM FAT; 30 G PROTEIN; 26 G FAT (9.7 G SAT.); 6 G CARBO (0.3 G FIBER); 616 MG SODIUM; 102 MG CHOL.

Harissa lamb with lemon mint chickpea salad

SERVES 4 | **TIME** 30 minutes

We cut the lamb into small pieces so it cooks quickly and so each one has some of the flavorful *harissa* crust when sliced.

¼ cup *harissa**
1 large garlic clove, minced
½ cup extra-virgin olive oil, divided
1 lb. bottom roast
2 cans (about 14.5 oz. each) chickpeas (garbanzos), drained and rinsed
⅔ cup fresh mint leaves
Zest of 1 lemon, thinly sliced
2 tbsp. lemon juice
½ tsp. kosher salt
¼ cup thinly sliced red onion

1. Heat grill to high (450° to 550°). In a small bowl, combine *harissa*, garlic, and ¼ cup oil; set some aside for serving. Cut lamb into 4 pieces, then brush 2 tbsp. of paste over each. Grill lamb, turning and brushing with a little more paste as you go, until done the way you like, about 10 minutes for medium-rare. Let rest 10 minutes, then slice.

2. For salad, mix together chickpeas, mint, zest, juice, salt, onion, and remaining ¼ cup oil. Serve lamb slices over or mixed into chickpea salad, with reserved *harissa* sauce on the side.

*Find in the international aisle of well-stocked grocery stores.

PER SERVING 621 CAL., 64% (395 CAL.) FROM FAT; 32 G PROTEIN; 45 G FAT (12 G SAT.); 22 G CARBO (6.1 G FIBER); 489 MG SODIUM; 99 MG CHOL.

*Harissa lamb
with lemon mint
chickpea salad*

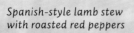

*Spanish-style lamb stew
with roasted red peppers*

Spanish-style lamb stew with roasted red peppers

SERVES 6 | **TIME** 2¼ to 2½ hours

We were inspired by the lamb stews at Basque restaurants in towns like Bakersfield, California, in creating this recipe. Catering to Basque immigrants who had gravitated to Idaho, Nevada, and California to work as sheepherders, these restaurants date to the turn of the last century. To this day, the meals in these places are usually served family-style, with portions ladled out into heaping bowlfuls.

3 lbs. lamb shoulder, fat trimmed and cut into 1½-in. chunks, or other lamb stew meat
Salt and pepper
About 1 tbsp. olive oil
1 medium onion, chopped
2 tbsp. *each* minced garlic and paprika
2 tsp. ground cumin
1 cup Syrah or other dry red wine
About 1½ cups reduced-sodium beef broth
3 tbsp. tomato paste
3 red bell peppers, halved, stemmed, and seeded
¼ cup chopped flat-leaf parsley
3 tbsp. *each* chopped pitted kalamata olives and chopped drained capers

1. Sprinkle lamb with salt and pepper. Pour 1 tbsp. olive oil into a large pot over medium-high heat. Working in batches, add lamb in a single layer; cook, turning as needed, until browned all over, 12 minutes per batch. Transfer to a bowl and add more oil between batches if necessary.

2. Reduce heat to medium; if pan is dry, add a little more oil. Add onion and cook, stirring occasionally, until soft, 5 minutes. Add garlic, paprika, and cumin; cook until fragrant, 2 minutes. Add wine, 1½ cups broth, and the tomato paste; bring to a boil, stirring to scrape up browned bits. Add lamb and juices; cover and simmer, stirring occasionally, until lamb is very tender when pierced, 1½ to 1¾ hours. Add more broth if mixture gets too dry.

3. Meanwhile, preheat broiler with oven rack 4 to 6 in. from heat. Set pepper halves skin side up on a baking sheet. Broil until blackened all over, about 8 minutes. Remove from oven and let stand at least 10 minutes, then peel and thinly slice lengthwise. In a small bowl, mix parsley, olives, and capers.

4. Stir roasted peppers into lamb mixture. If stew is too thick, add a little more broth. Cook, uncovered, until heated through. Season to taste with salt and pepper and top with parsley mixture.

PER SERVING 352 CAL., 43% (153 CAL.) FROM FAT; 39 G PROTEIN; 17 G FAT (5 G SAT.); 11 G CARBO (1.7 G FIBER); 578 MG SODIUM; 123 MG CHOL.

Charmoula lamb

SERVES 4 | **TIME** 30 minutes, plus at least 1 hour to marinate

Sometimes called the "pesto" of North Africa, charmoula is a blend of oil, herbs, and spices that is slathered on meat and fish. Its robust flavors really complement grilled foods, like these lamb kebabs.

⅓ cup olive oil
⅓ cup chopped cilantro
2 tbsp. lemon juice
1 tbsp. *each* ground cumin and sweet Hungarian paprika or regular paprika
2 tbsp. minced garlic
1 tsp. salt
½ tsp. pepper
1 lb. boned leg of lamb cut into 1½-in. chunks

1. Combine olive oil, cilantro, juice, cumin, paprika, garlic, salt, and pepper in a large bowl. Add lamb and mix until coated; chill at least 1 hour and up to 1 day.

2. Thread meat on metal or wooden skewers (soak wooden skewers at least 30 minutes in advance).

3. Prepare a hot charcoal or gas grill. Grill lamb, turning over once, 8 to 10 minutes for medium-rare (cut to test).

PER SERVING 319 CAL., 67% (213 CAL.) FROM FAT; 22 G PROTEIN; 24 G FAT (7.2 G SAT.); 1.9 G CARBO (0.6 G FIBER); 349 MG SODIUM; 79 MG CHOL.

Leg of lamb with figs and lemons

SERVES 8 | **TIME** About 1¾ hours

Is there anything more eye-catching than a roasted whole lamb leg? It's a great centerpiece for a celebratory meal, like a graduation or wedding feast, from late spring through early fall when ripe figs are in season. To make your own chicken broth, see page 276; to make your own crème fraîche, see page 279.

1 leg of lamb (5 to 6 lbs.), fat trimmed
Salt
1 tsp. fresh thyme leaves or dried thyme
4 or 5 rosemary sprigs (each 5 to 6 in. long) or 2 tsp. dried rosemary
12 ripe black figs (about 3 oz. each)
2 lemons (4 oz. each)
About 1 cup dry red wine, divided
2 tbsp. balsamic vinegar
2 tbsp. sugar
About ½ cup fat-skimmed chicken broth
¼ cup whipping cream or crème fraîche

1. Rinse lamb and pat dry. Sprinkle lightly with salt and set in a shallow 10- by 15-in. pan. Pat thyme all over meat; lay rosemary sprigs on the leg.

2. Rinse figs and lemons. Cut figs in half lengthwise through stems and lay, cut side up, around lamb. Trim off and discard ends of lemons, then thinly slice lemons crosswise and discard seeds. Scatter slices over and around figs. Pour about ½ cup wine and the vinegar into pan. Sprinkle fruit with sugar.

3. Bake in a 400° oven until an instant-read thermometer inserted through thickest part of meat to the bone reaches 130°, about 1½ hours. As liquid evaporates, add more wine to pan to prevent scorching. Occasionally, turn fruit gently. The edges of the pieces should get dark; if fruit starts to scorch, remove from pan.

4. Transfer roast and fruit to a platter and keep warm. Discard rosemary sprigs. Add enough broth to pan to make about ¾ cup total juices, then add cream. Bring to a rolling boil over high heat, stirring to release browned bits. Pour into a small bowl or pitcher.

5. Slice lamb and serve meat and fruit with pan juices. Season to taste with salt.

PER SERVING 313 CAL., 37% (117 CAL.) FROM FAT; 40 G PROTEIN; 13 G FAT (5.2 G SAT.); 9.1 G CARBO (1.7 G FIBER); 103 MG SODIUM; 130 MG CHOL.

Lamb burger pitas with two-pepper chutney

SERVES 4 | **TIME** 30 minutes

Using lamb instead of beef, pita bread instead of a bun, and chopped peppers as a condiment rather than ketchup, reader Susie Dahl, of Ojai, California, takes the grilled burger concept to a whole new level.

1 large red bell pepper, coarsely chopped
½ cup lightly packed mint leaves
2 tbsp. lemon juice
1 garlic clove
1 tsp. cayenne
2 tsp. pepper, divided
1 tsp. salt, divided
1 lb. ground lamb
½ cup chopped cilantro
1 tsp. *each* ground coriander and ground cumin
2 pita breads (6 in. wide), halved
Lettuce leaves

1. Heat grill to medium (350° to 450°). Put bell pepper, mint, lemon juice, garlic, cayenne, 1 tsp. pepper, and ½ tsp. salt into a food processor and pulse just until coarsely chopped. Set chutney aside.

2. Combine lamb, cilantro, remaining 1 tsp. pepper and ½ tsp. salt, the coriander, and cumin in a medium bowl until blended. Form into 4 patties, each about ½ in. thick.

3. Lightly oil grill and cook burgers, turning over once, until done the way you like, about 6 minutes total for medium. Cut burgers in half and put 2 halves into each pita piece, then tuck in lettuce leaves. Serve chutney on the side.

PER SERVING 361 CAL., 50% (180 CAL.) FROM FAT; 23 G PROTEIN; 20 G FAT (6.9 G SAT.); 22 G CARBO (3 G FIBER); 816 MG SODIUM; 76 MG CHOL.

Lamb burger pitas with two-pepper chutney

Lamb shoulder roast with roasted garlic sauce

Lamb shoulder roast with roasted garlic sauce

SERVES 8 | **TIME** 2¼ hours

Garlic lovers, gather round: This is a recipe for you. First, rub the meat with an aromatic herb and garlic oil, then roast it with lots more garlic to season the pan gravy. Even folks in Gilroy, California, the garlic capital of the West, would be impressed.

5 garlic cloves, peeled, plus 1 whole head
Zest of 2 lemons
½ cup fresh marjoram leaves, divided, plus sprigs for garnish
1 tsp. *each* kosher salt and pepper
3 tbsp. olive oil
1 boned lamb shoulder roast or boned leg of lamb (about 4 lbs.)
About 2½ cups reduced-sodium chicken broth
4 tsp. cornstarch

1. Preheat oven to 450°. In a food processor, whirl garlic cloves, zest, ⅓ cup marjoram leaves, and 1 tsp. *each* salt and pepper until minced. Blend in oil.

2. Remove any ties from lamb and open it up in a rimmed baking pan. Trim fat (leave a thin layer on the outside). Smear meat all over with marjoram mixture. Using kitchen twine, tie lamb crosswise at about 1½-in. intervals and lengthwise once or twice to form a neat roast. Set in pan fat side up.

3. Roast lamb until browned, 20 to 25 minutes. Meanwhile, cut garlic head in half crosswise, set cut sides down on an oiled piece of foil, and seal foil into a package.

4. Reduce heat to 300°; set garlic next to meat in pan and bake until very soft when squeezed, 50 to 60 minutes; stir ½ to 1 cup broth into drippings if needed to prevent scorching. Let garlic cool. Cook meat until an instant-read thermometer inserted in thickest part reaches 130° for medium-rare.

5. Transfer lamb to a cutting board (save pan drippings for sauce); tent with foil.

6. Squeeze garlic from peels into a blender. Stir cornstarch with 1½ cups broth until smooth; whisk into drippings, then purée in blender. Heat sauce in a pan, stirring, until boiling. Mince remaining marjoram leaves and stir into sauce. Pour into a gravy boat.

7. Snip twine from lamb, then cut thickly crosswise. Spoon some sauce on top and garnish with marjoram sprigs. Serve remaining sauce on the side.

PER SERVING 682 CAL., 63% (432 CAL.) FROM FAT; 54 G PROTEIN; 48 G FAT (19 G SAT.); 5.5 G CARBO (0.7 G FIBER); 412 MG SODIUM; 206 MG CHOL.

Spring lamb loin roasted with mint and garlic

SERVES 8 | **TIME** 1 hour

Chef Chris Cosentino, of San Francisco's Incanto restaurant, uses slender lamb loins and offers small plates of this recipe (see photo on page 13). The meat is amazingly tender and delicate but it can be expensive, so this is a good choice for a special occasion.

Anchovy butter
½ cup unsalted butter, at room temperature
½ cup minced yellow onion
1 salt-packed anchovy, rinsed and minced
3 tbsp. chopped mint leaves
Zest of 1 lemon
½ tsp. *each* sea salt and pepper

Lamb
2 tbsp. olive oil
2 boned lamb loins (4 lbs. total)
1 garlic head, cut in half crosswise
1 bunch mint, ends trimmed

1. Make anchovy butter: Put ingredients into bowl of a mixer and beat until smooth.

2. Prepare lamb: Preheat oven to 425°. Heat a large cast-iron frying pan over high heat until very hot. Add oil and swirl pan to coat. Put lamb in center of pan. Put garlic halves on either side of lamb, cut sides up, and lay mint over garlic. Cook lamb, turning over once, until well browned, about 4 minutes on each side. Put pan with lamb in oven; roast until an instant-read thermometer reaches 125°, 12 to 14 minutes for medium-rare.

3. Transfer lamb to a cutting board and tent with foil. Let rest 10 minutes before slicing. Serve with mint and garlic on the side and a dollop of anchovy butter on the warm lamb slices.

PER SERVING 647 CAL., 70% (456 CAL.) FROM FAT; 41 G PROTEIN; 51 G FAT (23 G SAT.); 4.7 G CARBO (0.8 G FIBER); 227 MG SODIUM; 189 MG CHOL.

Lamb stew with green chiles, cilantro, and peas

SERVES 4 to 6 | **TIME** About 4 hours

Niloufer Ichaporia King, the San Francisco–based author of *My Bombay Kitchen: Traditional and Modern Parsi Home Cooking*, shared this updated version of an old Parsi favorite with us. The Western touches are to use leeks instead of regular onions and to cook the peas for less time than is traditional. Fresh peas taste better, but if you use frozen, rinse off the ice crystals and add the peas right at the end. Serve the stew with quick-cooked pea shoots and small roasted potatoes if you like.

4 lamb shanks, sawed in halves or thirds by a butcher
1 tsp. finely shredded ginger (from about a 1-in. piece)
2 large garlic cloves, minced and mashed
    to a paste with ½ tsp. kosher salt
4 small leeks, white and pale green parts only,
    coarsely chopped (3 to 4 cups)
3 tbsp. vegetable oil
2 or 3 fresh green arbol, Thai, or serrano chiles,
    stems on and slit lengthwise
1 tsp. cumin seeds
About 1 tsp. kosher salt
Pinch of turmeric (optional)
2½ cups coarsely chopped cilantro, divided
2 cups freshly shelled peas (about 2 lbs. in the pod)

1. Trim the meat of as much fat and sinew as possible. Mix ginger and garlic paste together; rub onto meat and let the meat sit at room temperature at least 30 minutes.

2. Clean leeks (see page 94) and put in a colander to drain.

3. Heat oil in a deep, heavy 12-in. pot or a 12-in. frying pan with sides at least 2 in. high over medium-high heat. Add chiles. When they start to look blistered, add cumin seeds; stir for a few seconds, then add the leeks.

4. Lower heat to medium and cook, stirring occasionally, until leeks soften, about 10 minutes. Push leek mixture to the side and add meat, tossing it constantly so that it changes color without burning or sticking to the pan. Add splashes of water as necessary to keep from sticking.

5. Pour in about 7 cups water (or enough to almost cover the lamb). Add 1 tsp. salt, the turmeric, if using, and 2 cups cilantro. Bring to a boil, reduce heat to maintain a simmer, cover, and let meat cook until it's meltingly tender but not in shreds, 1½ to 2 hours. Season to taste with salt and skim excess fat from the gravy.

6. Transfer shanks to a plate and bring gravy to a boil just before serving. Cook until reduced by half, about 20 minutes. Return shanks to pan, add peas, cover, and cook until warmed through, about 5 minutes. Stir in remaining ½ cup cilantro and serve.

Make ahead Up to 2 days, chilled (chilling makes skimming the excess fat easier); add the peas just before serving.

PER SERVING 217 CAL., 39% (84 CAL.) FROM FAT; 17 G PROTEIN; 9.3 G FAT (1.6 G SAT.); 17 G CARBO (3.3 G FIBER); 392 MG SODIUM; 43 MG CHOL.

Using cilantro

Fresh cilantro (sometimes referred to as Chinese parsley) is used extensively to prepare Latin, Asian, Indian, and other dishes. The leaves come from the same plant that produces coriander seeds—hence its other name, fresh coriander. Always use fresh leaves, rather than dried, as they lose flavor quickly once cut. The stems are edible and can be finely chopped and added to longer-cooking recipes. The leaves are often sprinkled over a dish at the end for both flavor and color or as a garnish.

Lamb stew with green chiles, cilantro, and peas

CHICKEN

CHICKEN

This universally loved ingredient is as popular on the Western table as it is elsewhere in the U.S. (it is the number one meat consumed by Americans).

Chicken can go into endless preparations and can pair up with dynamite flavors, from Latin to Asian to Moroccan to all-American. Chicken quality and flavor can vary, mainly based on how the chickens were raised, fed, and processed.

SEASONAL AVAILABILITY We cook with chicken all the time and that's partly because it is available at grocery stores all year. Find free-range, organic chicken at farmers' markets and specialty-foods stores.

SELECTING AND STORING Being aware of a few labeling terms may help you select the chicken you want. The USDA requires all chickens to be raised without growth hormones, and no additives are allowed on fresh chicken. According to the USDA, *free range* means the chicken was allowed access to the outdoors, while *organic* indicates the chicken ate organically produced feed, was allowed access to pasture, and was not given antibiotics (vaccinations are allowed). You might see *air chilled* on the label: Some producers use air to chill chickens during processing

rather than submerging them in a chlorinated water bath. The safest way to store chicken is to keep it cold at all times, so shop for chicken last so it is at room temperature only a short time. Refrigerate chicken in its package until you use it, and cook fresh chicken within two days of purchase. You can freeze a whole chicken for up to one year, parts for about nine months, and ground chicken for up to four months.

USING Unlike the chicken-and-egg dilemma, what comes first with chicken is knowing how you are going to prepare it. If the dish you want to make is a slow-simmered braise, use succulent legs or thighs. If it's a quick sauté or grilled dish, boneless breasts are the way to go. For a fun appetizer, how about some wings? For a quick weeknight meal, ground chicken or that reliable deli roast chicken may be the solution. For a Sunday supper or celebration dinner, nothing beats a golden, crackling whole-roasted bird. We can think of a thousand uses for chicken, but here we offer a few favorites.

Margarita chicken wings

SERVES 4 to 6 | **TIME** 25 minutes, plus at least 3 hours to marinate

Apply the flavors of a Western classic—margaritas—to chicken wings and you get an appetizer that is tangy, salty, and very addictive. By separating each wing into two parts, you have a more manageable size. The marinade can also be used to jazz up flank steak, pork, and chicken thighs for grilling.

Margarita Marinade (recipe follows)
10 chicken wings (about 2 lbs.)
Lime wedges

1. Make the marinade. Then, rinse wings, pat dry, and cut apart at joints. Put in a resealable plastic bag with marinade. Seal and refrigerate, turning occasionally, at least 3 hours and up to overnight. Remove wings; reserve marinade.

2. Preheat oven to 500°. Line a large baking pan with aluminum foil and coat lightly with oil. Arrange wings skin side up and brush with reserved marinade.

3. Bake wings until golden brown, about 10 minutes. Turn wings over, brush with marinade, and bake 5 to 6 minutes more. Turn wings over once more, brush with marinade, and bake until skin is brown and glossy, 2 to 4 minutes. Serve warm, with lime wedges.

PER SERVING 246 CAL., 41% (100 CAL.) FROM FAT; 15 G PROTEIN; 11 G FAT (3.1 G SAT.); 4.9 G CARBO (0 G FIBER); 373 MG SODIUM; 48 MG CHOL.

MARGARITA MARINADE

MAKES 1¾ cups (enough for 2 lbs. chicken wings)

¾ cup *each* **tequila and triple sec**
¼ cup lime juice
2 tsp. coarse kosher salt (see "Kosher Salt 101," right)

In a bowl, whisk together tequila and triple sec. Add lime juice and salt and stir until salt dissolves.

Margarita chicken wings

Kosher salt 101

One of the best all-purpose seasonings for your kitchen is kosher salt, which is specially milled for "koshering" (purifying) food, but favored by many cooks for everyday use at home. Its clean taste and flaky texture make it great for pinching up from a ramekin to add to marinades, vinaigrettes, or just about anything you are cooking and for crusting the rim of a margarita glass.

Greek chicken pasta

SERVES 4 to 6 | **TIME** 30 minutes

Rotisserie chicken is one of the best kitchen secrets around: We use it in sandwiches, soups, tacos, and this easy pasta from reader Erin Tragert, of South Lake Tahoe, California. Use good-quality feta, preferably not already crumbled. With so few ingredients, each needs to pull its weight, and here it's the cheese that makes this dish shine.

6 oz. spaghetti
3 tbsp. olive oil
1 cup chopped onion
1 tbsp. minced garlic
8 oz. baby spinach
½ cup dry white wine, such as Pinot Grigio
½ tsp. red chile flakes
1 cup pitted kalamata olives, halved
1 cup toasted pine nuts (see "Toasting Nuts," page 224)
½ tsp. *each* kosher salt and pepper
2 cups shredded rotisserie chicken
3 oz. feta cheese, crumbled

1. Cook spaghetti as package directs.

2. Meanwhile, heat oil in a large frying pan over medium heat. Add onion and garlic and cook until softened, about 5 minutes. Stir in spinach, wine, chile flakes, olives, nuts, salt, and pepper.

3. Drain pasta, return to pot, and add the onion mixture and chicken. Stir to coat and cook over medium heat until warmed, about 4 minutes. Transfer to plates and top with cheese.

PER SERVING 538 CAL., 58% (312 CAL.) FROM FAT; 22 G PROTEIN; 35 G FAT (5.9 G SAT.); 35 G CARBO (4.3 G FIBER); 940 MG SODIUM; 56 MG CHOL.

Rainbow carrot, pea shoot, and chicken salad

SERVES 6 | **TIME** 1¼ hours

In carrot bunches sold as "rainbow," each color is actually a different variety, but they've been grown together. For the most beautiful salad, use carrots that are a mix of sizes and colors from light to dark. Slicing them is fastest on a classic French- or Japanese-style mandoline, but you can also use a vegetable peeler.

1½ lbs. rainbow carrots (preferably a mix of long and
    short ones)
4 oz. pea shoots*
2 cups sugar snap peas
⅓ cup extra-virgin olive oil
¼ cup Meyer lemon juice
1 large garlic clove, minced
About ½ tsp. kosher salt
¼ tsp. pepper
1 cup crumbled sheep's- or goat's-milk feta cheese
¾ cup mint leaves, cut into slivers
3 cups shredded cooked chicken

1. Scrub carrots gently (so you don't lose the bright outer color), using a brush under running water. With a mandoline or vegetable peeler, cut thin lengthwise ribbons to make 1 qt.; discard ends and tough cores.

2. Put dark and light carrot ribbons in separate bowls of ice water and soak about 15 minutes to crisp. Drain, roll in kitchen towels, and pat dry.

3. Discard tough or thick stems from pea shoots and tear sprigs into 4- to 5-in. pieces. Pull strings from straight sides of snap peas, then thinly slice peas lengthwise. In a large bowl, whisk oil, lemon juice, garlic, ½ tsp. salt, and the pepper.

4. Add carrots, pea shoots, snap peas, feta, mint, and chicken to bowl and toss gently. Season to taste with salt.

*Find at farmers' markets and Asian markets.

PER SERVING 395 CAL., 51% (202 CAL.) FROM FAT; 28 G PROTEIN; 23 G FAT (7 G SAT.); 22 G CARBO (4.6 G FIBER); 542 MG SODIUM; 85 MG CHOL.

Rainbow carrot, pea shoot,
and chicken salad

Chicken halves
with artichokes
and garlic

Chicken halves with artichokes and garlic

SERVES 6 | **TIME** 1 hour 15 minutes

Once you've pared the artichoke hearts, this recipe comes together in a snap. Adding a bit of water to the roasting juices creates a garlicky sauce that would be delicious spooned over mashed potatoes or rice.

2 tbsp. olive oil
1 chicken (4 lb.), halved, backbone removed
1½ tsp. kosher salt
6 garlic cloves, unpeeled
5 large artichokes, trimmed (see "Trimming Artichokes, page 20) and quartered
1 cup unpitted green olives
5 flat-leaf parsley sprigs

1. Preheat oven to 375°. Heat oil in a large dutch oven over medium-high heat. Sprinkle chicken all over with salt and lay it in hot oil, skin side down. Cook until browned, about 5 minutes. Turn chicken over and add 1 cup water, the garlic, and artichoke hearts.

2. Roast chicken in oven, uncovered, until cooked through, about 1 hour. Remove from oven, add olives and parsley, and serve.

PER SERVING 454 CAL., 51% (232 CAL.) FROM FAT; 43 G PROTEIN; 26 G FAT (6.3 G SAT.); 13 G CARBO (6.2 G FIBER); 767 MG SODIUM; 127 MG CHOL.

Thai chicken and noodle curry

SERVES 4 to 6 | **TIME** 45 minutes

The secret ingredient in this noodle dish is the curry paste—a complex, medium-hot blend made with lemongrass and chiles. Find it in the Asian foods aisle of well-stocked grocery stores, at Asian markets, or online. If Thai basil isn't available, substitute regular basil.

10 oz. wide rice noodles
2 tsp. vegetable oil
2 tbsp. minced garlic
¼ cup minced shallots
12 oz. boned, skinned chicken breast, thinly sliced crosswise
1½ tbsp. panang curry paste, such as Mae Ploy brand
1 can (14 oz.) coconut milk, divided
1 tbsp. *each* sugar, lime juice, reduced-sodium soy sauce, and Thai or Vietnamese fish sauce
½ cup *each* sliced green onions, cilantro leaves and small sprigs, and Thai basil leaves and small sprigs
1 lime, cut into wedges

1. Bring a medium pot of water to a boil. Add noodles and cook until softened, about 4 minutes. Drain and rinse with cold water. Set aside.

2. Heat oil in a wok or large frying pan over high heat. Add garlic and shallots and cook until fragrant, about 30 seconds. Add chicken, curry paste, and half the coconut milk. Stir well to dissolve paste and boil until liquid is slightly reduced, about 5 minutes. Stir in remaining coconut milk, the sugar, lime juice, soy sauce, and fish sauce, then bring to a boil. Reduce heat and simmer until liquid is slightly thicker, 2 to 3 minutes more.

3. Add noodles, toss to coat, and cook, stirring often, a few minutes until hot. Pour mixture into a serving bowl. Sprinkle with green onions, cilantro, and basil. Serve with lime wedges.

PER SERVING 414 CAL., 38% (159 CAL.) FROM FAT; 14 G PROTEIN; 18 G FAT (13 G SAT.); 50 G CARBO (0.6 G FIBER); 526 MG SODIUM; 36 MG CHOL.

Best brined roast chicken

SERVES 4 to 6 | **TIME** 2¼ hours, plus 8 hours to brine

Brining not only produces a stellar turkey, it delivers the best roast chicken you'll ever make. You have a choice of two schools of seasoning with this recipe: an Asian brine or a Mexican one. If you want to prepare a very small chicken and your butcher doesn't sell that size, try a market that roasts rotisserie birds on-site (they are often small) and ask if you can buy one uncooked. Plan a day ahead for overnight soaking of the bird.

Chinese Star Anise Orange Brine or Mexican Tropical Chile Brine, with accompaniments (recipes follow)
1 chicken (3 to 4½ lbs.), lumps of fat and tail removed, rinsed
About 1 tbsp. peanut or vegetable oil

1. Prepare brine. Put chicken breast-down in brine, weight with a small plate, cover, and chill at least 8 and up to 12 hours.

2. Drain chicken (discard brine) and pat completely dry inside and out. Rub chicken all over with oil, then set breast-up on a V-shaped rack in a 12- by 17-in. roasting pan; tuck wing tips under if you like. Let chicken stand at room temperature 30 minutes. Meanwhile, preheat oven to 400°.

3. Roast until an instant-read thermometer inserted horizontally through thickest part of the breast reaches 160°, 45 to 55 minutes for a smaller bird or 1 to 1¼ hours for a larger one. After 30 minutes, if any areas start to get dark, tent them with foil. Transfer chicken to a warm platter and let stand in a warm place about 10 minutes.

4. Serve chicken with suggested accompaniments.

PER SERVING FOR CHINESE CHICKEN 425 CAL., 52% (223 CAL.) FROM FAT; 43 G PROTEIN; 25 G FAT (6.8 G SAT.); 5.4 G CARBO (0.8 G FIBER); SODIUM N/A; 134 MG CHOL.

PER SERVING FOR MEXICAN CHICKEN 411 CAL., 55% (224 CAL.) FROM FAT; 43 G PROTEIN; 25 G FAT (6.8 G SAT.); 1.9 G CARBO (0.5 G FIBER); SODIUM N/A; 134 MG CHOL.

CHINESE STAR ANISE ORANGE BRINE

1½ cups dry sherry
⅔ cup kosher salt
¼ cup soy sauce
3 tbsp. sugar
1 cup coarsely chopped unpeeled fresh ginger
12 star anise
4 cinnamon sticks (2½ in. long)
2 tbsp. red chile flakes
Zest of 4 oranges or 8 tangerines
2 cups orange juice or tangerine juice

Pour 2½ qts. water into a deep pot. Add all the ingredients except the orange juice. Cover, bring to a boil, then reduce heat and simmer 30 minutes. Nest pot in ice water until cool. Discard cinnamon and stir in juice.

Accompaniments Orange or tangerine slices, sushi rice, and green onions cut into 2-in.-long slivers

MEXICAN TROPICAL CHILE BRINE

⅔ cup kosher salt
10 large garlic cloves, crushed
¼ cup ground ancho chiles
2 tbsp. dried Mexican oregano
Zest of 5 large limes
½ cup lime juice
⅔ cup thawed frozen pineapple juice concentrate

Pour 1 qt. water into a deep pot. Add salt and warm over high heat, stirring, until salt dissolves. Remove from heat and stir in 2 qts. cold water, the garlic, chiles, and oregano. Nest pot in ice water until cool. Stir in remaining ingredients.

Accompaniments Corn or flour tortillas, cilantro sprigs, lime wedges, and chopped white onion

Best brined roast chicken
with Chinese star anise
orange brine

Yogurt-marinated
chicken kebabs
with pearl couscous

Yogurt-marinated chicken kebabs with pearl couscous

SERVES 4 | **TIME** 45 minutes

Reader Margee Berry, of Trout Lake, Washington, uses garam masala, an Indian spice blend, and pearl couscous (see "Pearl Couscous 101," page 255) to give this dish an Eastern outlook. Find both at well-stocked grocery stores. To make your own yogurt, see page 278.

1½ cups plain low-fat yogurt, divided
2 tsp. garam masala
1 tsp. Madras curry powder
2 garlic cloves, minced
1 tsp. plus 1 tbsp. salt, divided
½ tsp. pepper
1½ lbs. boned, skinned chicken breast, cut into 1½-in. pieces
⅓ cup crumbled feta cheese
3 tbsp. minced red onion
1 tsp. lemon zest
2 tbsp. chopped fresh mint, divided
1½ cups pearl couscous
2 tsp. olive oil
2 medium red bell peppers, seeded and cut into 1½-in. pieces

1. Combine 1 cup yogurt, the garam masala, curry powder, garlic, 1 tsp. salt, and the pepper in a large resealable plastic bag. Add chicken, seal bag, and shake to coat. Let marinate 20 minutes at room temperature.

2. Stir together remaining yogurt, the feta, onion, lemon zest, and 1 tbsp. mint in a small bowl; set aside.

3. Bring 2 qts. water to a boil and add 1 tbsp. salt. Add couscous and cook until tender, 12 to 15 minutes. Drain, return to pot, and add olive oil. Cover to keep warm.

4. Heat grill to medium-high (about 450°). Thread chicken and bell pepper onto four 8-in. metal skewers and discard marinade. Grill kebabs, turning over once, until chicken is browned and cooked through, about 10 minutes. Pile couscous on a platter, sprinkle with remaining 1 tbsp. mint, and arrange kebabs around it. Serve with yogurt-feta sauce.

PER SERVING 569 CAL., 14% (77 CAL.) FROM FAT; 55 G PROTEIN; 8.6 G FAT (3.5 G SAT.); 64 G CARBO (3.4 G FIBER); 1,275 MG SODIUM; 114 MG CHOL.

Grilled lemon chicken

SERVES 8 | **TIME** 1 hour

We learned a great trick for this mostly make-ahead dish from Los Angeles chef Brandon Boudet (of Little Dom's and three other L.A. restaurants). He simmers the chicken ahead of time so that all it needs is a few minutes on the grill. Squeeze the soft, juicy grilled lemons over the cooked meat, or cut the lemons into pieces to eat skin and all. To make your own chicken broth, see page 276.

5 cups reduced-sodium chicken broth or beer
1½ tsp. red chile flakes, divided
8 bone-in chicken thighs with skin (3 lbs. total)
2 tbsp. olive oil
1 tsp. kosher salt
2 lemons, cut in half crosswise
Chopped thyme leaves and thyme sprigs

1. Heat grill, ideally charcoal, to medium (about 400°). Meanwhile, bring broth, ½ tsp. chile flakes, and the chicken to a simmer in a 5- to 6-qt. covered pot. Reduce heat and simmer until chicken is barely cooked through at bone, 12 to 15 minutes.

2. Transfer chicken to a bowl (save broth for other uses). Let stand a few minutes, then drain juices. Coat chicken with oil, remaining 1 tsp. chile flakes, and the salt. Coat lemons on cut sides with the oil in bowl.

3. Grill lemons on cut sides until softened and grill chicken, covered, turning over once, until browned, 5 to 10 minutes total; if chicken flares up, move to another spot. Transfer to a platter. Garnish chicken with thyme.

Make ahead Through step 2 up to 1 day, covered and chilled.

PER SERVING 240 CAL., 57% (137 CAL.) FROM FAT; 23 G PROTEIN; 15 G FAT (4.1 G SAT.); 2 G CARBO (0.6 G FIBER); 113 MG SODIUM; 84 MG CHOL.

BLT chicken burgers

SERVES 4 | **TIME** 30 minutes

If you think poultry burgers are dry and bland, these will change your mind. The patties get their moistness from a blend of ground breast (light) and leg (dark) meat that's mixed with cheese and garlic. Use a light hand when forming the burgers and be careful not to overmix.

1 lb. ground chicken, preferably a mixture of ½ white
    and ½ dark meat
½ cup shredded sharp cheddar cheese
⅓ cup grated parmesan cheese
1 tsp. minced garlic
½ tsp. *each* kosher salt and pepper
⅓ cup mayonnaise
¼ cup finely chopped fresh basil
1 tbsp. *each* lemon juice and lemon zest
4 onion kaiser rolls, split
8 strips bacon (about 8 oz. total), cooked until crisp
1 large tomato, thinly sliced
4 leaves romaine lettuce

1. Heat grill to medium (350° to 450°).

2. Meanwhile, in a large bowl, gently mix chicken, cheeses, garlic, salt, and pepper. Form into 4 burgers about ¾ in. thick, making a slight depression with your thumb in the center of each to help keep burgers flat as they cook. Put on a plate, cover, and chill until ready to grill.

3. Whirl mayonnaise, basil, lemon juice, and zest in a blender and refrigerate until ready to use. With a silicone brush or oiled paper towels, lightly oil cooking grate.

4. Grill burgers, covered, turning over once, until browned and no longer pink inside (cut to test), 8 to 10 minutes total. Transfer burgers to a clean plate and place rolls, cut sides down, on grill until lightly browned, 30 seconds.

5. Spread toasted sides of rolls with basil mayonnaise. Set a chicken patty on each roll bottom and top each with 2 strips bacon, a tomato slice, and a lettuce leaf. Cover with roll top.

PER BURGER 670 CAL., 56% (378 CAL.) FROM FAT; 38 G PROTEIN; 42 G FAT (12 G SAT.); 35 G CARBO (2.7 G FIBER); 1,121 MG SODIUM; 138 MG CHOL.

White wine coq au vin

SERVES 4 | **TIME** 45 minutes

Dark, meaty thighs are perfect for this herb-laced version of the classic French stew. To make your own broth, see page 276.

4½ tbsp. flour
¾ tsp. kosher salt, divided
½ tsp. pepper, divided
1 tsp. herbes de Provence
4 slices bacon (¼ lb. total), chopped
1½ lbs. boned, skinned chicken thighs, cut into 1-in. chunks
2 tbsp. olive oil
1½ cups peeled baby carrots
3 stalks celery
1 medium onion
1⅓ cups Chardonnay
2 cups reduced-sodium chicken broth
½ cup lightly packed flat-leaf parsley sprigs
¼ cup lightly packed fresh tarragon sprigs

1. Shake flour with ½ tsp. salt, ¼ tsp. pepper, and the herbes de Provence in a resealable plastic bag; set aside.

2. Cook bacon in a 5- to 6-qt. pan over medium-high heat, stirring occasionally, until browned, 6 to 7 minutes. Meanwhile, shake chicken chunks half at a time in flour to coat.

3. Transfer bacon with a slotted spoon from pan to paper towels. Brown half the chicken in bacon fat, stirring occasionally, 3 to 5 minutes. Transfer to a plate. Repeat with remaining chicken, adding oil to pan. Meanwhile, cut carrots in half lengthwise and cut celery into diagonal slices. Chop onion.

4. Add vegetables to pan with the remaining salt and pepper and cook until onion is golden, about 5 minutes. Meanwhile, in a microwave-safe bowl, microwave wine and broth until steaming, about 3 minutes.

5. Add broth mixture, chicken, and bacon to pan, stirring to loosen browned bits. Cover and bring to a boil over high heat. Reduce heat and simmer until vegetables are tender, about 15 minutes. Meanwhile, coarsely chop parsley and tarragon, then stir them into stew.

PER SERVING 544 CAL., 54% (295 CAL.) FROM FAT; 40 G PROTEIN; 33 G FAT (8.9 G SAT.); 21 G CARBO (3.1 G FIBER); 808 MG SODIUM; 133 MG CHOL.

White wine coq au vin

CRAB

CRAB

Blessed as we are with seafood on the West Coast, it is perhaps Dungeness crab that we look forward to the most. The name Dungeness comes from a small community in Washington state, where the crabs were first harvested and sold commercially in the 1800s.

Today, the crab harvest is big business, with traps set from central California to Alaska and customers eagerly waiting for the first boats to come in. Nothing compares to Dungeness crab's rich, delicate meat in salads, tacos, and crab cakes or savored straight from the shell.

SEASONAL AVAILABILITY While the official start date varies year to year, Dungeness crab is often in season by Thanksgiving and available winter, spring, and through most of the summer as the harvest moves northward into colder waters. The size of crabs fishermen can take from the sea is controlled to ensure a healthy yield year to year.

SELECTING AND STORING Dungeness crabs that you find in the market are generally from a little over 1 pound to 2½ pounds. A cooked, cleaned crab yields about 25 percent of its weight in sweet, juicy meat, or about ½ pound of succulent meat from a 2-pound crab (a single serving is about ⅓ pound). You can buy live crab; crabmeat already picked from the shell; or crab cooked,

cleaned, and cracked by the fishmonger or by you at home (see how-tos on page 190). For the freshest taste, cook live crabs yourself; our tips on page 186 make cooking them easier than you think. Ideally, eat fresh crab the day you buy it. If Dungeness is not available where you live, fresh or frozen meat from other kinds of crab can be substituted in recipes. You can keep freshly cooked crabmeat in the refrigerator up to two days.

USING Many of us on the West Coast rub our hands together in anticipation of our first annual crab feed after crab season opens. We set our table with bowls of cracked crab and the tools we need—claw or nutcrackers for the shells, crab forks or cocktail picks to get at the meat, extra bowls for discards—plus sourdough bread, melted butter or mayonnaise (the traditional accompaniment), Chardonnay, and lots and lots of napkins. It's hard to beat this experience, but we also love crabmeat in dips, soups, sandwiches, salads of all stripes, stews, and pasta dishes.

Crab salad cups

SERVES 8 | **TIME** 30 minutes

Behind the scoreboard at AT&T Park in San Francisco, the Crazy Crab'z stand sells to baseball fans a fresh, light crab salad similar to this one. We dress it up with avocado and parsley and spoon the salad into lettuce cups to make it a finger-friendly hors d'oeuvre.

1 lb. shelled cooked crab (see pages 186 and 190)
½ cup mayonnaise
2 tbsp. chopped flat-leaf parsley
¼ cup minced red onion
1 tsp. sugar
Kosher salt and pepper
16 medium butter lettuce leaves (from about 2 heads)
1 avocado, cut into 16 thin slices (see "Cutting an Avocado Safely," page 47)
2 tsp. prepared cocktail sauce
1 lemon, sliced into small wedges

1. Stir together crab, mayonnaise, parsley, onion, and sugar in a medium bowl until well combined. Season to taste with salt and pepper. Chill until ready to serve.

2. Arrange lettuce on a platter. Place about 2 tbsp. crab mixture onto center of each leaf. Top each with a slice of avocado, about ⅛ tsp. cocktail sauce, a lemon wedge, and salt and pepper to taste.

Make ahead Through step 1 up to 1 day, chilled and covered.

PER SERVING 207 CAL., 70% (144 CAL.) FROM FAT; 13 G PROTEIN; 16 G FAT (2.4 G SAT.); 5.4 G CARBO (1.4 G FIBER); 257 MG SODIUM; 65 MG CHOL.

Warm crab and artichoke dip with French bread

SERVES 8 | **TIME** 25 minutes

Here's a dish that will never go out of style: a warm mayonnaise dip that can be made on the spur of the moment because most of the ingredients are things you have on hand. Reader Patrick Sheridan, of Monterey, California, adds a crunchy topping of sliced almonds to this timeless recipe.

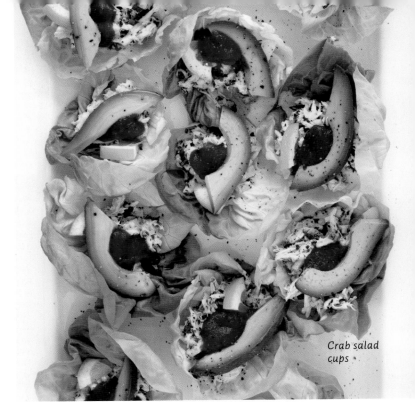

Crab salad cups

½ cup mayonnaise
1 tbsp. lemon juice
8 oz. frozen artichoke hearts, thawed and chopped
8 oz. shelled cooked crab (see pages 186 and 190)
¼ cup grated parmesan cheese
½ tsp. kosher salt
¼ cup sliced almonds
1 baguette (8 to 12 oz.)
4 tsp. olive oil
1 tsp. *each* fresh thyme and oregano leaves

1. Preheat oven to 375°. In a medium bowl, combine mayonnaise, lemon juice, artichokes, crab, parmesan, and salt. Pour into a greased medium gratin dish. Sprinkle with almonds and bake until browned and bubbling, about 15 minutes.

2. Score baguette 1 in. deep across loaf. Combine oil and herbs and brush over loaf, making sure to let oil soak into cuts. Toast in oven on a baking sheet for 5 minutes before serving with dip.

PER SERVING 255 CAL., 37% (95 CAL.) FROM FAT; 13 G PROTEIN; 11 G FAT (1.8 G SAT.); 27 G CARBO (2.9 G FIBER); 624 MG SODIUM; 38 MG CHOL.

Cooking live crabs

For the ultimate flavor and freshness, crabs should be cooked live right out of the water the day you buy them. To clean and crack the crabs, see page 190.

1. Keep live crabs chilled up to 12 hours in an open bowl or box covered with damp paper towels. Fill a large pot with enough water to cover crabs by 2 to 3 in., leaving 3 to 4 in. of clearance below pot rim; bring to a boil.

2. Cut the handles off a sturdy paper bag. If the crabs are wrapped in newspaper or another material, gently unwrap them into the bag, putting in no more than two at a time. If the crabs are loose in a box, use tongs (see photo below left) to lift each one up from the rear between the legs and put in the bag.

3. Hold the bag near the bottom and gently upend it (see photo above right) to let the crabs fall out into the water (avoid using tongs, which don't always keep a steady grip if your crab starts to move); cover the pot. Bring to a boil, lower heat to a simmer, and cook, 15 minutes for 1½- to 2½-lb. crabs, 20 minutes for bigger ones.

4. Lift out the crabs with tongs and rinse with cold running water until cool enough to handle.

Crab tacos

MAKES 8 tacos | **TIME** 40 minutes

Cooks often stuff crabmeat into tortillas and top it with salsa. This recipe by reader Judith S. Liebman came to us all the way from Urbana, Illinois. You can use crisp ready-made taco shells or soft tortillas.

4 Roma tomatoes, halved, seeded, and sliced
1 large garlic clove, minced
2 large jalapeño chiles, halved, seeded, and sliced, divided
½ cup fresh cilantro leaves, divided
3 tbsp. lime juice
Kosher salt and pepper
1 tsp. olive oil
½ cup chopped onion
8 oz. shelled cooked crab (see box at left and page 190)
8 taco shells or tortillas
1 cup Iceberg lettuce, thinly sliced
1 cup shredded jack or cheddar cheese
1 avocado, thinly sliced (see "Cutting an Avocado Safely," page 47)
¼ cup chopped green onion

1. Preheat oven to 350°. Put tomatoes, garlic, half of the jalapeño, ¼ cup cilantro, and the lime juice in a food processor and pulse a few times to chop. Add salt and pepper to taste. Set salsa aside.

2. Heat oil in a large skillet over medium heat. Cook onion and remaining jalapeño until soft, 4 minutes. Add crab and cook just until crab is warm, about 2 minutes.

3. Put taco shells or tortillas on a baking sheet and warm in oven, about 3 minutes. Arrange on a platter and fill with crab mixture, dividing evenly. Top crab with lettuce, cheese, and avocado. Sprinkle the tacos with green onion and the remaining ¼ cup cilantro. Serve with salsa on the side or on top.

PER TACO 200 CAL., 54% (108 CAL.) FROM FAT; 11 G PROTEIN; 12 G FAT (3.8 G SAT.); 13 G CARBO (1.7 G FIBER); 210 MG SODIUM; 43 MG CHOL.

Crab tacos

California crab sandwich

California crab sandwich

SERVES 4 | **TIME** 20 minutes

Sometimes the best way to indulge in fresh crabmeat is the simplest: Throw some on a sandwich with avocado and cream cheese, as does reader Tom Trapani, of Millbrae, California.

12 oz. shelled cooked crab (see pages 186 and 190)
4 oz. cream cheese, softened
2 tbsp. mayonnaise
3 green onions, chopped
1 tbsp. lemon juice
¼ tsp. *each* **kosher salt, pepper, and cayenne**
8 slices sourdough sandwich bread, toasted
1 avocado, sliced (see "Cutting an Avocado Safely," page 47)
1 cup alfalfa sprouts

1. Mix crab, cream cheese, mayonnaise, onions, lemon juice, salt, pepper, and cayenne in a bowl.

2. Spoon mixture onto 4 slices of toast. Top each with some avocado and sprouts and another slice of toast and cut in half.

PER SANDWICH 547 CAL., 39% (213 CAL.) FROM FAT; 30 G PROTEIN; 24 G FAT (8.1 G SAT.); 53 G CARBO (5.9 G FIBER); 1,003 MG SODIUM; 98 MG CHOL.

Panko-crusted crab cake bites with roasted pepper–chive aioli

SERVES 8 (makes 24) | **TIME** 35 to 40 minutes

What makes the perfect crab cake? A careful hand. Don't overmix the ingredients or pack them down when shaping the patties.

12 oz. shelled cooked crab (see pages 186 and 190)
¼ cup finely diced celery
¼ cup minced fresh chives
¼ cup mayonnaise
1 large egg
2 tsp. Dijon mustard
¼ tsp. hot sauce
1¼ cups *panko* **or fine dried bread crumbs, divided**
Roasted Pepper–Chive Aioli (recipe follows)
Fresh chives, rinsed and cut into 1-in. lengths

1. Preheat oven to 475°. Sort through crab and discard any bits of shell.

2. Combine celery, minced chives, mayonnaise, egg, mustard, and hot sauce in a large bowl; mix well with a fork. Add crab and ¼ cup *panko*; stir gently just to mix.

3. Put remaining 1 cup *panko* in a shallow bowl. Shape crab mixture into 24 cakes, each about 2 in. wide and ½ in. thick. Turn each cake in *panko* to coat on all sides, pressing gently to make crumbs adhere. Place cakes slightly apart in an oiled 12- by 17-in. baking pan.

4. Bake until golden brown, 15 to 18 minutes. With a spatula, transfer crab cakes to a platter. Spoon a dollop of aioli onto each cake. Garnish platter with fresh chives. Serve hot.

Make ahead Aioli, up to 2 days, covered and chilled; crab cakes, through step 3 up to 4 hours, covered and chilled.

PER SERVING 206 CAL., 61% (126 CAL.) FROM FAT; 11 G PROTEIN; 14 G FAT (2.2 G SAT.); 7.6 G CARBO (0.5 G FIBER); 290 MG SODIUM; 79 MG CHOL.

ROASTED PEPPER–CHIVE AIOLI
Mix together ⅓ cup **mayonnaise**, ¼ cup chopped and drained canned **roasted red peppers**, 1 tbsp. minced fresh **chives**, 2 tsp. **lemon juice**, and 1 tsp. minced **garlic** in a small bowl. Makes about ½ cup.

Panko

Panko are Japanese-style coarse bread crumbs, and they create an extra-crunchy, light crust on fried or baked foods. Cooks love them because they're crispier than regular bread crumbs, and they've jumped from Japanese recipes into all manner of American dishes. Find *panko* in well-stocked supermarkets (in the Asian section or with other bread-crumb products) and in Asian grocery stores.

Cleaning and cracking cooked crabs

1. Put a cooked crab, belly up, on a work surface. Pull off and discard the triangular flap and the pointy appendages underneath it plus the small paddles from front of crab.

2. Pry off the broad back shell. Discard liquid in shell. Scoop out and save the soft, golden "butter" and white fat from shell to eat if you like.

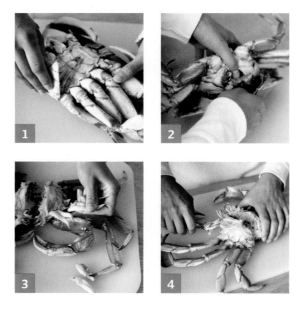

3. Turn crab over. Pull off and discard any reddish membrane. Scoop out any remaining "butter." Pull off the long, spongy gills from sides of body. Rinse body well.

4. Twist legs and claws off body. Using a nutcracker or wooden mallet, crack the shell of each leg and claw section. With a knife, cut body into quarters.

Crab salad on cucumber rounds

SERVES 8 | **TIME** About 35 minutes

Kaffir (also called makrut) lime and lemongrass are the citrusy notes in these Asian-inspired appetizers. Find those ingredients at an Asian market or the produce section of a well-stocked grocery store; kaffir lime leaves are often sold frozen. Or use lime zest as an easy substitute.

1 or 2 stalks fresh lemongrass (each 10 to 12 in. long)
    or 1 tbsp. lemon zest
12 fresh or thawed frozen kaffir lime leaf sections
    (each 1½ to 2 in. long) or 1 tbsp. lime zest
⅓ lb. shelled cooked crab (see page 186 and box at left)
¼ cup thinly slivered shallots
1 tbsp. finely shredded carrot
1 tbsp. *each* chopped fresh cilantro, fresh mint leaves,
    and green onion
2 tbsp. lime juice
1½ tsp. Thai roasted-chili paste
1 tsp. Thai or Vietnamese fish sauce or salt to taste
1 tsp. sugar
About 8 oz. English cucumber

1. Rinse lemongrass. Cut off and discard tough tops and root ends; peel off and discard tough outer green layers of stalks down to tender white parts. Finely chop enough to make ¼ cup.

2. Rinse kaffir lime leaves. Stack three or four leaves at a time and cut crosswise into very fine shreds.

3. Mix lemongrass, lime leaves, crab, shallots, carrot, cilantro, mint, and green onion in a bowl. In a small bowl, mix lime juice, chili paste, fish sauce (but not salt, if using), and sugar.

4. Stir lime juice mixture into crab mixture just before serving. If not using fish sauce, add salt to taste. Rinse cucumber and cut crosswise into about 24 rounds about ¼ in. thick. Top each slice with a scant 1 tbsp. crab mixture.

Make ahead Through step 3 up to 3 hours, crab mixture and lime-juice mixture chilled separately, covered.

PER SERVING 36 CAL., 18% (6.3 CAL.) FROM FAT; 4.4 G PROTEIN; 0.7 G FAT (0.1 G SAT.); 3.1 G CARBO (0.5 G FIBER); 84 MG SODIUM; 19 MG CHOL.

Crab salad on cucumber rounds

Quick crab
stew in fennel-
tomato broth

Quick crab stew in fennel-tomato broth

SERVES 4 | **TIME** 30 minutes

Reminiscent of cioppino, the heart of this easy meal is cooked, cleaned crabs from the fish market or the seafood counter at the grocery store (or to cook, clean, and crack them yourself, see pages 186 and 190). You'll want to have a crispy loaf of bread on hand to dip into the juices and some lemon wedges to garnish each portion.

3 celery stalks, trimmed and cut in half
½ small white onion, quartered
1 small fennel bulb, quartered
1 tbsp. olive oil
1 cup dry white wine
1 can (14 oz.) fire-roasted diced tomatoes
¼ tsp. red chile flakes
½ tsp. kosher salt
½ tsp. pepper
2 cooked crabs (1½ lbs. each), cleaned, cut into quarters
    and shells cracked (see pages 186 and 190)
Handful *each* fresh oregano leaves, flat-leaf parsley leaves,
    and small fennel fronds
1 loaf crusty Italian bread

1. Chop celery, onion, and fennel in a food processor. Heat oil in a large pot over medium heat; add vegetables and cook, stirring often, until softened, about 7 minutes.

2. Add wine, 1 cup water, tomatoes, chile flakes, salt, and pepper. Cook, covered, to let flavors develop, 8 to 10 minutes. Add crabs and cook, covered, stirring often, until warm and fragrant, about 5 minutes.

3. Transfer to a large serving bowl. Chop herbs together in a food processor, then sprinkle over crab and serve with warmed bread.

PER SERVING 364 CAL., 15% (56 CAL.) FROM FAT; 45 G PROTEIN; 6.3 G FAT (0.8 G SAT.); 20 G CARBO (5.1 G FIBER); 1,286 MG SODIUM; 145 MG CHOL.

Crab and hominy chowder

SERVES 4 to 6 (makes 2 qts.) | **TIME** About 30 minutes

Crab and corn are a beloved chowder combination, but there's usually no fresh corn in the market when Dungeness crab is in season. We use hominy instead, giving this soup a satisfying bite and playing up the Southwest vibe of the avocado and cilantro. To make your own chicken broth, see page 276.

3 slices bacon, chopped
1 large leek, white part only, halved lengthwise, thinly sliced,
    and cleaned (see "Cleaning Leeks," page 94)
½ cup dry white wine
2 cups reduced-sodium chicken broth
1 cup hominy, drained and rinsed
12 oz. red thin-skinned potatoes, cut into ½-in. chunks
1 tsp. salt, divided
¼ cup *each* vegetable oil and olive oil
1 cup cilantro, chopped
2 jalapeño chiles, stemmed and seeded
1 garlic clove
1 avocado
1 tsp. lime juice
¼ cup whipping cream
Pepper
8 oz. Dungeness crab, cooked and shelled (see pages 186 and 190)

1. In a 4- to 6-qt. pan over medium-high heat, cook bacon until fat starts to render. Discard all but 1 tsp. fat from pan. Add leek and cook, stirring, until soft. Add wine and boil until almost evaporated. Add broth, 2 cups water, the hominy, potatoes, and ½ tsp. salt. Bring to a boil, then reduce heat and simmer until potatoes are tender when pierced, about 10 minutes.

2. Meanwhile, whirl vegetable oil, olive oil, cilantro, jalapeños, garlic, and remaining ½ tsp. salt in a blender until smooth. Chop avocado (see page 47) and mix with lime juice in a small bowl.

3. Stir whipping cream and salt and pepper to taste into chowder. Add crab; cover and cook until heated through, stirring as little as possible to keep crab intact. Ladle chowder into bowls and top with a spoonful each of cilantro mixture (leftovers can be spread on toast for an easy appetizer) and avocado.

PER SERVING 312 CAL., 61% (190 CAL.) FROM FAT; 12 G PROTEIN; 21 G FAT (4.5 G SAT.); 20 G CARBO (2.6 G FIBER); 681 MG SODIUM; 52 MG CHOL.

Capt'n Bobino's fisherman-style crab

SERVES 4 to 6 | **TIME** 30 minutes

This recipe came from Pete Huckins (aka Capt'n Bobino when on his crab boat), of Mendocino County, California. His version was made with live crabs, while we opt for cooked ones for convenience. However, for the freshest possible flavor and the full crab experience, ask your seafood merchant to clean and crack the live crabs, or cook, clean, and crack them yourself (see pages 186 and 190).

¾ cup butter
¼ cup olive oil
¼ cup minced garlic
1 lb. boned, skinned, firm white-fleshed fish such as halibut, rinsed and cut into 1½-in. pieces
1 cup dry sherry or dry white wine
⅓ cup lemon juice
2 cooked Dungeness crabs (about 2 lb. each), cleaned and cracked
½ cup chopped parsley
Salt and pepper
8 oz. dried angel hair pasta
Lemon wedges
1 baguette (about 8 oz.), sliced

1. Bring 4 qts. water to a boil in a 5- to 6-qt. pan over high heat. Add butter and olive oil to a 12-in. frying pan (with sides at least 2½ in. high) or 14-in. wok over medium-high heat; when butter is melted, add garlic and stir just until fragrant, 1 to 2 minutes. Add fish and turn pieces occasionally until beginning to brown, 2 to 3 minutes.

2. Pour in sherry and lemon juice; gently add crabs. Sprinkle with parsley. Cover and simmer until crabs are hot and fish is opaque but still moist-looking in the center (cut to test), 5 to 6 minutes. Season to taste with salt and pepper.

3. Meanwhile, add pasta to boiling water; cook, stirring occasionally, until barely tender to bite, 3 to 4 minutes. Drain pasta well and spread in the bottom of a wide serving bowl. Pour crab mixture over pasta and garnish with lemon wedges. Serve with baguette slices to sop up the sauce.

PER SERVING 751 CAL., 44% (338 CAL.) FROM FAT; 39 G PROTEIN; 37 G FAT (16 G SAT.); 53 G CARBO (2.3 G FIBER); 723 MG SODIUM; 160 MG CHOL.

Cedar-planked salmon with crab and citrus beurre blanc

SERVES 4 | **TIME** 1 hour 20 minutes

In Washington state, Steve W. Little of Sequim's Dockside Grill pairs the best of the Pacific catch: He roasts salmon and serves it with a crab-laced sauce. Cooking on a cedar plank (find them at cookware stores and online) is actually quite simple as long as you set aside time to soak the wood in water. Make the beurre blanc while the salmon cooks.

4 pieces wild salmon fillet (6 to 8 oz. each and at least 2 in. wide)
1 tbsp. olive oil
2 tbsp. paprika-based BBQ rub
1 tbsp. butter
8 oz. Dungeness crab (ideally claw meat)
Citrus Beurre Blanc (recipe follows)

1. Soak a ½-in.-thick cedar plank in warm water at least 1 hour. Preheat oven to 450°. Rub salmon with oil and BBQ rub, set skin side down on plank, and roast directly on oven rack until almost opaque, 8 to 12 minutes.

2. Melt butter in a medium frying pan over medium-low heat. Add crab and heat until warm. Top each salmon piece with crab and drizzle with beurre blanc.

PER SERVING 592 CAL., 56% (331 CAL.) FROM FAT; 59 G PROTEIN; 37 G FAT (15 G SAT.); 4.2 G CARBO (1.2 G FIBER); 423 MG SODIUM; 227 MG CHOL.

CITRUS BEURRE BLANC

SERVES 4 | **TIME** 15 minutes

In a medium saucepan, whisk together 2½ tbsp. **dry white wine**; 1 tbsp. *each* **lemon**, **lime**, and **orange juices**; 1½ tsp. minced **shallots**; and ¼ cup **heavy cream**. Season to taste with **salt** and **white pepper**. Bring to a boil over medium heat, whisking occasionally, and boil until reduced by half. Reduce heat to low and whisk in 4 tbsp. **butter**, 1 tbsp. at a time. Immediately remove from heat.

*Cedar-planked salmon
with crab and citrus
beurre blanc*

BEER

The story of beer has followed an arc similar to that of chocolate and bread. Immigrants brought recipes and techniques from their homelands, the process was adapted to local ingredients and tastes, and a uniquely American tradition evolved.

A few of these early brewers became mass producers (think Anheuser-Busch), which in turn spawned an artisanal revival, and now there are more breweries in the United States than in any other country, making a wider variety of beers than anywhere else in the world.

Much of the credit for this shift goes to Fritz Maytag, a transplanted Midwesterner who in the mid-1960s bought San Francisco's Anchor Brewing Company and set out to restore beermaking traditions. Slowly but steadily, other small breweries opened in the West about the same time that home beermaking caught on, producing types of beer they could not buy.

TRADITIONAL STYLES

The range of styles in beer is huge (more than 117 in the world, by one estimate), but they fall into two main categories: ales and lagers. In broad terms, the differences between them are a matter of the kind of yeast used and the temperature at which the beer is fermented. Ales are fermented at warmer temperatures, producing rich, fruity aromas and flavors. Lagers are fermented at cooler temperatures and tend to be leaner and subtler.

BELGIAN BEERS

The latest fascination in beermaking and consumption seems to be the Belgian style and for good reason: Belgians truly venerate their beer, which is appropriate since some of Belgium's oldest brewing traditions began in monasteries. The monks picked fruit and herbs from their gardens and used them—along with hops, barley, water, and different strains of yeasts—to produce hearty, rich ales with a huge range of flavors. Even now, Belgian brews (and the Western beers modeled after them) are synonymous with creativity.

GOOD WITH FOOD

The abundance of top-quality beer today means pairing it with food is a hot frontier; some restaurants even have "beer sommeliers." The key to pairing food with beer: Pick lighter-bodied, milder lagers and ales to drink with delicate foods and darker, richer versions of either for heartier dishes. But here are more guidelines for making a good match.

Think geography Beers from a certain region tend to go well with foods from the same region. For instance, German beers pair well with sausages and smoked ham; English ales are great with beef and lamb roasts.

Think parallel flavors Pair the beer with a food that shares its flavor profile. For example, a well-seared steak with a browned and caramelized crust goes well with a sweet, malty amber ale.

Think opposites Sometimes flavors and textures that seem diametrically opposed can be electric together; a classic example is stout with raw oysters. Don't be afraid to experiment. Malty, sweet beers tone down the heat of spicy food. Acidic, hoppy beers like pilsners or American pale ales cut through the oil and butter in rich dishes like fried foods and cheeses.

With dessert Stouts and porters, with their malted sweetness, pair well with caramel, nuts, and chocolate; Belgian fruit lambics can be terrific with chocolate.

BEER

Beer-battered cod and onion rings

How beer is made

Mashing Ground-up malted grain (usually barley) is mixed with warm water to make a porridgelike mash.

Lautering The mash is strained to produce a sweet liquid, the wort.

Brewing The wort boils with hops (aromatic, bitter flowers), which balance the sweetness and add flavor.

Fermentation Yeast starts feeding on the wort's barley sugar, turning it into alcohol and carbon dioxide.

Secondary fermentation/aging The yeast keeps fermenting, at the top or the bottom of the vat. Warmer top-fermenting makes rich, fruity ales; cooler bottom-fermenting creates crisp, clean lagers.

Lime-chile beer

SERVES 2 | **TIME** 10 minutes

Here's a riff on the British shandy, a mixture of beer and lemonade.

⅓ cup lime juice, plus 2 lime wedges
2½ tsp. sugar
1 bottle (12 oz.) light-bodied wheat beer, such as
    New Belgium's Sunshine Wheat
¼ tsp. *each* kosher salt and chili powder

1. In a glass measuring cup, stir together lime juice, sugar, and ⅓ cup water until sugar dissolves. Fill 2 beer mugs with ice and pour half the beer into each. Top with lime mixture.

2. Sprinkle one side of each lime wedge with salt and the other with chili powder. Serve with beer.

PER SERVING 108 CAL., 1% (0.9 CAL.) FROM FAT; 0.8 G PROTEIN; 0.1 G FAT (0 G SAT.); 16 G CARBO (1 G FIBER); 253 MG SODIUM; 0 MG CHOL.

Beer-battered cod and onion rings

SERVES 4 | **TIME** About 1 hour

Coated in a beer batter, these fried fish and onion rings are ridiculously addictive. Serve with malt vinegar and tartar sauce if you like.

1 cup all-purpose flour
¾ tsp. baking powder
½ tsp. salt, plus more for sprinkling on onion rings and fish
¼ tsp. pepper
1 large egg
¾ cup (half a 12-oz. bottle) medium-bodied ale, such as
    New Belgium's Fat Tire
Vegetable oil for frying
1 yellow onion, sliced into ½-in.-thick rings
1½ lbs. skinless cod fillets, rinsed and cut into 2- by 4-in. pieces
1 lemon, sliced paper-thin
1 cup flat-leaf parsley sprigs, stems trimmed

1. In a large bowl, whisk flour, baking powder, ½ tsp. salt, pepper, egg, and beer.

2. Preheat oven to 200°. In a 6- to 8-qt. pot, heat 2 in. of oil to 375° over medium-high heat. Add onion to batter, turn to coat well, then put several onion rings in pot (do not crowd). Cook, turning often, until golden brown, about 6 minutes. Transfer to a rack set over a sheet pan, sprinkle with salt, and put in oven to keep warm. Repeat with remaining onions.

3. Allow oil to return to 375° and skim to remove any batter bits. Add fish to batter and turn to coat well. Cook fish in hot oil, turning and holding down as needed, until deep golden brown, about 7 minutes. Drain on rack and sprinkle with salt.

4. Add lemon slices and parsley to oil and cook until crisp, about 1 minute.

5. Pile fish and onion rings on a platter and garnish with fried lemon slices and parsley.

PER SERVING 427 CAL., 34% (144 CAL.) FROM FAT; 36 G PROTEIN; 16 G FAT (2.4 G SAT.); 33 G CARBO (3.5 G FIBER); 501 MG SODIUM; 126 MG CHOL.

Beeramisu

SERVES 6 to 8 | **TIME** 20 minutes, plus at least 8 hours to chill

Pieter Vanden Hogen, former chef at Oregon's Pelican Pub & Brewery, used the brewery's award-winning Tsunami Stout for his version of tiramisu.

8 oz. mascarpone cheese
3/4 cup heavy cream
1/4 cup coffee liqueur, such as Kahlúa
1 pkg. (7 oz.) Italian-style crunchy ladyfingers (*savoiardi*)
1½ cups Pelican Tsunami Stout beer or other non-hoppy stout beer
1 tbsp. cocoa powder

1. Line a 5- by 9-in. loaf pan with plastic wrap, leaving at least a 1-in. overhang on all sides. Combine mascarpone, cream, and liqueur and beat on low speed, then medium, until mixture is thick enough to spread (do not overbeat).

2. Set 1 ladyfinger vertically against a long edge of loaf pan and trim it flush with rim of pan. Use it as a guide to trim 12 more cookies, reserving trimmed ends. Soak 1 ladyfinger at a time in beer, about 1 second per side; then arrange in rows along the

Beeramisu

long sides of pan, picket fence–style. Arrange 4 ladyfingers lengthwise on bottom of pan.

3. Spoon half of the mascarpone mixture over bottom layer of ladyfingers and smooth evenly. Top with another layer of soaked ladyfingers (using reserved trimmed ends first), then top with remaining mascarpone mixture, smoothing evenly. Sift cocoa over top of mascarpone mixture. Wrap beeramisu and chill at least 8 hours and up to 24.

4. Use plastic wrap to lift cake out of the loaf pan. Unwrap and slice crosswise. Dust each slice with additional cocoa if you like.

PER SERVING 334 CAL., 57% (189 CAL.) FROM FAT; 4.3 G PROTEIN; 21 G FAT (14 G SAT.); 25 G CARBO (0.4 G FIBER); 85 MG SODIUM; 58 MG CHOL.

MUSHROOMS

MUSHROOMS

Nothing tastes quite like earthy, woodsy mushrooms, and that's why we consider them one of our treasured ingredients. Whether a common or exotic variety, mushrooms have a definite presence on the plate.

The Pacific Northwest has an ideal climate for growing wild mushrooms, but most of the mushrooms you buy in the market—from enoki, cremini, portabella, shiitake, and oyster mushrooms to the ubiquitous white common mushroom and its cousin the brown cremini—have been cultivated by farmers.

SEASONAL AVAILABILITY Cultivated fresh mushrooms and dried mushrooms of all kinds are on grocery shelves year-round. In season, you can find true wild, or foraged, mushrooms at farmers' markets and well-stocked or specialty-foods stores. The time of year we associate most with mushrooms is fall, when a hot, dry spell is followed by a good rain—as the Italians say, the earth "boils"—and the hills in the West burst with fungi, like chanterelles (August to January) and trumpets and hedgehogs (November to March). Morel mushrooms come to market usually beginning in March, lobster mushrooms in summer, and the king bolete (porcini) in fall and again in spring if we're lucky.

SELECTING AND STORING Even though mushrooms are a fungus, the one thing you want to avoid is selecting a moldy, soggy one. The caps should be firm and smooth, with stems that aren't dry or shriveled (although shiitake stems can look woody). For common mushrooms, look for caps that are closed tightly around the stem; if the gills are exposed, the mushrooms are old. Store mushrooms in the refrigerator unwashed in a paper bag; chill for up to four days. To clean mushrooms, follow the tips given on page 204.

USING Different varieties inspire different uses. Chefs prize the hedgehog for its spicy, almost peppery, flavor that can stand up to robust dishes. The yellow chanterelle is said to have a flavor reminiscent of apricots. A meaty porcini, sliced and grilled, is known as "poor man's steak." Mild common mushrooms absorb the flavor of the ingredients around them (they're wonderful stuffed with sausage or sautéed with butter and cream). To reverse this concept, the liquid of reconstituted dried mushrooms in soups, stocks, and risotto can make everything in the pot taste like mushrooms.

Mushroom puffs

MAKES About 24 puffs | **TIME** About 1 hour

Mushrooms are little magicians, soaking up the flavors around them and transforming a dish from plain to fancy, as in this elegant finger food. A touch of soy adds oomph.

½ tbsp. *each* butter and olive oil
1 tbsp. minced shallot (about 1 small)
1 tsp. minced garlic (1 or 2 cloves)
⅓ lb. common mushrooms, cleaned (see page 204)
    and finely chopped
2 tsp. minced fresh thyme or 1 tsp. dried
1 tbsp. Madeira
½ tbsp. soy sauce
½ lb. chilled puff pastry
1 large egg
¼ cup heavy cream

1. Melt butter with oil in a medium frying pan over medium-high heat. Add shallot and garlic and cook 30 seconds, stirring. Add mushrooms and thyme and cook, stirring occasionally, until mushrooms stop giving off liquid and start to brown, about 5 minutes. Add Madeira and soy sauce and cook just until liquid has evaporated, about 2 minutes. Let cool to room temperature.

2. Preheat oven to 400°. On a floured work surface and with a floured rolling pin, roll out pastry sheet to ⅛ in. thick. Cut pastry into rounds with a buttered and floured 2-in. biscuit or cookie cutter with fluted edges and arrange rounds ½ in. apart on 2 baking sheets.

3. Press the middle of each round with your finger to make a depression, leaving a ¼-in.-wide rim. Poke each center once with a fork and top with a scant tsp. of mushroom filling. Whisk egg and cream together and set aside.

4. Bake pastries until golden brown and beginning to puff, 8 to 12 minutes. Remove from oven and lower heat to 350°.

5. With the end of a small funnel, punch down pastry centers carefully while spooning about ½ tsp. of the egg-cream mixture through funnel (to help guide the liquid) and into pastry (spoon in more if the pastry will accept it without overflowing). Bake pastries until deep golden brown, 10 to 15 minutes more.

Mushroom puffs

Make ahead Filling, up to 1 day, chilled; pastry rounds, through step 2 up to 1 day, chilled, or up to 1 week, frozen on plastic-wrapped baking sheets (thaw in the refrigerator before filling and baking).

PER PUFF 81 CAL., 59% (48 CAL.) FROM FAT; 1.4 G PROTEIN; 5.3 G FAT (1.3 G SAT.); 6.8 G CARBO (0.3 G FIBER); 52 MG SODIUM; 13 MG CHOL.

Sausage mushroom caps

SERVES 12 | **TIME** About 20 minutes

Unlike the puffs on page 203, this appetizer puts the mush-rooms on the outside rather than the inside. Try spicy sausage if you want these little bites to have a kick.

24 medium-size common or cremini mushrooms
  (about 1 lb. total), cleaned (see below)
⅓ lb. seasoned bulk pork sausage
3 tbsp. seasoned dried bread crumbs
About 2 tbsp. extra-virgin olive oil
24 flat-leaf parsley leaves

1. Preheat broiler with oven rack 6 to 7 in. from heat. Scoop out mushroom stems with a small spoon; save for another use.

2. Mix sausage with bread crumbs in a small bowl. Mound sausage mixture in mushrooms, then place, filled side up, in a rimmed 10- by 15-in. baking sheet.

3. Broil until sausage is well browned, about 5 minutes. Lift mushrooms onto a platter, brush with oil, and top with parsley leaves.

PER SERVING 73 CAL., 70% (51 CAL.) FROM FAT; 2.8 G PROTEIN; 5.7 G FAT (1.4 G SAT.); 2.5 G CARBO (0.2 G FIBER); 116 MG SODIUM; 9 MG CHOL.

Cleaning mushrooms

Trim away tough or discolored ends from mushroom stems and any bruised spots or blemishes (for shiitakes and oysters, remove the entire fibrous stem). For firm mushrooms, such as portabellas, wipe dirt off cap with a damp cloth or place in a colander, rinse thoroughly under cool running water, and pat dry with towels. For delicate mushrooms that have lots of places for dirt to hide, such as chanterelles and hedgehogs, submerge in a bowl of cool water and gently agitate with your hands to loosen dirt. Drain, rinse carefully under running water, and gently pat dry with a towel.

Mushroom, chicory, and celery-root salad

SERVES 8 to 10 | **TIME** 1 hour

This is a good choice for a holiday or dinner party menu because you can prep the dressing and the vegetables the day before. The roasted mushrooms play nicely off of the bitter tones in the chicories.

1½ lbs. mixed wild and cultivated mushrooms such as maitake,
  oyster, and king trumpet, cleaned (see below left)
½ cup extra-virgin olive oil, divided
¾ tsp. kosher salt, divided
¼ tsp. pepper
1 garlic clove, peeled
2 tsp. whole-grain mustard
1 tsp. honey
½ tsp. fresh thyme leaves
¼ cup Champagne vinegar
8 oz. celery root
12 cups loosely packed chicories, such as escarole and radicchio,
  leaves torn into bite-size pieces

1. Preheat oven to 375°. Cut large mushrooms to make all pieces about the same size. Toss in a bowl with ¼ cup oil, ½ tsp. salt, and the pepper. Spread on a rimmed baking sheet. Bake, stirring occasionally, until browned, 30 to 45 minutes. Let cool.

2. Make dressing: Sprinkle garlic clove with remaining ¼ tsp. salt, mince, and then flatten with side of chef's knife into a paste. Scrape paste into a jar with a tight-fitting lid and add mustard, honey, thyme, vinegar, and remaining ¼ cup oil. Cap jar and shake until emulsified.

3. Peel celery root, then cut into matchsticks, dropping them into a bowl of water to prevent darkening. Pat dry, then put in a large salad bowl and add chicories and mushrooms. Toss gently with dressing.

Make ahead Dressing, up to 1 day, chilled; vegetables, up to 1 day (chill celery root matchsticks in water); dress just before serving.

PER SERVING 156 CAL., 64% (100 CAL.) FROM FAT; 3.5 G PROTEIN; 12 G FAT (1.7 G SAT.); 13 G CARBO (6.6 G FIBER); 159 MG SODIUM; 0 MG CHOL.

Mushroom, chicory,
and celery-root salad

Sausage
mushroom
caps

Mushroom and soft-cooked egg salad with hollandaise

Mushroom and soft-cooked egg salad with hollandaise

SERVES 4 | **TIME** 30 minutes

This mock hollandaise—thickened with crème fraîche rather than eggs cooked over a double boiler—is brilliant. When drizzled over the warm mushrooms, it melts just enough that you'll wonder if it's the real thing. Offer this as a light lunch or brunch entrée. To make your own crème fraîche, see page 279.

4 large eggs
3 tbsp. melted butter, divided
1 tbsp. extra-virgin olive oil
8 oz. cremini mushrooms, cleaned (see page 204), stems removed, and quartered
4 oz. *each* chanterelle and oyster mushrooms, cleaned and cut into 1-in. pieces
½ tsp. salt
½ cup crème fraîche
1½ tsp. Dijon mustard
1 tsp. *each* lemon juice and zest
About 6 cups watercress with tough stems removed
Pepper

1. Bring a medium saucepan of water to a boil. Using a slotted spoon, gently submerge eggs into water. Simmer 5 minutes, then carefully immerse eggs in cool water.

2. Heat 1 tbsp. butter with the oil in a 12-in. frying pan over medium-high heat. Add mushrooms and cook until browned, about 8 minutes, then season with salt.

3. Whisk together crème fraîche, mustard, and juice and zest in a small bowl. Gradually whisk in remaining 2 tbsp. butter to make hollandaise sauce.

4. Divide watercress among plates. Top with warm mushrooms, then drizzle with hollandaise. Crack an end of each egg and peel a quarter of shell. Using a spoon, carefully loosen eggs from their shells and scoop onto salads. Add a few turns of pepper on top.

PER SERVING 326 CAL., 77% (250 CAL.) FROM FAT; 11 G PROTEIN; 28 G FAT (15 G SAT.); 9.3 G CARBO (2.4 G FIBER); 494 MG SODIUM; 263 MG CHOL.

Mushrooms in sherry and shallot broth

SERVES 4 | **TIME** 35 minutes

For such a simple soup, this one is full of complex flavor. The key is to use at least four types of mushrooms to maximize their impact. To make your own broth, see page 276.

1 lb. mixed mushrooms, cleaned (see page 204)
2 tbsp. butter
1 cup chopped shallots
1 tsp. chopped fresh thyme leaves
1 cup dry sherry
4 cups chicken or vegetable broth
¼ tsp. *each* salt and pepper
8 to 12 thyme sprigs or several flat-leaf parsley leaves

1. Slice mushrooms into bite-size pieces. If using shiitakes, discard stems.

2. Melt butter in a large saucepan over medium-high heat. Stir in shallots and cook until lightly browned, about 4 minutes. Add mushrooms and thyme. Cook, stirring often, until mushrooms are lightly browned, 8 to 10 minutes. Add sherry and broth; cook, stirring, until soup boils. Cover and simmer to blend flavors, 2 to 3 minutes. Add salt and pepper.

3. Divide soup among 4 bowls and top each with a few fresh thyme sprigs or parsley leaves.

PER 1½-CUP SERVING 195 CAL., 31% (61 CAL.) FROM FAT; 4.5 G PROTEIN; 6.8 G FAT (3.6 G SAT.); 16 G CARBO (2.1 G FIBER); 1,176 MG SODIUM; 21 MG CHOL.

Pot roast with wild mushrooms and fresh thyme

SERVES 6 | **TIME** About 4¼ hours

When added to this slow braise, mushrooms infuse both the meat and the sauce with their woodsy flavors. Plus, the same ingredients that complement the pot roast—wine, onions, thyme—are naturals with mushrooms.

1 boned, tied beef chuck roast (3½ to 4 lbs.)
Kosher salt and pepper
About ⅓ cup all-purpose flour
3 tbsp. olive oil
1½ cups *each* coarsely chopped onions, celery, and peeled carrots
4 cups reduced-sodium beef broth
1 bottle (750 ml.) Merlot or other dry red wine
3 fresh thyme sprigs plus 1 tbsp. chopped leaves
2 tbsp. butter
¾ cup chopped shallots
2 lbs. mixed mushrooms, such as chanterelle, trumpet, enoki, cremini, and common, cleaned (see page 204) and cut into bite-size pieces
1 tsp. orange zest

1. Preheat oven to 325°. Sprinkle roast lightly with salt and pepper; coat generously with flour. Pour oil into a large (at least 6-qt.), heavy ovenproof pot over medium-high heat. Add beef and cook, turning as needed, until browned all over, about 15 minutes total. Transfer to a plate.

2. Add chopped vegetables to pot and cook, stirring often, until beginning to brown, 10 to 12 minutes. Add broth, wine, thyme sprigs, and beef. Cover and bring to a boil, then transfer pot to oven. Bake until beef is tender when pierced, 3 to 3¼ hours, turning roast over once.

3. Meanwhile, melt butter in a large frying pan over medium-high heat. Add shallots and cook, stirring often, until beginning to brown, 3 to 4 minutes. Add mushrooms, increase heat to high, and cook, stirring often, until liquid has evaporated and mushrooms are beginning to brown, 12 to 14 minutes. Stir in thyme leaves and salt and pepper to taste.

4. Transfer beef to a platter; cover with foil and keep warm in a 200° oven. Pour braising liquid through a strainer into a wide frying pan. Skim off fat. Boil over high heat until reduced by about half, about 20 minutes. Stir in zest and salt and pepper to taste. Pour sauce into a bowl.

5. Cut beef into ½-in. slices and drizzle with a little sauce. Spoon mushrooms around meat and serve with remaining sauce on the side.

PER SERVING 583 CAL., 36% (212 CAL.) FROM FAT; 67 G PROTEIN; 24 G FAT (8.2 G SAT.); 25 G CARBO (3.8 G FIBER); 474 MG SODIUM; 129 MG CHOL.

Mushroom pâté

MAKES About 2 cups | **TIME** 40 minutes

For a nonmeat alternative to liver or duck pâté, mushrooms are really satisfying, and using a variety of fungi gives the pâté more layers of flavor. To serve, spread on toasted bread.

½ cup butter
2 lbs. mixed cremini, oyster, or common mushrooms, cleaned (see page 204) and coarsely chopped
1 cup chopped shallots
4 garlic cloves, peeled and minced
1½ tsp. *each* ground cumin and ground coriander
Salt and pepper
Chopped parsley
Toasted baguette slices

1. Melt butter in a 6-qt. pan over high heat. Add mushrooms, shallots, garlic, cumin, and coriander. Cook, stirring often, until liquid has evaporated and mixture is lightly browned, 20 to 30 minutes.

2. Whirl mushroom mixture in a food processor until smooth. Season to taste with salt and pepper. Mound in a bowl. Sprinkle with chopped parsley.

Make ahead Up to 1 day, covered and chilled; serve at room temperature.

PER 2 TBSP. 72 CAL., 72% (52 CAL.) FROM FAT; 1.7 G PROTEIN; 5.8 G FAT (3.6 G SAT.); 4.2 G CARBO (0.4 G FIBER); 63 MG SODIUM; 16 MG CHOL.

Pot roast with
wild mushrooms
and fresh thyme

*Veal scaloppine
with mushroom
marsala sauce*

Veal scaloppine with mushroom marsala sauce

SERVES 4 | **TIME** 30 minutes

For weeknight dinners or weekend parties, this recipe from reader Sherry Huff, of Sacramento, California, impresses everyone. Serve with sautéed spinach and mashed potatoes.

1/3 cup flour
About 1 tsp. *each* salt and pepper
1 tsp. dried oregano
1 lb. veal cutlets, pounded to about 1/4 in. thick
2 tbsp. olive oil
3 tbsp. butter
12 oz. mushrooms, cleaned (see page 204) and sliced
3 tbsp. chopped garlic
2/3 cup sweet marsala wine
1/2 cup *each* reduced-sodium beef broth and whipping cream

1. Combine flour, 1 tsp. *each* salt and pepper, and the oregano in a bowl. Lightly dust veal with flour mixture and set on a plate.

2. Heat olive oil in a large frying pan over medium-high heat. Working in 2 batches, brown veal in oil, turning once, about 4 minutes per side. Transfer to a platter.

3. Melt butter in the same pan, add mushrooms and garlic, and cook 5 minutes. Add marsala and broth. Cook over high heat until slightly reduced, 5 minutes. Add cream and season to taste with salt and pepper. Return to a boil. Pour sauce over veal.

PER SERVING 508 CAL., 53% (270 CAL.) FROM FAT; 28 G PROTEIN; 30 G FAT (15 G SAT.); 21 G CARBO (1.7 G FIBER); 817 MG SODIUM; 153 MG CHOL.

Pan-roasted sablefish with mushrooms and sour cream

SERVES 4 | **TIME** 30 minutes

Most people don't think of eating mushrooms with seafood, yet the distinctive texture and flavor of shiitakes are perfect with rich sablefish fillets. Pan-roasting is a cooking method that starts on the stove and finishes in the oven.

1/2 lb. shiitake mushrooms, cleaned (see page 204), stemmed, and cut into 1/2-in.-thick slices
1 1/2 tsp. chopped fresh thyme leaves
About 1/2 tsp. kosher salt
1/4 tsp. pepper
1/4 cup olive oil, divided
1/2 cup dry white wine
1 1/2 tbsp. finely chopped garlic
4 skinned sablefish fillets (each about 1 in. thick; about 1 lb. total), rinsed and patted dry
3 tbsp. sour cream

1. Preheat oven to 375°. In a large, ovenproof (not nonstick) frying pan over medium-high heat, cook mushrooms, thyme, 1/2 tsp. salt, and the pepper in 2 1/2 tbsp. oil until mushrooms are crisp and brown, 8 to 10 minutes. Add wine and garlic and cook 1 minute more. Transfer to a bowl.

2. Wipe out pan; pour in 1 1/2 tbsp. oil. Salt fish lightly on skinned side and set skinned side down in pan. Cook 5 minutes on stove, then bake until fish is almost opaque, 3 to 6 minutes.

3. Transfer fish to plates. Pour out liquid from pan, scrape pan clean, and set over medium-low heat. Reheat mushrooms, pour off any excess liquid, and stir in sour cream. Spoon mushrooms over fish.

PER SERVING 364 CAL., 74% (269 CAL.) FROM FAT; 17 G PROTEIN; 30 G FAT (6.1 G SAT.); 5.3 G CARBO (1.3 G FIBER); 266 MG SODIUM; 60 MG CHOL.

Portabella burgers

SERVES 4 | **TIME** 15 to 20 minutes

Swap out meat for mushrooms in these juicy vegetarian burgers. Buy portabellas with the stems trimmed, or cut off the stems and save them for another use, such as the soup on page 207.

4 portabella mushroom caps (about 5 in. wide; 1 to 1¼ lbs. total), cleaned (see page 204)
1 to 2 tbsp. olive oil
⅔ to ¾ cup canned peeled roasted red peppers, coarsely chopped
¼ lb. thin-sliced Swiss cheese
4 round sandwich buns (about 4 in. wide; ¾ lb. total)
Butter or margarine (optional)
Salt and pepper
1 to 2 cups watercress leaves, rinsed and drained

1. Heat grill to high (450° to 550°). Rub mushrooms lightly with oil.

2. Lay the mushroom caps, cup (gill) sides down, on the grill. Cook, covered, until juices start to drip from the mushroom caps, about 5 minutes. Turn caps over and continue to cook until mushrooms are flexible and no longer firm when pressed, 5 to 7 minutes more.

3. Lay an equal portion of the red peppers in each cap and cover with cheese. Cook until cheese melts, about 3 minutes.

4. Meanwhile, split buns, butter if desired, and lay cut sides down on grill until lightly toasted.

5. Set a mushroom cap on each bun base, season to taste with salt and pepper, add a mound of watercress, and cover with the bun top.

PER SERVING 417 CAL., 35% (144 CAL.) FROM FAT; 18 G PROTEIN; 16 G FAT (6.6 G SAT.); 52 G CARBO (3.4 G FIBER); 603 MG SODIUM; 26 MG CHOL.

Drunken mushroom gratins

SERVES 6 as a first course | **TIME** About 45 minutes

Mushrooms and Pinot make a fabulous pair. Just choose a Pinot that's on the earthy (some might even say "mushroomy") side.

1 cup Pinot Noir or other dry red wine
½ oz. dried morel mushrooms
2 tbsp. butter
½ cup minced shallots
2 tbsp. minced garlic
1½ lbs. cremini or common mushrooms, cleaned (see page 204) and thickly sliced
½ cup whipping cream
1 tbsp. chopped fresh thyme leaves or 1 tsp. dried thyme
1 tbsp. lemon juice
Kosher salt and pepper
1½ cups (about 6 oz.) shredded asiago or jack cheese

1. Bring wine to a boil in a small saucepan over high heat. Remove from heat, add morels, and let stand until soft, about 20 minutes. Lift morels from liquid, squeezing out any excess, and finely chop. Reserve morels and liquid.

2. Meanwhile, melt butter in a large frying pan over medium-high heat. Add shallots and garlic and cook, stirring often, until soft, about 3 minutes. Increase heat to high, add creminis, and cook, stirring often, until almost all their liquid has evaporated and creminis are beginning to brown, 8 to 10 minutes.

3. Pour wine carefully into pan, leaving behind any sediment from morels. Boil until reduced by about half, 4 to 5 minutes. Add chopped morels, cream, and thyme, and boil, stirring occasionally, until sauce is slightly thickened, 4 to 5 minutes. Stir in lemon juice and season to taste with salt and pepper.

4. Preheat broiler with oven rack 4 to 6 in. from heat. Spoon mushroom mixture into 6 small ramekins. Sprinkle with cheese and set on a baking sheet.

5. Broil just until cheese is melted and starting to brown, 2 to 3 minutes.

PER SERVING 280 CAL., 64% (180 CAL.) FROM FAT; 12 G PROTEIN; 20 G FAT (13 G SAT.); 11 G CARBO (1.7 G FIBER); 379 MG SODIUM; 58 MG CHOL.

Drunken mushroom gratins

Mushroom ragout

Mushroom ragout

SERVES 10 to 12 | **TIME** 3 hours, including soaking

At Tilth in Seattle, Washington, chef Maria Hines smokes mushrooms to go with hearty beans in her vegetarian stew.

½ lb. dried cannellini or small lima beans
1 *each* whole carrot and whole celery stalk
½ onion plus 1 chopped onion
4 whole garlic cloves plus 3 chopped cloves
2 sprigs flat-leaf parsley plus ½ cup chopped leaves
2 sprigs thyme
6 black peppercorns
3 tbsp. olive oil, divided
2½ lbs. wild mushrooms, cleaned (see page 204)
    and cut into bite-size pieces
About 1 tsp. salt
3 tbsp. sherry vinegar
Pepper

1. Put beans in a medium pot, cover with water, and bring to a boil. Cover and turn off heat. Let sit 1 hour.

2. Drain beans, then return to pot; add carrot, celery, half onion, whole garlic cloves, parsley sprigs, thyme, and peppercorns. Cover with water by 1 in. and bring to a boil. Reduce heat to maintain a steady simmer and cook until beans are tender, 1 to 1½ hours. Discard vegetables and herbs and let beans cool. Drain, reserving liquid, and set liquid and beans aside.

3. Put 1 tbsp. oil, the mushrooms, and 1 tsp. salt in a large (not nonstick) frying pan over high heat. Cook, stirring, until mushrooms stop giving off liquid and start to brown. Transfer to a large bowl.

4. Add remaining 2 tbsp. olive oil and the chopped onion to the same frying pan over medium-high heat. Cook until onion is soft, 3 minutes. Add chopped garlic and cook, stirring, until fragrant, about 1 minute. Add vinegar and cook, scraping up any browned bits, until pan is almost dry. Return mushrooms to pan along with reserved beans and ¼ cup reserved bean cooking liquid. Cook, stirring, until well combined and hot. Stir in chopped parsley and season to taste with salt and pepper. Serve hot or warm.

PER SERVING 128 CAL., 26% (33 CAL.) FROM FAT; 6.6 G PROTEIN; 3.7 G FAT (0.5 G SAT.); 19 G CARBO (3.7 G FIBER); 200 MG SODIUM; 0 MG CHOL.

Wild mushroom and butternut squash bread pudding

SERVES 8 to 10 | **TIME** About 1¾ hours

This would be a wonderful Thanksgiving side dish, but it works as a vegetarian main dish too.

3 cups cubed (¾ in.) butternut squash
1 tbsp. extra-virgin olive oil
1½ tsp. kosher salt, divided
1 tsp. pepper, divided
About 4 tbsp. unsalted butter, divided
3 leeks, white and light green parts only, thinly sliced and cleaned
2 garlic cloves, minced
¾ lb. mixed wild mushrooms, cleaned and sliced
1 tbsp. fresh thyme leaves
6 cups cubed (1 in.) rustic white bread, lightly toasted
3 cups half-and-half
4 large eggs
1 tbsp. flour
¼ cup shredded parmesan cheese
1 cup shredded gruyère cheese

1. Preheat oven to 375°. Heap squash on a rimmed baking sheet, drizzle with oil and ½ tsp. *each* salt and pepper, and toss to coat. Bake, stirring occasionally, until tender and golden brown, about 35 minutes. Transfer to a bowl.

2. Melt 2 tbsp. butter in a large frying pan over medium heat. Add leeks with ¼ tsp. salt; cook until softened. Add garlic, cook 2 minutes, and add mixture to squash.

3. Melt remaining 2 tbsp. butter in same pan. Add mushrooms and ¼ tsp. *each* salt and pepper, and increase heat to medium-high. Cook, stirring, until mushrooms have released their liquid and are beginning to brown, about 6 minutes. Remove from heat and stir in thyme. Add mushrooms to squash-leek mixture. Stir in bread; scoop into a buttered 9- by 13-in. baking dish.

4. In a bowl, whisk half-and-half, eggs, remaining salt and pepper, the flour, and parmesan. Pour custard over bread mixture and let stand 10 minutes. Top with gruyère. Bake, uncovered, until cheese is melted and browning and custard is just set (poke with a knife to check), 30 to 35 minutes.

PER SERVING 329 CAL., 58% (190 CAL.) FROM FAT; 12 G PROTEIN; 21 G FAT (12 G SAT.); 24 G CARBO (2.2 G FIBER); 508 MG SODIUM; 137 MG CHOL.

NUTS

NUTS

Orchards in the West bloom riotously in spring with the pink and white blossoms of nut trees, a sign of the huge harvest of walnuts, almonds, hazelnuts, and more to come in fall.

Almond trees were introduced to California by Franciscan missionaries in the 1700s; now the state produces 80 percent of the world's crop. French settlers brought hazelnuts (also called filberts) to Oregon and now those orchards grow nearly the entire U.S. crop. California can make the same claim for walnuts and is the second largest producer of pistachios in the world. Look to Hawaii as the source for macadamias. Pine nuts are harvested from natural stands (not orchards) of piñon pines, widespread throughout the Colorado Plateau and stretching west to California and north to Wyoming. Even pecans are grown in California. With so many local nuts to choose from, we find plenty of sweet and savory ways to use them.

SEASONAL AVAILABILITY Raw or toasted shelled nuts are available year-round. Almonds are sold whole, blanched (skinned), sliced, slivered, and sometimes ground; hazelnuts come whole, skinned, chopped, and sometimes ground; walnuts and pecans come in halves or pieces; macadamias and pine nuts are sold whole; and pistachios come with the shell partially opened (a sign that the nut inside is ripe) or shelled. In the fall to early winter, you can find fresh almonds, walnuts, and pecans in the shell.

SELECTING AND STORING When buying nuts in the shell, look for shells that aren't cracked, soft, or moldy. Nuts in the shell have sweet meats that stay fresh longer than shelled nuts, but they are less convenient. Buy nuts packaged or in bulk from a store that has a lot of turnover because nuts get rancid if stored too long (what causes nut rancidity is the oil in the meat, which also gives nuts their distinctive flavor). Because of their open shells, pistachios go rancid fast, so consume them quickly. Unshelled nuts can be stored in a cool, dry, and dark place for up to one year. Store shelled nuts in an airtight container at room temperature for up to two months, in the refrigerator for up to six months, or in the freezer for up to one year.

USING We all know the phrase "from soup to nuts," but perhaps it should be "from nuts to nuts" because nuts are a great way to start and finish a meal. Nuts can be served as an appetizer (plain, salted, or with seasonings), ground into spreads, and mixed with other ingredients. You can start your day with nut-filled muffins or finish it with a nutty dessert. In between, nuts not only add texture and flavor to soups, salads, and main dishes, but protein, potassium, iron, and other vital nutrients.

Mediterranean pistachios and fruits

MAKES 3 cups | **TIME** 20 minutes

Stir spoonfuls of this intriguing blend of sticky dried fruits, nuts, and seeds into your favorite cereal or yogurt to wake up the whole bowl.

1½ cups unsalted pistachios
¼ cup dried pomegranate seeds or dried cranberries
½ cup chopped dried apricots, preferably Blenheim*
¼ tsp. *each* **ground allspice and ground or freshly grated nutmeg**
½ tsp. cinnamon
2 tsp. sugar

Toast pistachios (see "Toasting Nuts," page 224) and let cool completely. Toss pistachios with remaining ingredients until well coated.

*Order California dried Blenheim apricots from B&R Farms (*brfarms.com*).

Make ahead Up to 3 days; up to 1 week if you add dried fruit just before serving.

PER ¼ CUP 116 CAL., 55% (64 CAL.) FROM FAT; 3.5 G PROTEIN; 7.1 G FAT (0.9 G SAT.); 11 G CARBO (2.1 G FIBER); 2.4 MG SODIUM; 0 MG CHOL.

Apricots with basil–goat cheese and almonds

MAKES 40 appetizers | **TIME** 15 minutes

Dark orange dried Blenheim apricots (tangier and sweeter than Turkish ones) and stubby Marcona almonds are worth seeking out for this recipe because the flavors are so simple that each ingredient really stands out. You can find them at some natural-foods and well-stocked grocery stores or online (see right).

4 oz. fresh goat cheese, such as Laura Chenel, at room
    temperature
About 2 tsp. milk
2 tbsp. finely chopped fresh basil leaves
40 dried apricots, preferably Blenheim*
40 almonds, preferably Marcona or Marchini*
2 tsp. honey

Apricots with basil–goat cheese and almonds

1. With a wooden spoon, mix together cheese, 2 tsp. milk, and the basil until spreadable. Thin with more milk if necessary.

2. Spread a heaping ¼ tsp. cheese on each apricot and top each with an almond. Drizzle with honey.

*Order California dried Blenheim apricots from B&R Farms (*brfarms.com*) and California-grown Marchini almonds, which are similar to Spanish Marcona almonds, from J. Marchini Farms (*marchinialmond.com*).

Make ahead Up to 1 day, chilled; serve at room temperature drizzled with honey.

PER SERVING 36 CAL., 31% (11 CAL.) FROM FAT; 1 G PROTEIN; 1.2 G FAT (0.5 G SAT.); 5.4 G CARBO (1 G FIBER); 11 MG SODIUM; 1.3 MG CHOL.

Spicy sesame nut mix

SERVES 8 (makes 6 cups) | **TIME** 35 minutes

Offer this addictive nibble instead of chips and watch it disappear in minutes. Flavored with sage and cinnamon, it's especially good for fall and winter holidays.

1 large egg white
2 tbsp. honey
1 tbsp. sesame seeds
4 tsp. dried rubbed sage
3/4 tsp. cinnamon
1/4 tsp. cayenne
1/2 tsp. salt
13/4 cups salted peanuts
13/4 cups pecan halves
1 cup pine nuts

1. Preheat oven to 300°. In a small bowl, whisk egg white until frothy; whisk in honey, sesame seeds, sage, cinnamon, cayenne, and salt. Add nuts and stir. Divide mixture between 2 large nonstick or parchment-lined baking pans and spread into an even layer.

2. Bake, stirring often with a wide spatula, until nuts are golden and fragrant, 20 to 25 minutes. To prevent the mixture from sticking, turn often with spatula as it cools. Serve warm or cool.

PER SERVING 480 CAL., 83% (400 CAL.) FROM FAT; 14 G PROTEIN; 44 G FAT (5 G SAT.); 15 G CARBO (6.2 G FIBER); 254 MG SODIUM; 0 MG CHOL.

Hazelnut-butter muffins

MAKES 18 muffins | **TIME** 45 minutes

Add nutty nutrition to your breakfast by swapping hazelnut butter for regular butter to boost monounsaturated fat and decrease saturated fat. You can buy hazelnut flour, milk, and butter at natural-foods or well-stocked grocery stores. You can substitute other nut flours, milks, and butters, such as almond.

1 cup *each* hazelnut flour (also called hazelnut meal),
    whole-wheat flour, and all-purpose flour
1 tbsp. baking powder
3/4 tsp. salt
1/2 cup hazelnut butter
1 cup hazelnut milk
2 large eggs
1/4 cup vegetable oil
1 tsp. cinnamon
1 tsp. vanilla extract
1/2 cup packed light brown sugar
1/4 cup honey
6 tbsp. roughly chopped toasted hazelnuts
    (see "Toasting Nuts," page 224)

1. Preheat oven to 375°. In a medium bowl, whisk together flours, baking powder, and salt.

2. In a large bowl, whisk together hazelnut butter, hazelnut milk, eggs, oil, cinnamon, vanilla, brown sugar, and honey until blended.

3. Fold flour mixture gently into wet ingredients until just combined. Divide mixture evenly among 18 paper-lined muffin cups and sprinkle 1 tsp. chopped hazelnuts over each muffin. Bake until golden and a toothpick inserted in centers comes out clean, about 20 minutes. Cool on a wire rack.

PER MUFFIN 222 CAL., 52% (117 CAL.) FROM FAT; 4.8 G PROTEIN; 13 G FAT (1.24 G SAT.); 24 G CARBO (2.9 G FIBER); 130 MG SODIUM; 24 MG CHOL.

Hazelnut-butter muffins

*Mango chicken
boats with
macadamia nuts*

Mango chicken boats with macadamia nuts

SERVES 8 to 10 | **TIME** 25 minutes

Use shredded meat from a rotisserie chicken for the easiest preparation of these appetizers. To dice a mango, see page 47; to make your own crème fraîche, see page 279.

3 cups shredded cooked chicken
1 cup diced mango
½ cup chopped celery
⅓ cup chopped green onions
¼ cup chopped fresh tarragon
⅓ cup lemon juice
¼ cup *each* crème fraîche (or sour cream) and mayonnaise
1 tsp. salt
½ tsp. pepper
Belgian endive spears from 3 large heads
¼ cup chopped roasted, salted macadamia nuts

1. Combine chicken, mango, celery, green onions, and tarragon in a large bowl.

2. In another bowl, whisk together lemon juice, crème fraîche, mayonnaise, salt, and pepper. Add to chicken mixture and stir gently to combine.

3. Spoon chicken salad onto endive spears, then sprinkle with macadamia nuts.

PER SERVING 205 CAL., 66% (135 CAL.) FROM FAT; 12 G PROTEIN; 15 G FAT (4 G SAT.); 5.3 G CARBO (1.2 G FIBER); 311 MG SODIUM; 44 MG CHOL.

Belgian endive 101

A member of the chicory family, Belgian endive is a small, torpedo-shaped head of compact, pointed leaves that's grown in darkness to keep it pale. The leaves are creamy white with yellow-green or red tips. Belgian endive has a slightly bitter flavor and crunchy leaves that are good for stuffing, scooping, or dipping; you can also cut them crosswise and toss them in with salad greens. They can also be braised or grilled whole and become sweeter as they cook.

Walnut red pepper dip

Walnut red pepper dip

MAKES 2 cups | **TIME** 10 minutes

Similar to Spanish romesco sauce, this dip, from reader Lynn Lloyd, of Santa Cruz, California, is great with toasted bread or sliced veggies and is a happy change from spinach dip or other tired standbys for your next gathering.

2 cups shelled walnuts
½ tsp. *each* ground cumin, sugar, and salt
1 jar (12 oz.) roasted red peppers, drained
1 garlic clove, minced
2 tbsp. olive oil
2 tsp. lemon juice

In a food processor, pulse walnuts, cumin, sugar, and salt until walnuts are finely ground. Add peppers, garlic, oil, and lemon juice. Whirl until smooth.

PER TBSP. 59 CAL., 85% (50 CAL.) FROM FAT; 1.1 G PROTEIN; 5.5 G FAT (0.5 G SAT.); 2.2 G CARBO (0.4 G FIBER); 51 MG SODIUM; 0 MG CHOL.

Toasting nuts

It is often recommended to toast nuts before adding them to recipes, which intensifies their natural flavors and aromas and makes them crunchier. In the case of thin-skinned nuts like hazelnuts, it also makes removing their skins easier.

To toast a small amount Place nuts in a small frying pan over medium-high heat and cook, stirring frequently, until they smell fragrant and are a light golden brown (they will continue to toast a bit more when removed from heat).

To toast larger batches Spread the nuts in a single layer in a shallow baking pan and toast in a 375° oven until the nuts are light golden brown and smell rich and toasty, about 10 minutes.

To skin nuts after toasting Place them in a clean kitchen towel and rub vigorously. Most of the skins will slough off. Don't worry if a few bits still cling here and there; they won't harm the flavor or texture.

Chicken soup with saffron and almonds

SERVES 4 (makes 6½ cups) | **TIME** 45 minutes

Hints of the Mediterranean, where saffron and almonds are often cooked together, come through in this light soup. To make your own chicken broth, see page 276.

¼ tsp. saffron threads
½ cup sliced almonds
About 2 tbsp. extra-virgin olive oil, divided
1 lb. boned, skinned chicken breasts,
    cut into 1-in. chunks
1½ cups quartered mushrooms
1½ tbsp. chopped garlic
1 qt. reduced-sodium chicken broth
Zest of 1 lemon
¼ tsp. pepper
1 cup Yukon Gold potatoes, cut into ¾-in. cubes
4 oz. baby spinach
1½ tbsp. lemon juice
Kosher salt

1. Toast saffron in a 5- to 6-qt. pan over medium heat until fragrant, about 4 minutes; scrape out of pan and set aside. Add almonds and 1 tbsp. oil to pan and cook, stirring occasionally, until golden, about 4 minutes. With a slotted spoon, transfer nuts to a bowl.

2. Add remaining 1 tbsp. oil and the chicken to pan and increase heat to medium-high. Cook until chicken is brown on underside, about 3 minutes. Stir in mushrooms and garlic. Cook, stirring occasionally, until chicken is no longer pink, about 3 minutes. With a slotted spoon, transfer to a bowl.

3. Add broth, zest, pepper, saffron, and potatoes to pan. Cover and bring to a boil, then reduce heat and simmer 5 minutes. Return chicken mixture to pan and simmer, covered, until flavors are blended, about 5 minutes. Stir in spinach and cook until wilted, 1 to 2 minutes. Add lemon juice and season to taste with salt. Ladle into bowls, drizzle with oil, and sprinkle with almonds.

PER 1½-CUP SERVING 338 CAL., 37% (124 CAL.) FROM FAT; 37 G PROTEIN; 14 G FAT (1.8 G SAT.); 16 G CARBO (3.7 G FIBER); 514 MG SODIUM; 66 MG CHOL.

Chicken soup with
saffron and almonds

Nut-stuffed delicata squash

Nut-stuffed delicata squash

SERVES 4 | **TIME** 1 hour

As a cold-weather vegetarian main dish, these stuffed squash will satisfy even carnivorous types. Some kind of alchemy takes place with the onions, sage, and nuts to create a distinctly sausagelike flavor.

3 tbsp. butter
2 medium yellow onions, finely chopped
3 garlic cloves, minced
¾ tsp. salt
1 tbsp. chopped fresh sage
⅓ cup *each* chopped walnuts, pistachios, almonds, and pine nuts
⅓ cup plain low-fat yogurt
2 large eggs, lightly beaten
About ½ cup shredded parmesan cheese
2 delicata squash (about 2 lbs. total), halved
    lengthwise and seeded

1. Preheat oven to 350°. Melt butter in a large frying pan over medium-high heat. Add onions, garlic, and salt. Cook, stirring occasionally, until onions are soft, about 3 minutes. Stir in sage and cook until fragrant, about 1 minute. Stir in nuts. Set aside.

2. Combine yogurt, eggs, and ½ cup parmesan in a large bowl. Stir in nut mixture. Divide stuffing among squash halves, sprinkle with more parmesan, and bake until tender when pierced with a fork and tops are browning, about 45 minutes.

PER SQUASH HALF 526 CAL., 65% (342 CAL.) FROM FAT; 21 G PROTEIN; 38 G FAT (11 G SAT.); 32 G CARBO (7.6 G FIBER); 812 MG SODIUM; 140 MG CHOL.

Romanesco and toasted almond pasta

SERVES 4 to 6 | **TIME** 30 minutes

Romanesco broccoli, a beautiful lime-green vegetable with a dense, heavy head covered in spiraling points, is widely grown in Italy and is showing up more often in farmers' markets. Compared to its close cousin the cauliflower, the flavor is milder and gently sweet and goes particularly well with almonds.

12 oz. campanelle or penne pasta
7 tbsp. olive oil, divided

Romanesco and toasted almond pasta

2 heads Romanesco broccoli, roughly chopped
¾ tsp. kosher salt, divided
3 garlic cloves, finely chopped
½ tsp. red chile flakes
Zest of 1 lemon
½ cup toasted sliced almonds (see "Toasting Nuts," page 224)
¼ cup shredded asiago cheese

1. Cook pasta as package directs. Meanwhile, heat 3 tbsp. oil in a large frying pan over medium heat. Add Romanesco and ½ tsp. salt and cook, stirring occasionally, until tender-crisp, about 5 minutes. Add 1 tbsp. more oil to pan along with the garlic and chile flakes. Cook until garlic is fragrant and light golden and Romanesco is tender, about 5 minutes.

2. Drain pasta, reserving 1 cup pasta water, and return pasta to pot. Stir in Romanesco mixture, zest, almonds, cheese, remaining 3 tbsp. oil and ¼ tsp. salt, and enough pasta water to moisten (about ¾ cup).

PER SERVING 438 CAL., 46% (202 CAL.) FROM FAT; 13 G PROTEIN; 22 G FAT (3.5 G SAT.); 51 G CARBO (6.5 G FIBER); 257 MG SODIUM; 5 MG CHOL.

*Glazed carrots
with pecans*

Glazed carrots with pecans

SERVES 10 | **TIME** 30 minutes

Make this pretty side dish, created by reader Oceana Magee, of Port Townsend, Washington, to go with pork chops or roast poultry.

1 tbsp. olive oil
6 cups diagonally sliced (¼ in.) peeled carrots
1 tsp. minced fresh ginger
1 cup packed brown sugar
1½ cups toasted pecan halves (see "Toasting Nuts," page 224)

Heat oil in a nonstick frying pan over medium-high heat. Add carrots and cook, stirring frequently, 4 minutes. Stir in ginger and sugar and cook, stirring, until sugar melts, about 2 minutes. Add pecans and cook until carrots are tender when pierced and mixture is glazed in sugar, 3 to 5 minutes.

PER ½-CUP SERVING 245 CAL., 51% (125 CAL.) FROM FAT; 2.3 G PROTEIN; 14 G FAT (1.4 G SAT.); 31 G CARBO (3.7 G FIBER); 59 MG SODIUM; 0 MG CHOL.

Pork chops with butternut squash, escarole, and walnuts

SERVES 4 | **TIME** 45 minutes

The colors tell the story, don't they? A one-pan dinner of meat, greens, nuts, and hard-shell squash epitomizes the best of the autumn farmers' market. To make your own chicken broth, see page 276.

1 tbsp. extra-virgin olive oil
4 boned pork chops (sometimes called pork cutlets;
    about 1¼ lbs. total)
¾ tsp. *each* kosher salt and pepper, divided
1 bunch escarole (about 12 oz.)
¼ cup reduced-sodium chicken broth, divided
2 tbsp. apple cider vinegar
1 tbsp. packed light brown sugar
5 shallots, cut in half
1 bag (12 oz.) peeled, cubed butternut squash
2 tbsp. roughly chopped fresh sage
¼ cup roughly chopped walnuts

1. Preheat oven to 450°. Heat oil in a large ovenproof frying pan over medium-high heat. Rub pork chops with ½ tsp. *each* salt and pepper and cook until golden brown on one side, about 3 minutes. While the pork cooks, core and roughly chop escarole. Transfer pork to a plate.

2. Add 2 tbsp. broth, the vinegar, sugar, and remaining ¼ tsp. *each* salt and pepper to frying pan and simmer 1 minute. Add shallots, squash, sage, and escarole to pan. Cook until escarole has wilted, about 5 minutes, mixing occasionally with tongs.

3. Put frying pan in oven and bake, uncovered, until squash is just tender, about 20 minutes. Remove from oven and fit pork, browned side up, between vegetables. Drizzle remaining broth over mixture and sprinkle walnuts on top. Return to oven and bake, uncovered, until vegetables begin to turn golden and pork is cooked through, 5 to 10 minutes.

PER SERVING 373 CAL., 43% (159 CAL.) FROM FAT; 35 G PROTEIN; 18 G FAT (4.2 G SAT.); 20 G CARBO (4.9 G FIBER); 456 MG SODIUM; 80 MG CHOL.

Pork chops with butternut squash,
escarole, and walnuts

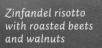

Zinfandel risotto with roasted beets and walnuts

Zinfandel risotto with roasted beets and walnuts

SERVES 6 to 8 | **TIME** 2 hours

Famed author and cooking teacher Joanne Weir features this recipe in her book *Wine Country Cooking*. Together, the fruity dark wine and the ruby-hued beets tint the risotto a festive shade of red. If you're serving this for a dinner party or holiday, you can make most of it ahead of time. To make your own vegetable broth, see page 276.

1 lb. baby or large red beets (about 3 lbs. if buying with greens)
4 tbsp. extra-virgin olive oil, divided
½ cup walnut halves
2 cups Zinfandel or other fruity red wine
1 qt. reduced-sodium vegetable broth
1 small onion, chopped
2 cups Carnaroli, Vialone Nano, or Arborio rice
    (see "Choosing the Right Rice," right)
2 tbsp. unsalted butter
1 tsp. freshly grated nutmeg
1 cup freshly grated parmigiano-reggiano cheese, divided
Salt and pepper

1. Preheat oven to 375°. Trim any beet greens (save for another use) and wash beets. Put beets in a baking pan and drizzle with 1 tbsp. oil. Cover with foil and bake until tender, about 1 hour. When cool enough to handle, peel and cut into ½-in. wedges.

2. Meanwhile, toast the walnuts (see "Toasting Nuts," page 224) on another rack of the oven. Let cool, then chop coarsely and set aside.

3. In a medium saucepan, bring wine and broth to a simmer. Meanwhile, heat remaining 3 tbsp. olive oil in a wide, heavy-bottomed pot over medium heat. Add onion and cook, stirring often, until translucent, about 7 minutes.

4. Stir in rice and cook until just beginning to stick to bottom of pan, 2 to 4 minutes. Add 1 cup wine mixture and cook, stirring, until liquid is almost absorbed. Add another ½ cup wine mixture and cook the same way. Continue adding wine mixture ½ cup at a time, stirring until each addition has been absorbed before adding the next, until all of it has been used and rice is almost tender to the bite, about 20 minutes (use hot water if you run out of wine).

5. Remove pan from heat and add butter, nutmeg, ½ cup cheese, and the beets. Stir quickly, cover, and let sit 4 to 5 minutes.

6. Season to taste with salt and pepper and transfer to a large, shallow serving bowl or platter. Sprinkle with remaining ½ cup cheese and the toasted walnuts.

Make ahead Up to 1 day. In step 3, heat only 1 cup wine with the broth. Cook rice through step 4, but do not add any hot water (rice will still be quite crunchy). Spread rice on a rimmed baking sheet. Cover and chill; 15 minutes before serving, bring remaining 1 cup wine to a simmer and warm the chilled risotto in a large pot over medium heat. Add hot wine ½ cup at a time to risotto and stir until each addition has been absorbed before adding the next, until rice is almost tender to the bite, 8 to 10 minutes (use hot water if you run out of wine). Continue with recipe from step 5.

PER SERVING 395 CAL., 36% (144 CAL.) FROM FAT; 11 G PROTEIN; 16 G FAT (5.2 G SAT.); 44 G CARBO (4.1 G FIBER); 280 MG SODIUM; 18 MG CHOL.

Choosing the right rice

The key to risotto's characteristic creaminess and chewiness is the rice itself, and risotto rice is no ordinary rice. It contains two different starches: an amylopectin exterior, which softens, especially under the pressure of constant stirring, to create a creamy sensation in the mouth; and an amylose interior, which stays relatively firm during cooking to give you that al dente bite. Widely available **Arborio** is the starchiest of the three popular risotto types, and it's the most prone to getting gummy as it cooks; inside, the grains tend to be chalky and crumbly. **Carnaroli** is our favorite; it has longer, narrow grains that cook the most evenly and have the best texture—creamy without being gluey and a good chewy interior. **Vialone Nano** rice grains are smaller, oval-shaped, and produce a delicate risotto with a nutty flavor; it is generally the most expensive of the three.

Chocolate–macadamia nut clusters

MAKES About 42 cookies | **TIME** About 45 minutes

These drop cookies will remind you of chocolate-covered macadamia nut candies, which is the effect reader Elsie Chan, of Leucadia, California, was after when she developed them. Take care not to overbake the cookies; their centers should remain soft and chewy.

8 oz. bittersweet or semisweet chocolate, chopped
¼ cup butter
1 cup sugar
2 large eggs
1½ tsp. vanilla
3 tbsp. all-purpose flour
¼ tsp. baking powder
1½ cups unsalted roasted macadamia nuts (7.5 oz.)
1 cup semisweet chocolate chips
1 cup sweetened flaked dried coconut (3 oz.)

1. Put chopped chocolate and butter in a heatproof bowl set over a pan of barely simmering water (bottom of bowl should not touch water) and stir often until chocolate is melted and mixture is smooth. Remove from over water and let cool to room temperature, about 15 minutes.

2. Preheat oven to 350°. In a large bowl with a mixer on high speed, beat sugar, eggs, and vanilla until smooth. Add chocolate mixture and beat until well blended. Stir in flour and baking powder, then beat just until moistened. Stir in nuts, chocolate chips, and coconut.

3. Drop dough in 1-tbsp. portions, about 2 in. apart, onto buttered or cooking parchment–lined 12- by 15-in. baking sheets.

4. Bake cookies until firm on the edges but still soft when pressed in the middle, 8 to 10 minutes; if baking more than one pan at a time, switch pan positions halfway through baking. Let cookies cool on sheets for 5 minutes, then use a wide spatula to transfer to racks to cool completely.

PER COOKIE 132 CAL., 65% (86 CAL.) FROM FAT; 1.5 G PROTEIN; 9.6 G FAT (4.6 G SAT.); 12 G CARBO (0.5 G FIBER); 20 MG SODIUM; 13 MG CHOL.

Hazelnut shortbread bars

MAKES 32 bars | **TIME** About 1¾ hours

Chopping some of the nuts and leaving others whole creates a mosaic effect on the tops of these irresistible cookies. They are an easy gift to whip up in December or serve with tea or coffee anytime.

3 cups raw, skin-on hazelnuts, divided
¾ tsp. cinnamon, divided
2 cups flour
1 cup plus 3 tbsp. cold butter, cubed
¾ cup granulated sugar, divided
½ tsp. salt, divided
7 tbsp. maple syrup
3 tbsp. packed light brown sugar

1. Preheat oven to 375°. Toast hazelnuts and remove half of skins (see "Toasting Nuts," page 224). Finely chop ½ cup nuts in a food processor. Reduce heat to 325°.

2. Put chopped nuts, ½ tsp. cinnamon, the flour, 1 cup butter, ½ cup granulated sugar, and ¼ tsp. salt in a large bowl. Beat on low speed with a mixer until well blended.

3. Grease a 9-in. square baking pan, line with foil (let it hang over edges), then grease foil. Press dough evenly into bottom of pan. Bake until golden and firm, about 45 minutes. Meanwhile, very roughly chop half of remaining nuts to make 1 cup.

4. In a small saucepan, bring remaining ¼ tsp. cinnamon, 3 tbsp. butter, ¼ cup granulated sugar, ¼ tsp. salt, the maple syrup, and the brown sugar to a boil, whisking frequently. Remove from heat and stir in 1 cup whole hazelnuts and the chopped nuts (2 cups total; you may have leftover nuts). Pour over crust and spread evenly. Bake until set when pan is tilted, about 18 minutes.

5. Let cool on a rack. Lift foil with cookie to a board. Cut cookie into 16 squares, then cut each square in half diagonally.

PER BAR 203 CAL., 65% (132 CAL.) FROM FAT; 2.8 G PROTEIN; 15 G FAT (4.9 G SAT.); 17 G CARBO (1.5 G FIBER); 98 MG SODIUM; 18 MG CHOL.

Hazelnut shortbread bars

Almond torte

Almond torte

SERVES 8 | **TIME** About 1 hour

A classic for Passover, when most foods made from wheat flour are not eaten, a version of this recipe dates back to at least 1855 and is probably much older. When baked, the batter forms a dense (but not heavy) torte, like a soufflé—only with an earthy side. We serve it with a simple raspberry sauce that can be made ahead (the sauce is great over plain pound cake and turns vanilla ice cream into a cheery sundae). Or just top each piece with sliced strawberries.

¾ cup whole almonds*
Vegetable-oil spray
1 tbsp. plus ½ cup sugar
4 large eggs, separated
1 tsp. almond extract
¼ tsp. salt
Raspberry Coulis (recipe follows)

1. Bring a large pot of water to a boil. Add the almonds and cook 2 minutes. Drain, rinse almonds with cold water, and slip off and discard skins. Pat dry with a kitchen towel and set aside.

2. Preheat oven to 375°. With vegetable-oil spray, lightly coat inside of a 10-in. pan with removable rim or any other 2-qt. baking dish with sides at least 2 in. high. Sprinkle inside of dish with 1 tbsp. sugar, tilting and turning the dish to coat evenly. Discard any excess. Set dish aside.

3. Whirl almonds in a blender or food processor until finely ground (be careful not to grind them into almond butter). Set aside. In a large bowl, whisk egg yolks with remaining ½ cup sugar for several minutes until pale yellow and thick. Gently stir in ground almonds and almond extract. Set aside.

4. In a large clean bowl, beat together egg whites and salt until firm peaks form. Stir one-third of the whites into the yolk-almond mixture to combine thoroughly, then gently fold in remaining whites. Pour batter into prepared dish and bake until set and golden brown on top, about 30 minutes. Let cool 15 minutes, slice, and serve with raspberry coulis.

*****Using whole blanched almonds saves time, allowing you to skip step 1; find them in gourmet and Middle Eastern markets.

PER SERVING 166 CAL., 49% (82 CAL.) FROM FAT; 5.6 G PROTEIN; 9.1 G FAT (1.4 G SAT.); 17 G CARBO (1.4 G FIBER); 108 MG SODIUM; 106 MG CHOL.

RASPBERRY COULIS

MAKES 1 cup | **TIME** 20 minutes

2 cups fresh or frozen raspberries
About ½ cup sugar
About 1 tbsp. lemon juice

1. Bring raspberries and ½ cup sugar to a boil in a medium saucepan over medium-high heat. Reduce heat and simmer, stirring occasionally, until mixture starts to thicken, about 15 minutes.

2. Press mixture through a fine-mesh strainer, using a spatula to extract as much liquid as possible. Discard seeds and skins. Stir in 1 tbsp. lemon juice. Taste and add more sugar or lemon juice if you like. Serve coulis warm or at room temperature.

Make ahead Up to 1 week, covered tightly and chilled; reheat over low heat if you like.

PER 2 TBSP. 64 CAL., 3% (1.8 CAL.) FROM FAT; 0.3 G PROTEIN; 0.2 G FAT (0 G SAT.); 16 G CARBO (1.4 G FIBER); 0.5 MG SODIUM; 0 MG CHOL.

COFFEE

Wake up and smell the coffee! The West has been doing that for nearly two centuries. In 1825, coffee plants were brought from Brazil to the island of Oahu. Today, Hawaii is a major grower of coffee, the beans in the Kona districts of the Big Island being the best known.

Many of the revolutionary moments in American coffee history have happened in the West. During the Gold Rush, a 15-year-old named James A. Folger worked for the Pioneer Steam Coffee and Spice Mills in San Francisco and started carrying coffee samples to exhausted miners in the gold fields. He eventually bought and renamed the company, and J.A. Folger & Co. became one of the first national coffee brands. A unique coffee culture grew up in San Francisco's North Beach, where Italian immigrants began serving espresso at Caffe Trieste in 1956. Then in the mid '60s, a Dutch immigrant named Alfred Peet opened Peet's Coffee in Berkeley. He popularized a dark-roast style and later trained the founders of Starbucks, which opened its first store in Seattle in 1971 and went on to become America's largest coffeehouse chain.

COFFEE CONSCIOUSNESS

In the past decade, coffee consumption in the West has grown even more conscientious, with companies such as Stumptown Coffee Roasters of Portland, Oregon, and San Francisco's Blue Bottle winning accolades not just for their beans and individual drip coffees, but for focusing on free-trade standards, a movement that has global impact. Coffee is the developing world's second most-valuable export commodity after petroleum. Shade-grown coffee supports greater biodiversity. Fair-trade coffee guarantees growers a living wage. And drinking coffee in your local coffee shop fosters a sense of community in small towns and big cities alike.

IT'S GOOD FOR YOU TOO

But there are other reasons to enjoy drinking coffee. New research suggests it may protect against diabetes, increase levels of HDL (the good cholesterol), reduce inflammation and the risk of some cancers, and even give you extra zip when you work out.

HOW TO MAKE A GOOD CUP OF COFFEE

Buying Coffee loses freshness shortly after roasting, so get your beans in small quantities from a store that regularly roasts its own (or gets frequent deliveries) and can tell you exactly when the beans were roasted.

Storing Keep beans in an airtight container at room temperature up to 2 weeks. You can store them longer in the refrigerator or freezer, but both methods dry out the coffee's flavorful oils. Never freeze coffee after it's been ground; it will lose flavor fast.

Grinding Because grinding beans releases the oils that hold aroma and flavor, grind fresh daily. Check the manufacturer's guidelines for the best grind for your equipment.

Brewing A good guideline to start with is 2 tbsp. freshly ground coffee to 6 oz. water. The key is water temperature: For electric coffeemakers, start with cold water; for most other methods, bring water to a boil, then let it sit about 30 seconds (water that's boiling hot extracts bitter flavors).

COFFEE

Coffee-braised
spoon lamb

Cardamom coffee

A spiced drink from southern India that will remind you of chai, but with that coffee kick. Serves 1.

Simmer crushed seeds from 1 cardamom pod and ¾ cup low-fat milk in a small saucepan over medium-low heat for about 5 minutes, stirring occasionally.

Heat ⅔ cup water almost to boiling. Put 3 tbsp. finely ground coffee in a drip cone set on a large mug. Pour water over grounds.

Strain milk into coffee. Stir in sugar if you like.

PER CUP 80 CAL., 20% (16 CAL.) FROM FAT; 6.5 G PROTEIN; 1.8 G FAT (1.2 G SAT.); 9.2 G CARBO (0 G FIBER); 85 MG SODIUM; 9.2 MG CHOL.

Coffee and brown sugar bacon

SERVES 8 | **TIME** 40 minutes

Coffee's not just for drinking with breakfast; rub some right on bacon strips (along with brown sugar), and you'll be eating it for breakfast too.

1 lb. thick-cut bacon
1 tbsp. ground coffee
½ cup packed brown sugar
2 tbsp. freshly brewed coffee

1. Preheat oven to 375°. Line a rimmed baking sheet with parchment paper and set a flat rack on top.

2. Lay bacon strips on rack, overlapping slightly if needed. Sprinkle top of strips evenly with ground coffee. In a small bowl, combine brown sugar and brewed coffee, stirring just to blend to a paste. Brush top of strips with half of sugar mixture.

3. Bake 15 minutes. Turn bacon over and brush with remaining sugar glaze. Bake until crispy, 10 minutes.

PER SERVING 144 CAL., 49% (70 CAL.) FROM FAT; 4.9 G PROTEIN; 7.8 G FAT (2.8 G SAT.); 14 G CARBO (0 G FIBER); 259 MG SODIUM; 13 MG CHOL.

Coffee-braised spoon lamb

SERVES 8 | **TIME** 6¼ hours

Yes, it's that tender: lamb braised so low and slow you can cut it with a spoon. The acidity of the coffee offsets the richness of the meat. Serve with polenta or potatoes to sop up the luscious sauce.

6 garlic cloves, divided
1 bone-in leg of lamb (about 7 lbs.), outside fat trimmed
Kosher salt and pepper
1 large onion, quartered
4 large carrots, cut into chunks
2 shallots
1 tomato, quartered
¼ cup olive oil
1 cup dry red wine
3 cups freshly brewed strong coffee, divided
¼ cup chopped flat-leaf parsley

1. Preheat oven to 400°. Mince 2 garlic cloves and rub onto lamb, spreading evenly. Generously sprinkle lamb with salt and pepper. Put lamb on a V-shaped rack in a large roasting pan. Surround rack with onion, carrots, shallots, tomato, and remaining 4 garlic cloves. Drizzle oil over vegetables and lamb.

2. Roast 30 minutes. Then reduce heat to 350° and cook 30 minutes longer.

3. Reduce heat to 250°. Transfer lamb to a plate and lift rack from pan. Set the roasting pan on a burner over high heat, add wine, and boil, using a wide metal spatula to stir and scrape caramelized vegetables from bottom of pan, until wine has reduced by half. Stir in 2 cups coffee. Remove from heat. Set lamb back in pan (without rack); spoon juices over it. Cover tightly with foil. Return to oven and cook until lamb is tender and pulling away from the bone, about 5 hours, turning lamb once halfway through cooking.

4. Transfer lamb to a platter and cover with foil. Reheat remaining 1 cup coffee and pour with liquid and vegetables from pan into a blender, working in batches if needed. Pulse until smooth. Pour sauce through a strainer set over a bowl, using the back of a spoon or ladle to push it through if needed. Season sauce with salt and pepper. Pour half of sauce over lamb and serve the rest alongside. Sprinkle lamb with parsley.

PER SERVING 469 CAL., 42% (198 CAL.) FROM FAT; 55 G PROTEIN; 22 G FAT (6.2 G SAT.); 10 G CARBO (0 G FIBER); 156 MG SODIUM; 170 MG CHOL.

Coffee and almond milk granitas

SERVES 8 | **TIME** 30 minutes, plus about 14 hours to steep and freeze

The great thing about granita is you don't need an ice cream maker to create it. This tastes like a frozen almond latte—creamy, nutty, and refreshing.

1½ cups whole unblanched almonds
3 cups milk
⅔ cup sugar, divided
2½ cups freshly brewed coffee

1. Toast the almonds (see "Toasting Nuts," page 224).

Coffee and almond milk granitas

2. Meanwhile, heat milk in a saucepan over high heat until hot. Stir in hot almonds and ⅓ cup sugar; let cool. Chill, covered, at least 8 hours or overnight.

3. Pour almond-infused milk through a strainer into a metal loaf pan; discard nuts.

4. In another metal loaf pan, stir coffee and remaining ⅓ cup sugar until sugar dissolves. Wrap both pans airtight; freeze. After 2 hours, stir slushy liquid with a fork, scraping sides of pans to create larger granita flakes. Return pans to freezer until completely frozen, about 4 hours.

5. Chill 8 bowls. Remove pans from the freezer 5 to 10 minutes before you want to serve the granitas. Using a fork, scrape tops of the granitas to break into flakes. Spoon about ½ cup coffee granita into each chilled bowl and ½ cup almond milk granita alongside.

Make ahead Up to 4 days.

PER SERVING 266 CAL., 54% (144 CAL.) FROM FAT; 7.9 G PROTEIN; 16 G FAT (3.2 G SAT.); 26 G CARBO (2.7 G FIBER); 49 MG SODIUM; 13 MG CHOL.

DRIED FRUIT

DRIED FRUIT

They taste like captured sunshine: raisins, currants, dried figs, dried apricots, dates, and prunes. Picked at their ripest and preserved for longevity, dried fruit, with its chewy, luscious flavor, inspires us in the kitchen and out on the trail.

Growers start with ripe plums, grapes, figs, and apricots and dry them—in dehydrators or in the sun—which removes the moisture and concentrates the flavor, but keeps the nutrients. Prunes are dried plums; raisins are dried grapes, which come in black and golden hues; and currants are dried tiny Zante grapes. Dates fall into a category of their own: They are the fruit of date palm trees, which are grown in the deserts of California and Arizona. Most dates are harvested when ripe and then fully dried before they are sold, but at some farmers' markets, you can find ripe dates at varying stages of dryness.

SEASONAL AVAILABILITY Dried fruits store extremely well, which means they are available at grocery stores all year.

SELECTING AND STORING Prunes and dates are available with or without pits, and dates are also sold chopped and even in paste, mostly for baking. Typically, two sources of dried apricots are available: California-grown apricots are halved before they are dried (we

particularly like Blenheim); Mediterranean or Turkish ones are dried whole without the pits. Various figs are grown and dried in the West, so you may have a choice of dark purple or amber-colored varieties. In many ways, dried fruit are the ultimate convenience food: ready to transport and ready to eat. You can tote them around in a backpack or your car, as they don't have to be refrigerated. But they don't keep forever—packages of dried fruit usually have a best-by date—but drying fruit was an ancient way of preserving one year's harvest until the next harvest came around. Store dried fruit airtight at room temperature for up to one month or refrigerated for up to six months.

USING Dried fruit was historically a Mediterranean and Middle Eastern mainstay, so many of the dried fruit recipes that we use today have roots in those cultures. But we enjoy them in American ways too: Where would trail mix be without raisins and apricots or Newtons without dried figs? We add dried fruit to our breakfasts, snacks, appetizers, salads, and more.

Quick ginger bran muffins

MAKES 8 | **TIME** 25 minutes

Here's a healthy breakfast on the go, dreamed up by reader Ginger Johnson, of Reno, Nevada.

¾ cup bran cereal (flakes or another shape)
¼ cup unprocessed bran
1 tbsp. *each* vegetable oil, honey, and molasses
½ cup milk
1 large egg
½ cup whole-wheat flour
½ tsp. baking soda
⅛ tsp. salt
½ tsp. cinnamon
¾ tsp. ground ginger
½ cup dried fruit, such as raisins, cherries, or cranberries
Cooking-oil spray

1. In a large bowl, mix together both brans with ¼ cup boiling water. Let cool. In a small bowl, combine oil, honey, molasses, milk, and egg, then stir into the bran mixture. Add flour, baking soda, salt, spices, and dried fruit and stir until just combined.

2. Spray a microwave-safe ½-cup bowl or ramekin with cooking spray and spoon in ¼ cup batter. Microwave until the muffin springs back when touched but isn't hard, about 45 seconds for a single muffin or 90 seconds for 4 muffins cooked together. Repeat with remaining batter.

Make ahead Through step 1 up to 4 days, chilled.

PER MUFFIN 128 CAL., 24% (31 CAL.) FROM FAT; 3.6 G PROTEIN; 3.6 G FAT (0.8 G SAT.); 24 G CARBO (4 G FIBER); 150 MG SODIUM; 28 MG CHOL.

Hot fruit and spice cereal

SERVES 2 | **TIME** 20 minutes

Instead of granola, layer cooked amaranth, a gluten-free grain, with dried cherries and apricots for this parfaitlike breakfast. You can cook the amaranth ahead and assemble the dish at serving time, but we also like the grain served hot as a contrast to the cool yogurt. Look for amaranth in boxes or in bulk at well-stocked grocery and natural-foods stores. To make your own yogurt, see pge 278.

Quick ginger bran muffins

½ cup amaranth grain
½ cinnamon stick
¼ cup *each* dried cherries and chopped dried apricots
2 tbsp. honey
½ cup nonfat Greek yogurt

1. Bring amaranth, cinnamon, and ⅔ cup water to a boil in a saucepan. Reduce heat and simmer, covered, 10 minutes. Let cool slightly. Discard the cinnamon.

2. In a microwave-safe container, microwave fruit, honey, and 2 tbsp. water until warm, about 30 seconds. Mix 1 tbsp. honey liquid from the fruit into yogurt. Divide yogurt between 2 dishes, top each with half of amaranth, and then half of honeyed fruit.

PER SERVING 359 CAL., 8% (29 CAL.) FROM FAT; 13 G PROTEIN; 3.2 G FAT (0.8 G SAT.); 74 G CARBO (8.7 G FIBER); 34 MG SODIUM; 0 MG CHOL.

*Martina's
energy balls*

1. Bring honey and soy milk to a boil in a medium saucepan over high heat; boil 1 minute. Set aside. Put coconut on a plate or in a shallow bowl and set aside.

2. Pulse oats, sesame seeds, nuts, and figs in a food processor until finely ground. Add to honey mixture in saucepan and stir together. Wet your hands with water and roll 1-tbsp. portions of mixture into balls; then roll in coconut.

PER BALL 83 CAL., 40% (33 CAL.) FROM FAT; 1.9 G PROTEIN; 3.7 G FAT (1.6 G SAT.); 12 G CARBO (1.5 G FIBER); 12 MG SODIUM; 0 MG CHOL.

Warm dates with soft blue cheese and prosciutto

SERVES 12 | **TIME** 30 minutes

This contemporary take on date-and-bacon appetizers is an unforgettable combo of sweet, creamy, and salty. You can assemble the dates ahead and heat them just before serving.

½ cup (2 oz.) loosely packed crumbled mild blue cheese,
    such as Danish
½ cup mascarpone or cream cheese
12 Medjool dates, halved and pitted
2 oz. thinly sliced prosciutto (4 to 5 slices), cut into
    24 thin (½ in.) strips
1 tbsp. vegetable oil

1. Mash blue cheese and mascarpone in a bowl with a fork until smooth. Fill each date cavity with a rounded ½ tsp. cheese, then wrap each half with a strip of prosciutto.

2. Warm oil and 1 tbsp. water in a medium nonstick frying pan over low heat. Add dates and cook, covered, until warmed through and softened, about 3 minutes. Serve warm.

PER 2 DATE HALVES 185 CAL., 58% (108 CAL.) FROM FAT; 4.1 G PROTEIN; 12 G FAT (5.7 G SAT.); 18 G CARBO (1.6 G FIBER); 156 MG SODIUM; 27 MG CHOL.

Martina's energy balls

MAKES 14 to 16 balls | **TIME** About 15 minutes

The Martina behind this snack of dried figs, nuts, oatmeal, and honey is none other than tennis star Martina Navratilova, who said of them, "They keep me going at matches…and I snack on them before and during a workout." Use any kind of nut you like—almonds, walnuts, pecans, or pine nuts. Peanuts (technically a legume, not a nut) will work too. Although Navratilova uses raw nuts, we found that toasting them amps the flavor (see "Toasting Nuts," page 224).

⅓ cup honey
¼ cup plain (not unsweetened) soy milk
Unsweetened flaked or shredded dried coconut
1 cup regular ("old-fashioned") rolled oats
1 tbsp. sesame seeds
¼ cup nuts, chopped
4 dried figs, chopped (soak in water if necessary to make
    them pliable)

Warm dates with soft blue cheese and prosciutto

*Fig, onion, and
lemon haroseth*

*Cranberry
apricot chutney*

Fig, onion, and lemon haroseth

MAKES 3 cups (serves 12 as a relish) | **TIME** 50 minutes

Amy Giaquinta, of Napa Valley, uses lemons from her garden along with dried figs, rather than the more commonly used apples, to make this for Passover. Serve with matzo.

1½ cups chopped dried Mission figs
1¼ cups red wine
3 cups finely chopped onions
¼ cup olive oil
¾ tsp. pepper
¼ cup honey
¼ tsp. salt
Juice and finely shredded zest of 1½ Meyer lemons or
    1 regular lemon
½ cup toasted pine nuts (see "Toasting Nuts," page 224)

1. Bring figs and wine to a boil in a small saucepan; cover, reduce heat, and simmer until tender, about 25 minutes. After cooking, figs should be barely covered with liquid; spoon out excess if necessary.

2. Meanwhile, cook onions in oil in a large frying pan over medium heat, stirring often, until very soft, 20 minutes.

3. Stir fig mixture, pepper, honey, salt, lemon juice, and ½ of zest into onions. Let cool.

4. Stir in pine nuts just before serving and garnish with the remaining zest.

Make ahead Through step 3 (adding all of zest) up to 1 day, chilled airtight.

PER ¼ CUP 158 CAL., 43% (68 CAL.) FROM FAT; 2.5 G PROTEIN; 7.6 G FAT (1.1 G SAT.); 23 G CARBO (2.8 G FIBER); 53 MG SODIUM; 0 MG CHOL.

Cranberry apricot chutney

MAKES About 5 cups | **TIME** About 20 minutes, plus at least 1 hour to cool

Dried fruit lift this condiment out of the typical cranberry-orange holiday doldrums. It's wonderful with turkey, pork, or ham.

1 pkg. (12 oz.) fresh or frozen cranberries
1 cup sugar
⅓ cup *each* coarsely chopped dried apricots, dried currants,
    and golden raisins
2 tbsp. balsamic vinegar
2 tangerines (about ¼ lb. each)
½ cup chopped pecans

1. Sort cranberries, discarding any bruised or decayed fruit. Rinse berries.

2. In a 3- to 4-qt. pan over medium-high heat, bring 1 cup water, cranberries, sugar, apricots, currants, raisins, and vinegar to a boil, stirring often. Reduce heat and simmer, stirring occasionally, until cranberries begin to pop, 5 to 8 minutes.

3. Meanwhile, remove peel and white pith from tangerines and separate segments (see "Cutting Citrus Segments," page 268) and coarsely chop, reserving juice and discarding seeds. Add tangerines and juice to the pan; simmer to blend flavors, 2 to 3 minutes.

4. Stir in pecans. Serve at room temperature or chilled.

Make ahead Up to 3 days, chilled airtight, or up to 1 month, frozen.

PER ¼ CUP 88 CAL., 19% (17 CAL.) FROM FAT; 0.6 G PROTEIN; 1.9 G FAT (0.1 G SAT.); 19 G CARBO (1.4 G FIBER); 1.1 MG SODIUM; 0 MG CHOL.

Cornbread stuffing with sage and dried fruit

SERVES 10 to 12 | **TIME** 1½ hours

Instead of the expected cornbread match with chile, cheese, and corn, we've used caramelized onions and chopped dried fruit to enrich this stuffing. The sweetness of the final product will depend on the cornbread recipe you use; we like Savory or Sweet Cornbread (see page 277), which gives you the choice. To make your own chicken broth, see page 276.

2 qts. cubed day-old cornbread
2 tbsp. olive oil
1 large white onion, halved and sliced
½ cup *each* dried cranberries and chopped dried apricots
1½ cups reduced-sodium chicken broth
2 large eggs
½ tsp. kosher salt
2 tbsp. chopped fresh sage leaves

1. Preheat oven to 350°. Spread cornbread on a large rimmed baking sheet. Bake until cornbread is dry and starting to crisp, about 15 minutes, turning pieces over once halfway through; set aside. Keep oven on.

2. Meanwhile, heat oil in a large frying pan over medium heat. Cook onion, stirring often, until golden brown and sticky, about 20 minutes. Transfer to a large mixing bowl. Add dried fruit.

3. Pour in broth, eggs, salt, and sage and mix well to combine. Add cornbread and toss gently just to moisten. Transfer mixture to a greased 9- by 13-in. baking dish.

4. Bake stuffing until firm to the touch and the top is starting to brown, about 40 minutes.

PER ¾-CUP SERVING 185 CAL., 31% (57 CAL.) FROM FAT; 3.5 G PROTEIN; 6.4 G FAT (1.5 G SAT.); 30 G CARBO (1.6 G FIBER); 368 MG SODIUM; 42 MG CHOL.

Radicchio salad with citrus, dates, almonds, and parmesan cheese

MAKES About 25 servings | **TIME** 25 minutes

Succulent citrus and dates pair up with crimson radicchio for this salad. Tangelos and blood oranges would work well here along with, or instead of, the grapefruit and navel oranges.

1 garlic clove, minced and mashed to a paste with ½ tsp. coarse kosher salt
½ tsp. pepper
3 tbsp. balsamic vinegar
6 tbsp. extra-virgin olive oil
3 grapefruit
3 navel oranges
1½ cups (about 15) pitted whole Medjool dates
2 large heads radicchio, torn into bite-size pieces
1 cup shaved parmesan cheese
¾ cup roasted almonds

1. Combine garlic paste, pepper, vinegar, and oil in a small jar with a tight-fitting lid. Cap jar and shake vigorously until dressing is emulsified.

2. Cut grapefruit and oranges into segments (see "Cutting Citrus Segments," page 268). Put segments in a large bowl. Pour off juices (or just pour into a glass and drink) to keep salad from getting soggy.

3. Slice dates thinly and add to bowl along with radicchio, ½ cup parmesan shavings, and ¼ cup almonds. Pour dressing over salad; toss thoroughly to coat. Turn salad onto a large platter or into a bowl and top with remaining ½ cup parmesan and ½ cup almonds.

Make ahead Through step 1 up to 1 week, chilled.

PER ⅔-CUP SERVING 130 CAL., 52% (68 CAL.) FROM FAT; 3.8 G PROTEIN; 7.6 G FAT (1.7 G SAT.); 13 G CARBO (2 G FIBER); 161 MG SODIUM; 3.9 MG CHOL.

Radicchio salad with citrus, dates, almonds, and parmesan cheese

*Red wine and onion
braised brisket*

Red wine and onion braised brisket

SERVES 12 | **TIME** 6 hours, plus overnight to chill

We were thrilled to get this recipe for slow-braised brisket with prunes from Evan Bloom and Leo Beckerman of the extremely popular Wise Sons Jewish Delicatessen in San Francisco, who prepared it as part of a Passover feast. The ideal cooking fat is schmaltz (chicken fat); find it at the meat counter of some markets or at a butcher shop. To make your own chicken broth, see page 276.

About 1 tbsp. kosher salt
About 2 tsp. pepper
1 tbsp. deli-style brown mustard
2 tsp. dried thyme leaves
1 beef brisket (about 5 lbs.), trimmed but with
**   some fat still attached**
2 tbsp. vegetable oil or schmaltz
3 cups reduced-sodium chicken broth, divided
½ bottle (375 ml.) dry red wine, such as Cabernet Sauvignon
12 whole dried prunes
1 tbsp. packed light brown sugar
2½ lbs. onions, thinly sliced
8 garlic cloves, smashed
1 lb. medium carrots, peeled, cut crosswise
**   into 2-in. lengths**
Prepared horseradish

1. Preheat oven to 350°. In a small bowl, mix 1 tbsp. salt, 2 tsp. pepper, mustard, and thyme together. Rub mixture all over brisket. Heat oil in an oval oven roaster (about 12 in. by 17 in.) or a wide 8-qt. pot* over medium-high heat. Add brisket and cook, turning over once, until a dark brown crust forms, 4 to 5 minutes per side. Transfer brisket to a plate.

2. Add 2 cups broth to pot and bring to a boil, scraping any browned bits from bottom of pot. Stir in wine, prunes, and brown sugar. Return brisket to pot, fat side down, and cover with onions and garlic. Cover pot and put in oven. Cook for 3 hours, turning meat halfway through. Turn meat again and add remaining 1 cup broth and the carrots to pot. Cook, covered, until carrots are tender, 30 to 45 minutes. Let cool, then chill overnight to firm meat.

3. Preheat oven to 350°. Skim fat from pan juices and discard it. Transfer brisket to a cutting board and slice across the grain. Fan out meat slices in a large roasting pan. Using a slotted spoon, arrange onions, carrots, and prunes over meat.

4. Boil juices remaining in the pot over high heat about 10 minutes to reduce somewhat. Season to taste with salt and pepper. Pour 2 cups of juices over meat (save the rest for soup), cover roasting pan tightly with foil, and bake until meat is hot, about 45 minutes.

5. Transfer meat to a large platter, using a wide spatula. Spoon onions, carrots, prunes, and some of juices on top and serve with horseradish.

*If you don't have a pot big enough for the whole brisket, cut the meat in half and stack the two halves in the pot; when you add the onions, add enough additional liquid (about 2 more cups broth and the rest of the bottle of wine) so the meat is covered by three-quarters.

Make ahead Up to 3 days, chilled.

PER SERVING 574 CAL., 55% (319 CAL.) FROM FAT; 36 G PROTEIN; 35 G FAT (14 G SAT.); 21 G CARBO (3.4 G FIBER); 577 MG SODIUM; 128 MG CHOL.

Buying brisket

When buying brisket, you may have two cuts to choose from because most butchers divide a whole brisket into the flat half, or first cut, which is lean and squarish, and the point cut, which is fattier, triangular, and more flavorful and tender. Or you can buy the whole brisket. No matter how you slice it, brisket requires a long, slow braise to become meltingly tender.

Pork shoulder roast with figs, garlic, and Pinot Noir

SERVES 6 or 7 | **TIME** 3¼ hours

Stuffing this roast with figs and garlic slivers will make you feel like a modern-day Julia Child, and the results are stunning: mosaic-like slices infused with rich fruit and wine flavors. Polenta and braised winter greens make good accompaniments.

1½ cups (10 oz.) dried Mission figs, stems removed, halved
    lengthwise
1 tbsp. sugar
½ tsp. anise seeds
2 tbsp. plus ½ tsp. chopped fresh thyme leaves,
    plus thyme sprigs
1 bottle (750 ml.) Pinot Noir, divided
1 boned pork shoulder (butt) roast (about 3½ lbs.)
8 garlic cloves, peeled and cut into large slivers
About 1½ tsp. kosher salt
About ½ tsp. pepper
3 tbsp. olive oil
About 1 tsp. fresh lemon juice (optional)

1. Put figs, sugar, anise, 1 tbsp. thyme, and 1 cup wine in a medium saucepan. Cover and bring to a boil over high heat. Reduce heat and simmer until figs are just tender when pierced, 10 to 12 minutes. Let cool.

2. With a small, sharp knife, make 16 evenly spaced lengthwise cuts into roast, each cut about 1 in. long and 1 in. deep. Insert a garlic sliver, then a fig half into each cut, closing meat over figs; make cuts a little bigger if needed. Set aside remaining garlic and figs and their liquid.

3. Preheat oven to 325°. Using kitchen twine, tie pork crosswise at about 1½-in. intervals and lengthwise twice to form a neat roast. In a small bowl, combine 1 tbsp. thyme, 1½ tsp. salt, ½ tsp. pepper, and the oil. Rub all over roast.

4. Heat a 12-in. frying pan over medium-high heat. Brown pork all over, turning as needed, 8 to 10 minutes total; adjust heat if needed to keep meat from scorching. Transfer pork fat side up to a 9- by 13-in. baking pan.

5. Reduce heat to medium. Add reserved garlic to frying pan; cook, stirring often, until light golden, about 1 minute. Pour in remaining wine from bottle and bring to a boil, scraping up browned bits with a wooden spoon. Pour mixture over pork and cover tightly with foil.

6. Bake pork until almost tender when pierced, 2½ hours. Stir reserved fig mixture into pan juices; bake, covered, until meat is tender, 15 to 20 minutes more.

7. Spoon pan juices over pork to moisten, then transfer meat to a cutting board and tent loosely with foil. Skim fat from pan juices. Pour juices with figs into a large frying pan and boil over high heat until reduced to 2 cups, about 5 minutes. Stir in ½ tsp. thyme. Taste and season with lemon juice and more salt and pepper if you like. Pour into a gravy boat. Remove twine from pork, then cut meat crosswise into thick slices. Garnish with thyme sprigs and serve with sauce.

Make ahead: Prepare through step 3 and chill airtight up to 1 day.

PER SERVING 498 CAL., 50% (247 CAL.) FROM FAT; 32 G PROTEIN; 28 G FAT (8.4 G SAT.); 32 G CARBO (4.2 G FIBER); 526 MG SODIUM; 107 MG CHOL.

Pork shoulder roast with figs,
garlic, and Pinot Noir

Pearl couscous with
fall vegetables and
caramelized onions

Pearl couscous with fall vegetables and caramelized onions

SERVES 6 to 8 | **TIME** 2½ hours

Golden raisins, chunky vegetables, and tangy-sweet onions give enough heft to this recipe, from Joanne Weir's *Wine Country Cooking*, to make it a main dish.

Caramelized onions

2 medium onions, sliced thinly
1 tbsp. olive oil or butter
¾ cup golden raisins
¾ tsp. ground cinnamon
½ tsp. *each* salt and pepper
1 tbsp. honey

Couscous and vegetables

3 tbsp. olive oil or butter
1½ tsp. salt, divided
½ tsp. pepper
1 tsp. saffron threads
¾ tsp. cumin
2 cinnamon sticks
7 cups reduced-sodium vegetable stock
3 to 4 medium carrots, cut in half and then into
    1½-in. pieces
4 small turnips, peeled and quartered
1 jalapeño chile, halved (seeded if you want less heat)
1½ lbs. butternut squash*, peeled, seeded, and
    cut into 1-in. chunks
3 medium zucchini, cut in half and then into 1½-in. pieces
2 cups pearl couscous (see "Pearl Couscous 101," right)
About 1 tsp. *harissa**
½ cup chopped cilantro

1. Make caramelized onions: Put onions in a large frying pan with ½ cup water, cover, and bring to a boil. Reduce heat to low and cook, covered, until softened, about 30 minutes. Remove cover and cook, stirring occasionally, until liquid has evaporated and onions are golden. Increase heat to medium-high, add oil, and cook, stirring, until deep golden. Meanwhile, soak raisins in hot water 15 minutes; drain.

2. Add spices and honey to pan; then stir in raisins and cook, stirring, until nutty brown, about 5 minutes. Set aside.

3. Make couscous and vegetables: Heat olive oil in a large pot over medium heat. Add 1 tsp. salt, the pepper, saffron, cumin, and cinnamon sticks and fry, stirring, 1 minute. Add vegetable stock and bring to a boil. Add carrots, turnips, and jalapeño; simmer, covered, 15 minutes. Add squash and zucchini and cook, covered, until all vegetables are soft but not falling apart, about 20 minutes.

4. Transfer 2 cups hot stock from vegetable pot to a 4-qt. saucepan. Add 1 cup water and remaining ½ tsp. salt. Bring to a boil, stir in couscous, and cook, covered, until tender, 6 to 8 minutes.

5. Transfer 2 cups stock from vegetable pot to a pitcher and stir in *harissa* to taste.

6. Spread couscous on a platter, making a well in the center. Using a slotted spoon, arrange vegetables, including cinnamon sticks, in the well; discard jalapeño. Scatter onions on top and sprinkle with cilantro. Moisten the couscous with some stock and strain the rest into a second pitcher.

7. Serve couscous and vegetables with the two stocks (plain and spicy) on the side.

*Using packaged cubed butternut squash will save you time. The heat level of *harissa* varies wildly depending on the brand, so taste before adding.

Make ahead Through step 7 up to 1 day, caramelized onions, vegetables, couscous, *harissa*-spiked stock, and plain stock chilled separately; 10 minutes before serving, reheat in a microwave and serve as directed.

PER SERVING 407 CAL., 16% (65 CAL.) FROM FAT; 11 G PROTEIN; 7.2 G FAT (1 G SAT.); 77 G CARBO (7.4 G FIBER); 861 MG SODIUM; 0 MG CHOL.

Pearl couscous 101

While some may think of couscous as a grain, it is actually pasta made from semolina (coarsely ground durum wheat). Pearl couscous, also known as Israeli couscous, has larger-size pellets than regular couscous, so it takes longer to cook, but it absorbs lots of liquid and flavor. Look for pearl couscous in well-stocked grocery stores or in specialty and Middle Eastern markets.

Fig gingerbread cakes

MAKES 18 | **TIME** About 1¾ hours

Perfect for the holidays, these moist little cakes are baked in two Perfect Brownie Baking Pans (*amazon.com*) to form exact squares, then "wrapped" in strips of Australian crystallized ginger, found in the baking aisle of most grocery stores.

1 cup chopped dried figs
Cooking-oil spray
¾ cup packed dark brown sugar
½ cup plus 6 tbsp. butter, at room temperature
¼ cup molasses (not blackstrap)
1¾ tsp. vanilla extract, divided
1 large egg plus 1 large egg yolk, at room temperature
1½ tsp. ground ginger
½ tsp. cinnamon
¼ tsp. *each* ground nutmeg, cloves, cardamom, and salt
1 cup plus 6 tbsp. flour
1¼ tsp. baking powder
¼ tsp. baking soda
About 1½ cups powdered sugar
1½ tbsp. milk
22 to 25 Australian crystallized ginger discs (8 to 10 oz.)
Granulated sugar, for sprinkling

1. Preheat oven to 350°. Put figs in a small bowl and pour in boiling water to cover.

2. Spray pans with cooking spray. In a bowl, using a mixer on medium speed, beat brown sugar with ½ cup butter until fluffy and pale, then add molasses, 1 tsp. vanilla, the egg, egg yolk, spices, and salt and beat well.

3. Whisk together flour, baking powder, and baking soda in a bowl. With mixer on low speed, gradually add flour mixture to wet mixture and beat until smooth; then beat in ¾ cup boiling water. Drain figs and stir into batter.

4. Divide batter among pans and bake until a toothpick inserted in centers comes out clean, 20 minutes. Cool cakes 10 minutes, then invert onto a rack, using a small knife to loosen.

5. Beat 6 tbsp. butter in a bowl until creamy, with mixer on medium speed. Add 1½ cups powdered sugar, ¾ tsp. vanilla, and the milk and beat until smooth. You should be able to

stand a spoon in it; if not, beat in a little more powdered sugar to thicken.

6. Slice thin strips of ginger from discs using a vegetable peeler. Dip peeler in hot water and dry off between slices to keep ginger from sticking. You'll need 70 to 100 strips to top cakes. Spread frosting onto cakes and arrange ginger strips in a bow pattern on tops of cakes. Sprinkle with granulated sugar to finish.

PER CAKE 282 CAL., 30% (86 CAL.) FROM FAT; 1.9 G PROTEIN; 9.7 G FAT (5.9 G SAT.); 48 G CARBO (1.2 G FIBER); 163 MG SODIUM; 47 MG CHOL.

Apricot-chocolate-almond biscotti

MAKES About 24 biscotti | **TIME** 1½ hours

The trick to making biscotti is to bake them once in log form, then slice and bake again. You get crumbly delivery systems for chewy apricot bits, hunks of dark chocolate, and crunchy almonds.

1¾ cups flour
1 cup sugar
½ tsp. baking powder
¼ tsp. salt
6 tbsp. unsalted butter, melted and cooled
½ tsp. vanilla extract
2 large eggs
¾ cup diced dried apricots, preferably Blenheim
⅔ cup slivered almonds
4 oz. chopped bittersweet chocolate

1. Preheat oven to 350°. Line a large baking sheet with parchment paper. In a food processor, whirl flour, sugar, baking powder, and salt to blend. In a small bowl, whisk together butter, vanilla, and eggs; add to flour mixture and whirl to form a dough. Transfer dough to a mixing bowl. Mix in apricots, almonds, and chocolate.

2. Put dough on baking sheet and form into two 12-in.-long logs. Flatten tops slightly and bake until golden, 25 to 30 minutes.

3. Remove logs from oven and reduce heat to 325°. Let logs cool 5 minutes, then cut on the diagonal into ½- to ¾-in.-thick slices. Lay slices flat on baking sheet and bake until lightly golden, 10 to 15 minutes. Cool completely on racks.

PER BISCOTTO 152 CAL., 41% (62 CAL.) FROM FAT; 2.7 G PROTEIN; 6.9 G FAT (3 G SAT.); 21 G CARBO (0.8 G FIBER); 41 MG SODIUM; 25 MG CHOL.

Fig gingerbread cakes

CITRUS

CITRUS

From the Pixie mandarin groves of Ojai, California, to the thousands of Meyer lemon trees that dot backyards from Arizona to Hawaii, the West is home to a spectacular array of citrus that adds tang and sparkle to every menu, from salad to dessert.

The fun of citrus in the West is the numerous varieties grown here beyond the grocery-store standards. The popular Meyer lemon, a lemon-orange hybrid, has a lovely aroma and is less acidic than a regular lemon. Blood oranges offer sweet red flesh and juice that have a raspberry flavor. Yuzu is a mandarin hybrid that tastes lemony, with a hint of lime and pine.

SEASONAL AVAILABILITY Because different kinds of lemons, limes, grapefruits, and oranges grow at different times, citrus is available in the market year-round. Traditionally, it was a winter treat, coming from climates with hot summers and mild winters. Those neon-colored orbs lit up the darkest time of year and were given as symbolic gifts at the holidays. December to March is still the best time for navel oranges and blood oranges; thinner-skinned Valencias ripen in the summer. For the mandarin family, including tangerines, tangelos (a tangerine-grapefruit cross), Pixies, and more, look for some varieties beginning in November. Lemons and grapefruit are available all year, but they are at their best in the winter; conventional (Bearss) limes are also available throughout the year, but the main crop is from winter to late spring.

SELECTING AND STORING In the case of all citrus, look for fruit that are heavy for their size with peels that are free of soft, dull, or moldy spots. Citrus fruit doesn't ripen off the tree, so choose with care. Store at room temperature for about one week or store in the refrigerator for two to four weeks. You can also squeeze the juice, freeze it in ice cube trays, and store the frozen cubes in an airtight container. Zest (the colored surface of citrus skin that is rich in flavorful oils) also freezes well—either finely shredded or as strips—up to four months, also airtight.

USING Little kumquats, with their sweet peel and tart flesh, are great for popping in your mouth whole or sliced into salads. The intensely aromatic, almost resinous zest and juice of Kaffir lime add an exotic note to butter cookies and simple icings. The quirky Buddha's Hand, with its fingerlike sections, has no pulp or juice; use its fragrant zest to infuse vodka, flavor sugar or salt (see page 277), or in place of lemon zest in recipes. Meyer lemons, yuzu, mandarins, and navel oranges are also good for infusing light spirits and flavoring salt. You can squeeze, slice, segment, or sugar citrus—and that's just a few of the wonders it can work in your kitchen.

Beets and preserved lemon bruschetta

SERVES 8 | **TIME** 20 minutes

Salt-cured lemons and chives add complexity to this appetizer, but you can keep preparation very simple by picking up the roasted beets at a specialty grocery store deli. Find preserved lemons at well-stocked grocery stores or make your own (see page 279); salt-preserved Meyer lemons are especially delicious (find at *robertlambert.com*).

1 cup diced roasted beets
1 to 2 tbsp. minced preserved lemon
2 tbsp. snipped chives, plus longer chive pieces for garnish
3 tbsp. extra-virgin olive oil
Salt and pepper
16 baguette slices, brushed with olive oil and grilled

Combine beets, preserved lemon to taste, snipped chives, and oil in a bowl. Season to taste with salt and pepper. Spread a heaping tbsp. of beet mixture on each baguette toast. Garnish with chive pieces.

PER 2-TOAST SERVING 143 CAL., 31% (45 CAL.) FROM FAT; 4.3 G PROTEIN; 5.3 G FAT (0.8 G SAT.); 21 G CARBO (1.5 G FIBER); 541 MG SODIUM; 0 MG CHOL.

Quinoa salad with chicken, avocado, and oranges

SERVES 4 to 6 as a main course | **TIME** 40 minutes

Lime and oranges punch up the citrus power in this easy, healthy salad. High-protein quinoa is widely available, but millet would also be good.

1¼ cups quinoa
1 tsp. chili powder
3 tsp. minced garlic, divided
Zest of 1 lime
2 tsp. plus 3 tbsp. olive oil
1 tsp. *each* kosher salt and pepper, divided
1 lb. boned, skinned chicken thighs
¼ cup lime juice
½ cup chopped fresh cilantro

Quinoa salad with chicken, avocado, and oranges

4 large oranges, peeled and segmented (see "Cutting Citrus Segments," page 268)
2 ripe avocados, cubed (see "Cutting an Avocado Safely," page 47)

1. Cook quinoa as package directs and fluff with a fork. Transfer to a large bowl and let cool.

2. Preheat broiler with oven rack set 4 to 6 in. from heat. In a large bowl, stir together chili powder, 2 tsp. garlic, the lime zest, 2 tsp. oil, and ½ tsp. *each* salt and pepper. Add chicken and toss to coat. Put chicken on a baking sheet and broil, turning over once, until browned and cooked through, about 12 minutes total. Let cool slightly, then slice and add to the reserved quinoa.

3. Add remaining ingredients to quinoa and chicken and toss to coat.

PER 1½-CUP SERVING 490 CAL., 48% (236 CAL.) FROM FAT; 21 G PROTEIN; 26 G FAT (4.4 G SAT.); 44 G CARBO (10 G FIBER); 311 MG SODIUM; 50 MG CHOL.

Southeast Asian
grapefruit and
shrimp salad

Southeast Asian grapefruit and shrimp salad

SERVES 4 | **TIME** 30 minutes

The dressing on this main dish salad balances hot, sour, sweet, and salty elements and is so vibrant that it needs no oil for richness. Find sambal badjak, a sweet-spicy Indonesian condiment, in the international foods aisle. To cut grapefruit into segments, see page 268.

¼ cup lime juice
2 tbsp. Thai or Vietnamese fish sauce
2 tbsp. *each* chopped cilantro and chopped fresh
    mint leaves
1 tbsp. minced fresh ginger
1 lb. (26 to 30 per lb.) peeled, deveined cooked
    shrimp
2½ cups pink or ruby grapefruit segments (from
    2½ lbs. fruit), plus their juice
About 1 tsp. sambal badjak or ¼ tsp. cayenne
2 cups lightly packed watercress sprigs

1. Combine lime juice, fish sauce, cilantro, mint, and ginger in a large bowl.

2. Split shrimp in half lengthwise, then add to bowl and gently toss with dressing to coat.

3. Spoon grapefruit segments into a wide, shallow serving bowl, using a slotted spoon. Pour ¼ cup grapefruit juice into the bowl with shrimp. Add sambal to taste, gently mixing to combine (save remaining grapefruit juice for another use).

4. Spoon shrimp and dressing onto fruit. Add watercress and gently toss.

PER SERVING 177 CAL., 7.3% (13 CAL.) FROM FAT; 26 G PROTEIN; 1.4 G FAT (0.4 G SAT.); 16 G CARBO (1 G FIBER); 967 MG SODIUM; 221 MG CHOL.

Spiced orange and date salad

SERVES 4 | **TIME** 15 minutes

Oranges and dates are often served after meals in Morocco, but reader Candice Etz, of Santa Barbara, California, tosses them into a simple salad that could be served alongside Charmoula Lamb (see page 161) or even as breakfast with morning yogurt.

5 oranges
½ cup pitted, chopped Medjool dates
¼ cup chopped toasted almonds (see "Toasting Nuts," page 224)
¾ tsp. cinnamon

Juice 1 orange. Peel and cut the remaining 4 into chunks. In a large bowl, mix juice, orange pieces, dates, almonds, and cinnamon until combined.

PER 1-CUP SERVING 220 CAL., 20% (44 CAL.) FROM FAT; 4.3 G PROTEIN; 4.9 G FAT (0.4 G SAT.); 45 G CARBO (7.5 G FIBER); 0.6 MG SODIUM; 0 MG CHOL.

Cranberry Meyer lemon relish

SERVES 10 (makes 2 cups) | **TIME** 15 minutes

Years ago, we got this recipe from a reader in Palo Alto, California, who grew Meyer lemons, which could be found only in backyard gardens at the time. Now that they're available everywhere, we highly recommend making this relish for the holidays or to spoon on roasted or grilled pork.

1 bag (12 oz.) fresh or thawed frozen cranberries
2 Meyer lemons (½ lb. total), ends trimmed
1 cup sugar

1. Discard any soft or decayed cranberries. Cut lemons into 1-in. chunks and discard seeds.

2. In a food processor, pulse lemon chunks until coarsely chopped. Add cranberries and pulse until the berries are barely chopped.

3. Mix fruit and 1 cup sugar in a medium saucepan. Bring to a boil over high heat. Reduce heat and simmer, stirring often, until flavors blend, about 5 minutes.

Make ahead Up to 1 week, covered and chilled.

PER 3-TBSP. SERVING 97 CAL., 1% (0.9 CAL.) FROM FAT; 0.4 G PROTEIN; 0.1 G FAT (0 G SAT.); 26 G CARBO (2.5 G FIBER); 1.5 MG SODIUM; 0 MG CHOL.

Orange and basil mussels

Heat oil in a large pot over medium heat. Cook garlic until fragrant, about 30 seconds. Add wine, juice, tomatoes, salt, pepper, and chile flakes and let simmer 5 minutes. Add mussels and half the basil; cook, covered, until mussels have opened, about 5 minutes. Transfer to a serving bowl and top with remaining basil.

PER SERVING 170 CAL., 27% (46 CAL.) FROM FAT; 9.1 G PROTEIN; 5.2 G FAT (0.8 G SAT.); 15 G CARBO (0.6 G FIBER); 504 MG SODIUM; 18 MG CHOL.

Oysters on the half shell with chile, cilantro, and Meyer lemon salsa

MAKES ½ cup salsa | **TIME** 7 minutes, plus chilling time

Part salsa, part mignonette—vinegar sauce for oysters—this topping is spicy, tart, and irresistible.

1½ red jalapeño or red Fresno chiles, seeded and finely diced
2 tbsp. finely chopped cilantro leaves
2 tbsp. red wine vinegar
¼ cup Meyer lemon juice
About ¼ tsp. fine sea salt
24 oysters on the half-shell

Mix all ingredients except oysters in a bowl and chill, covered, until cold (up to 6 hours). Season to taste with salt. Serve with oysters.

PER OYSTER WITH 1 TSP. SALSA 42 CAL., 25% (10 CAL.) FROM FAT; 4.8 G PROTEIN; 1.2 G FAT (0.3 G SAT.); 2.8 G CARBO (0 G FIBER); 75 MG SODIUM; 25 MG CHOL.

Orange and basil mussels

SERVES 4 | **TIME** 30 minutes

We were inspired by a bracing dose of freshly squeezed orange juice and a handful of basil in a dish similar to this at Kuleto's Italian Restaurant in San Francisco. Serve with warm crusty Italian bread.

1 tbsp. olive oil
1 large garlic clove, sliced
⅔ cup dry white wine
1½ cups orange juice
½ cup canned diced tomatoes
½ tsp. kosher salt
¼ tsp. pepper
¼ tsp. red chile flakes
2 lbs. mussels in shells, scrubbed, beards pulled off
⅓ cup sliced fresh basil leaves, divided

Buying oysters

You can shuck oysters yourself, but most fishmongers sell them on the half-shell to order (ask that they keep the liquid in the shells) or shucked completely, which is far more convenient. Make sure the sell-by date on shucked oysters, which are usually sold in a jar, is current. Whether jarred or on the half-shell, oysters should be refrigerated as soon as possible and used within two days of purchase. Serving oysters on the half-shell on a bed of chipped ice holds them steady, keeps them nice and cold, and looks fantastic.

Oysters on the half shell with chile, cilantro, and Meyer lemon salsa

Cod with citrus
chili glaze

Cod with citrus chili glaze

SERVES 4 | **TIME** 30 minutes

When reader Gregory Groth, of Napa, California, found a bumper crop of lemongrass in his garden, he was inspired to use it both in the steamer with the fish and in the sauce for this recipe. A reduction of rice wine, orange and lime juices and zests, chili, and ginger forms the spectacular sauce.

½ cup sake (rice wine)
¼ cup mirin* (sweet sake)
2 stalks lemongrass, outer layers removed
3 tbsp. chopped onion
1 tbsp. minced garlic
Juice and zest of 1 orange and 1 lime
¼ cup sweet Asian chili sauce, such as Mae Ploy brand*
4 quarter-size slices fresh ginger
4 pieces (4 oz. each) Pacific cod
Cooked brown rice
½ cup cilantro sprigs

1. Set a steamer in a wok or pot with 2 in. water underneath. Bring water to a boil.

2. Meanwhile, in a small saucepan over medium-high heat, boil sake and mirin until reduced by half. Mince 1 tbsp. lemongrass and cut the rest into thin 3-in. strips. Add minced lemongrass to sake mixture, reduce heat to medium, and add onion, garlic, juices, and zests. Cook 3 minutes; add chili sauce and cook until thickened, 10 minutes.

3. Put lemongrass strips and ginger in steamer. Top with fish; cook, covered, until just opaque in center, 8 minutes. Serve over rice with a drizzle of sauce and the cilantro.

*Find in the Asian foods aisle.

PER SERVING 242 CAL., 8% (20 CAL.) FROM FAT; 22 G PROTEIN; 2.3 G FAT (0.4 G SAT.); 18 G CARBO (0.7 G FIBER); 190 MG SODIUM; 40 MG CHOL.

Halibut steamed with ginger, orange, and lime

SERVES 4 | **TIME** About 30 minutes

Chef Jim Gallivan, formerly of Red Mountain Spa in Ivins, Utah, taught us the secrets to this entrée: Cook the fish in citrus-flavored steam, then concentrate the liquid for a sauce. The juice in the base, as well as the zest added at the end, accents all the other ingredients. Another trick is combining fresh and dry versions of ginger to intensify its impact.

3 cups orange juice
⅓ cup lime juice
1 tbsp. ground ginger
4 pieces (4 oz. each) boned, skinned halibut fillet
1 tbsp. cornstarch
2 tsp. minced fresh ginger
Salt
Cayenne
Asian chili oil (optional)
Thin shreds lime zest

1. Combine juices and ground ginger in the bottom of an 11- to 12-in.-wide steamer or in a deep 5- to 6-qt. pan. Set a nonstick or oiled rack at least 1 in. above surface of juice (elevate, if necessary, on the rim of a cheesecake pan or three clean, empty 2- to 3-in.-high cans with both ends removed). Cover pan and bring juice to a boil over high heat.

2. Rinse fish. Set pieces slightly apart on rack over boiling juice; cover pan and reduce heat to medium. Steam until fish is barely opaque but still moist-looking in center of thickest part (cut to test), 8 to 10 minutes. Lift out rack. With a wide spatula, lift fish from rack and set on a warm plate; cover to keep warm. Increase heat to high and boil pan juices, uncovered, until reduced to about 1½ cups, 10 to 12 minutes.

3. Mix cornstarch with 3 tbsp. water in a small bowl. Add mixture and fresh ginger to reduced pan juices; stir until boiling. Season to taste with salt and cayenne.

4. Divide sauce evenly among 4 plates. Lay 1 piece of fish in sauce on each plate. Garnish each portion with a few drops of chili oil and shreds of zest.

PER SERVING 226 CAL., 11% (25 CAL.) FROM FAT; 25 G PROTEIN; 2.8 G FAT (0.4 G SAT.); 24 G CARBO (0.4 G FIBER); 67 MG SODIUM; 36 MG CHOL.

Cutting citrus segments

For a beautiful presentation, follow these steps for segmenting grapefruit, oranges, lemons, and limes without any trace of bitter white pith on the fruit. Loose-skinned tangerines and mandarins can just be peeled and separated.

1. Cut ends off fruit, down to the flesh, with a small, sharp knife.

2. Set fruit cut side down on a cutting board. Following the curve of fruit with the knife, slice off peel and white pith. Trim away any missed patches of pith.

3. Hold fruit over a small bowl to catch juice, and slice between inner membranes and fruit to release segments; drop segments into bowl and squeeze juice from membranes into bowl.

Honey lime grilled pork tenderloin with citrus salsa

SERVES 4 | **TIME** 45 minutes

A full spectrum of citrus—lime, orange, lemon, and grapefruit—brightens a quick salsa that's as good with chicken or fish as it is with pork. To cut citrus into segments, see box at left.

1 pork tenderloin (about 1 lb.)
2½ tsp. extra-virgin olive oil, divided
1½ tsp. lime zest
⅓ cup lime juice (from about 3 limes)
¼ cup honey
1¼ tsp. kosher salt, divided
1 small Meyer lemon, cut in half horizontally, ends trimmed
Segments from 4 pink grapefruit, drained
Segments from 2 navel oranges, drained
1 tsp. chopped fresh thyme leaves
¼ cup chopped roasted, unsalted pistachios

1. Heat grill to medium (350° to 450°). Rub pork with ½ tsp. oil. In a bowl, whisk together zest, juice, honey, and ¾ tsp. salt; divide between 2 bowls.

2. Grill lemon, turning occasionally, until very soft, about 8 minutes. Grill pork, turning occasionally and brushing with half of the lime glaze, until a thermometer inserted in the thickest part reaches 145°, about 20 minutes.

3. Let lemon cool, remove seeds and central white core, and chop finely. Transfer pork to a platter, tent with foil, and let rest about 10 minutes.

4. Meanwhile, boil remaining glaze in a small saucepan, stirring occasionally, until thickened, about 5 minutes. Set aside.

5. Combine remaining 2 tsp. oil, grapefruit and orange segments, thyme, remaining ½ tsp. salt, chopped lemon, and pistachios in a bowl.

6. Slice pork, brush with thickened lime glaze, and serve with citrus salsa.

PER SERVING 414 CAL., 26% (108 CAL.) FROM FAT; 28 G PROTEIN; 12 G FAT (2.7 G SAT.); 54 G CARBO (6.1 G FIBER); 660 MG SODIUM; 75 MG CHOL.

Honey lime grilled pork tenderloin with citrus salsa

Roasted pork
spareribs with
citrus-soy sauce

Roasted pork spareribs with citrus-soy sauce

SERVES 6 to 8 | **TIME** 2½ hours

Bloggers Todd Porter and Diane Cu use whatever citrus they can find—even yuzu—to embellish these Asian-inflected ribs. Some Asian markets sell fresh yuzus in the fall; bottled yuzu juice is available year-round at Asian markets.

Citrus-soy sauce
3 tbsp. mirin* (sweet sake)
¾ cup prepared dashi* (seaweed soup stock)
2 tbsp. mixed citrus zest (yuzu, grapefruit, lemon, and/or lime)
¾ cup citrus juice (yuzu, grapefruit, lemon, and/or lime)
7 tbsp. soy sauce

Ribs
12 pork spareribs (about 4 lbs.)
1 tbsp. finely shredded ginger
¾ cup packed dark brown sugar
Lime wedges

1. Preheat oven to 350°. Make sauce: Whisk together sauce ingredients in a medium bowl (makes about 2 cups).

2. Prepare ribs: Arrange ribs in a roasting pan in a single layer. Pour 1¼ cups sauce over ribs. Cover pan with foil and bake 1½ hours.

3. Combine remaining ¾ cup sauce, the ginger, and brown sugar in a small saucepan. Cook over medium heat, stirring often, until sugar is dissolved, about 5 minutes. Remove from heat and set aside.

4. Remove foil from pan. Pour off juices and discard; pour brown sugar mixture over ribs and turn to coat. Bake 30 minutes more, uncovered, turning ribs over halfway through baking. Remove ribs from oven.

5. Preheat broiler with oven rack set about 7 in. from heat. Broil ribs, meaty side up, until browned, turning over after 7 minutes and broiling 3 minutes more. Turn ribs in remaining pan juices to coat. Serve with lime wedges.

*Find mirin and dashi in the Asian foods aisle.

PER SERVING 513 CAL., 56% (288 CAL.) FROM FAT; 31 G PROTEIN; 32 G FAT (12 G SAT.); 23 G CARBO (0.2 G FIBER); 886 MG SODIUM; 128 MG CHOL.

Oven-roasted asparagus with lemon olive oil

SERVES 6 | **TIME** About 15 minutes

Lemon zest elevates this side dish, created by chefs Caprial and John Pence in Portland, Oregon.

1½ lbs. asparagus, trimmed
2 tsp. extra-virgin olive oil
Salt and pepper
2 tsp. lemon zest
1 tbsp. lemon-flavored olive oil or extra-virgin olive oil

Preheat oven to 400°. Spread asparagus in a 10- by 15-in. baking pan. Drizzle with plain olive oil, then shake pan lightly to coat asparagus. Sprinkle with salt and pepper. Bake asparagus until tender-crisp, 9 to 10 minutes. Transfer to a platter. Sprinkle with zest; drizzle with lemon-flavored oil. Serve warm or at room temperature.

PER SERVING 54 CAL., 67% (36 CAL.) FROM FAT; 2.8 G PROTEIN; 4 G FAT (0.6 G SAT.); 3.5 G CARBO (1 G FIBER); 1.9 MG SODIUM; 0 MG CHOL.

Creamy lime slaw

SERVES 8 | **TIME** 30 minutes

Slaw becomes something memorable when you add lime juice, lime zest, and cilantro.

4 green onions
½ head *each* napa cabbage and red cabbage, sliced thinly
½ cup cilantro leaves
2 limes
½ cup nonfat Greek yogurt
1½ tbsp. sugar
1 tsp. kosher salt
½ tsp. pepper

1. Slice green onions long and diagonally. In a large bowl, toss together onions, cabbages, and cilantro.

2. Zest both limes and juice 1 lime. In a bowl, mix lime zest and juice, yogurt, sugar, salt, and pepper. Pour dressing over cabbage mixture; stir to combine.

PER 1-CUP SERVING 49 CAL., 2% (1 CAL.) FROM FAT; 2.9 G PROTEIN; 0.1 G FAT (0 G SAT.); 9.5 G CARBO (2.2 G FIBER); 268 MG SODIUM; 0 MG CHOL.

Sparkling orangeade

MAKES 2 qts. | **TIME** 6 minutes

This tastes best with freshly squeezed juice, but in a pinch, feel free to go for juice made from concentrate.

2 cups orange juice
¼ cup *each* lime juice and sugar
1 liter chilled sparkling water
Orange slices (optional)

1. In a large pitcher (at least 2 qts.), stir orange juice, lime juice, and sugar until sugar is dissolved.

2. Add 2 cups ice cubes and the sparkling water and stir to blend. Pour into tall glasses, adding orange slices if desired.

Make ahead Through step 1 up to 1 day, covered and chilled; add the ice and sparkling water just before serving.

PER 1-CUP SERVING 54 CAL., 2% (1.2 CAL.) FROM FAT; 0.5 G PROTEIN; 0.1 G FAT (0 G SAT.); 13 G CARBO (0.2 G FIBER); 0.8 MG SODIUM; 0 MG CHOL.

Spiced tangerine tea

MAKES 2 qts. | **TIME** 10 minutes

Chai-flavored tea mixed with freshly squeezed juice yields a soothing hot or cold drink.

5 chai spice or cinnamon tea bags
1 qt. fresh tangerine juice
½ cup firmly packed brown sugar
Tangerine slices

1. Bring 4 cups water to a boil in a 4- to 5-qt. pan over high heat. Add tea bags, remove from heat and let steep 5 minutes. Press tea bags against pan side to extract as much flavor as possible; discard bags.

2. Add juice and sugar to pan and whisk until sugar is dissolved. *To serve hot:* Return pan to low heat and stir often until tea is steaming (don't let it simmer or boil); float some tangerine slices in pan for decoration. *To serve cold:* Pour tea over ice in tall glasses and garnish rims with tangerine slices.

PER CUP 106 CAL., 0.1% (9 CAL.) FROM FAT; 0.6 G PROTEIN; 0.2 G FAT (0 G SAT.); 26 G CARBO (0 G FIBER); 11 MG SODIUM; 0 MG CHOL.

Tangerine crème brûlée

SERVES 8 | **TIME** 2¼ hours, plus 4 hours to chill

To achieve that brittle, glassy topping, a mini blowtorch is your best tool (find kitchen torches online and at cookware stores). You'll see what we mean after you taste this dessert, brought to us by bloggers Todd Porter and Diane Cu.

3 large eggs
5 large egg yolks
½ cup tangerine juice
¼ cup sugar, plus 16 tsp. sugar for topping
2½ cups heavy whipping cream
Finely shredded zest from 8 large tangerines (about ½ cup)
½ tsp. salt
1 tsp. vanilla extract

1. In a medium bowl, mix eggs, egg yolks, tangerine juice, and ¼ cup sugar until blended. In a medium saucepan, heat cream and zest over medium-low heat, stirring occasionally, until just about to boil. Remove from heat and let steep for 30 minutes. Reheat cream until almost boiling again. Add hot cream to the egg mixture a ladleful at a time, stirring constantly.

2. Add salt and vanilla to hot custard mixture and stir to combine. Pour custard through a fine-mesh strainer into a bowl or measuring cup with a pouring spout.

3. Preheat oven to 350°. Put 8 ramekins (6 oz. each) in a roasting pan and divide custard among ramekins (about ½ cup per ramekin). Add enough boiling water to pan to come about three-quarters up the sides of ramekins. Cover pan with foil and bake custards until just set, about 20 minutes (start checking early). Remove custards from water bath with tongs and let cool about 20 minutes. Chill custards at least 4 hours.

4. Sprinkle 2 tsp. sugar evenly over each custard. Use a kitchen blowtorch to melt and set the topping*. Serve immediately.

Make ahead Through step 3 up to 4 days, tightly covered.

*For even browning, rotate custard while flaming. The custard can be broiled under a gas broiler, as close to the heating element as possible without touching, but the results won't be as consistent as with a blowtorch.

PER SERVING 390 CAL., 75% (291 CAL.) FROM FAT; 5.6 G PROTEIN; 32 G FAT (19 G SAT.); 21 G CARBO (0.7 G FIBER); 204 MG SODIUM; 314 MG CHOL.

Tangerine crème brûlée

*Triple-decker
citrus popsicles*

Triple-decker citrus popsicles

MAKES 8 popsicles | **TIME** About 30 minutes, plus about 4¼ hours to freeze

The better the fruit, the more delicious these popsicles will be. Lisa Brenneis, of Churchill-Brenneis Orchard in Ojai, California, uses the farm's Oroblanco grapefruit, Gold Nugget and Page tangerines, and Moro blood oranges for her popsicles—but you can use any combination of citrus. You will need 8 popsicle molds (⅓- to ½-cup capacity), available at cookware and hardware stores.

1 cup *each* freshly squeezed blood orange juice (from 2 to 3 blood oranges), tangerine juice (from 3 to 4 large tangerines), and white grapefruit juice (from 1 to 2 grapefruit)
About ¼ to ½ cup superfine sugar*
1 to 2 tbsp. lemon juice

1. Taste the blood orange juice. Add 2 tbsp. sugar and 1 tsp. lemon juice and stir until sugar is completely dissolved. Taste again to see if it has the sweetness and tartness you like, bearing in mind that, when frozen, the juice will taste more subdued. If needed, add up to 1 tbsp. sugar and 1 tsp. lemon juice. Repeat with tangerine and grapefruit juices, using the same range of sugar and lemon juice for each.

2. Fill each of 8 popsicle molds one-third full with blood orange juice and freeze, making sure they're level and upright, until firm to the touch, about 45 minutes.

3. Fill each mold one-third more with tangerine juice and freeze just until firm to the touch, another 45 minutes. Carefully insert sticks, leaving 1½ to 2 in. of each sticking out. Freeze until sticks feel solidly anchored, about 45 minutes.

4. Fill each mold to top with grapefruit juice, cover, and freeze 2 hours or overnight.

5. Run warm water over the individual molds to unmold, just until popsicles release from sides, 5 to 15 seconds.

*Superfine sugar, available at most grocery stores, dissolves more quickly and thoroughly than regular sugar.

PER POPSICLE 77 CAL., 2% (1.8 CAL.) FROM FAT; 0.5 G PROTEIN; 0.2 G FAT (0 G SAT.); 19 G CARBO (0.1 G FIBER); 1.5 MG SODIUM; 0 MG CHOL.

Candied citrus peel

MAKES 6 cups | **TIME** 5 hours, plus 8 hours to dry

Citrus fruit is winter's gift, and candying the peels is an old holiday tradition.

5 lbs. oranges (or grapefruit, lemons, limes, or other citrus), washed and dried
8 cups sugar, divided

1. Cut fruit in half and juice; reserve juice for another use. Put fruit halves in a large pot and cover with cold water. Bring to a boil and cook 3 minutes. Drain. Return peels to pot, cover with cold water, bring to a boil, cook 3 minutes, and drain. Repeat once more.

2. Spread peels on baking sheets and let stand until cool enough to handle, 20 minutes. With a soup spoon, scrape inner membranes from peels and discard. Cut peels into ¼-in. strips; set aside.

3. Bring 8 cups water and 6 cups sugar to a boil in a large, heavy-bottomed pot over high heat. Add peels, then reduce heat to maintain a steady, gentle simmer; cook, stirring occasionally, until peels are tender, sweet, and translucent, about 3 hours. Don't let sugar brown or caramelize.

4. Drain peels and spread on racks set over baking sheets. Let stand until dry, at least 8 hours.

5. Toss a handful of peels at a time with remaining 2 cups sugar. Shake off excess sugar and put peels in an airtight container.

PER ¼-CUP PEEL 126 CAL., 1% (0.9 CAL.) FROM FAT; 0.2 G PROTEIN; 0.1 G FAT (0 G SAT.); 32 G CARBO (0 G FIBER); 0 MG SODIUM; 0 MG CHOL.

BASIC RECIPES

Here are a few homemade staples to use in recipes
in this book or to enliven your pantry.

Easy chicken broth

MAKES About 2 qts. | **TIME** 4 hours

Homemade broth is a cooking fundamental, useful as a base
for everything from soups to sauces. This recipe is simple to
make and creates enough broth for multiple dishes. Freeze up
to 6 months.

**About 2 lbs. chicken bones (from 1 large chicken)
    or chicken wings**
1 large onion, roughly chopped
3 medium carrots, peeled and roughly chopped
3 celery stalks, roughly chopped

1. Put all ingredients in a large pot and add 4 qts. water. Bring
to a boil and spoon off any foam that forms on top. Reduce
heat and simmer until broth is reduced by half, 2½ to 3 hours.

2. Pour mixture through a strainer into a bowl and let broth
cool; discard what is in the strainer.

3. Use broth or freeze by ladling into quart-size resealable
freezer bags or containers (for soup) and/or ice cube trays
(for sauces); transfer cubes to freezer bags once they're solid.

PER CUP 41 CAL., 33% (14 CAL.) FROM FAT; 5.6 G PROTEIN; 1.5 G FAT (0.4 G SAT.);
1.3 G CARBO (0 G FIBER); 32 MG SODIUM; 1.5 MG CHOL.

VARIATION: EASY RICH DARK CHICKEN BROTH
This variation on Easy Chicken Broth (above) gets a deeper
flavor and color from roasting the bones and vegetables, which
takes only 30 minutes. The result is a good substitute for beef
broth in soups and stews.
    Preheat oven to 350°. Put bones and vegetables in a roast-
ing pan and toss with 1 tbsp. **olive oil**. Roast until browned,
about 30 minutes. Proceed with recipe from Step 1.

Easy vegetable broth

MAKES About 2 qts. | **TIME** 4 hours

This nonmeat broth is particularly good in risotto (see pages
146 and 231) and vegetarian recipes. Don't leave out the
mushrooms; they give this broth its complexity. Freeze up
to 6 months.

1 large onion, roughly chopped
3 medium carrots, peeled and roughly chopped
3 celery stalks, roughly chopped
**2 large leeks, white and light green parts only, roughly chopped,
    cleaned (see "Cleaning Leeks," page 94)**
8 oz. mushrooms, cleaned (see page 204)
1 bunch parsley

1. Put all ingredients in a large pot and add 4 qts. water. Bring
to a boil and spoon off any foam that forms on top. Reduce
heat and simmer until broth is reduced by half, 2½ to 3 hours.

2. Pour mixture through a strainer into a bowl and let broth
cool; discard what is in the strainer.

3. Use broth or freeze by ladling into quart-size resealable
freezer bags or containers (for soup) and/or ice cube trays
(for sauces); transfer cubes to freezer bags once they're solid.

PER CUP 14 CAL., 5% (0.7 CAL.) FROM FAT; 0.6 G PROTEIN; 0.1 G FAT (0 G SAT.);
3 G CARBO (0 G FIBER); 19 MG SODIUM; 0 MG CHOL.

Savory or sweet cornbread

SERVES 9 | **TIME** 40 minutes

You can customize this recipe to suit your needs. Add less sugar to use the cornbread as a base for stuffing (see page 248). Add more sugar to serve out of the pan as an accompaniment to chili, posole, or pork chops.

1 cup all-purpose flour
1 cup yellow cornmeal
2 tbsp. or ⅓ cup sugar*
2½ tsp. baking powder
¾ tsp. salt
2 large eggs
1 cup buttermilk
About ¼ cup cooled melted butter or margarine

1. Preheat oven to 400°. Mix flour, cornmeal, sugar, baking powder, and salt in a bowl. In another bowl, beat eggs to blend with buttermilk and ¼ cup butter. Pour liquids into flour mixture and stir just until evenly moistened.

2. Scrape batter into a buttered 8-in. square pan and spread smooth.

3. Bake until bread springs back when lightly pressed in the center and begins to pull away from pan sides, about 25 minutes (20 minutes in a convection oven).

4. Cut bread into squares. Lift from pan with a slender spatula. Serve hot or cool.

*For bread that is sweeter and more tender, use the larger measure of sugar.

PER SERVING 196 CAL., 35% (69 CAL.) FROM FAT; 5.1 G PROTEIN; 7.5 G FAT (4.1 G SAT.); 27 G CARBO (1.2 G FIBER); 431 MG SODIUM; 64 MG CHOL.

Toasted fresh bread crumbs

MAKES About ¾ cup | **TIME** About 30 minutes

The secret to making evenly browned crumbs is to cook them in a skillet and stir constantly as they absorb the oil and darken. Sprinkle this as a garnish over pasta or soup instead of parmesan cheese.

One 4-in. length (4 oz.) of an Italian-style bread with crust, such as *pane pugliese*
2 tbsp. extra-virgin olive oil

1. Preheat oven to 300°. Cut bread into cubes and scatter on a rimmed baking sheet in 1 layer. Bake 15 minutes or until cubes feel dry on the outside but still moist inside. Let cool.

2. Put bread cubes in a food processor and pulse into fine crumbs. Set aside ¾ cup firmly packed bread crumbs; save remaining for another use.

3. Heat oil just until warm (not hot) in a 10-in. frying pan over medium heat. Add reserved bread crumbs and stir to coat with oil. Cook, stirring constantly, until bread crumbs are evenly golden brown and crunchy, about 5 minutes.

PER 2 TBSP. 91 CAL., 53% (48 CAL.) FROM FAT; 1.7 G PROTEIN; 5.3 G FAT (0.8 G SAT.); 9.5 G CARBO (0.6 G FIBER); 110 MG SODIUM; 0 MG CHOL.

Citrus salt

MAKES 1¼ cups | **TIME** 15 minutes, plus 8 hours to dry

Seasoned salts are popular with Western chefs as a finishing ingredient—sprinkled on dishes at the last minute, often in combination with a drizzle of olive oil. Made with the zest of lemons, limes, or oranges, this salt is particularly delicious on cooked fish or composed salads. The zest's color will fade over time, but that won't affect the taste.

1 cup flake salt, such as Maldon, or coarse salt
3 tbsp. citrus zest (any kind)

Mix salt and zest in a bowl; work zest into salt with your fingers to release oils and flavor. Spread on a rimmed baking sheet. Air-dry until dried completely, 8 hours to overnight.

Make ahead Up to 2 months, covered airtight at room temperature.

PER ¼ TSP. 0 CAL., 0% FROM FAT; 0 G PROTEIN; 0 G FAT; 0 G CARBO; 384 MG SODIUM; 0 MG CHOL.

Basic vanilla ice cream

MAKES 1 qt. | **TIME** 45 minutes, plus 5 hours to steep and freeze

What better item to have on hand than vanilla ice cream? It goes with everything, from fudge sauce (see below) to fruit crisps to pies. Or eat it straight from the freezer!

2 cups whipping cream
2 cups whole milk
1 vanilla bean, split lengthwise
4 large egg yolks
1 cup sugar

1. Heat cream, milk, and vanilla bean together in a 4-qt. pot. When liquid boils, remove from heat and cover. Steep about 1 hour to develop flavors.

2. Strain liquid into a bowl and return to the pot. Heat liquid over high heat until it reaches a simmer.

3. In a large bowl, whisk together yolks and sugar just as liquid reaches a simmer. Working in ½-cup increments, add hot liquid to yolk and sugar mixture until mixture is warm and the consistency of milk. Pour custard into pot and cook over high heat, stirring constantly, until slightly thickened, about 5 minutes. Do not let boil.

4. Strain custard into a bowl; nestle in another bowl filled with ice water, stirring occasionally, until cold to the touch.

5. Churn custard in an ice cream maker according to manufacturer's instructions. Freeze in an airtight container until firm, about 4 hours.

PER ½ CUP 327 CAL., 60% (196 CAL.) FROM FAT; 4.5 G PROTEIN; 22 G FAT (13 G SAT.); 30 G CARBO (0 G FIBER); 50 MG SODIUM; 161 MG CHOL.

Hot fudge sauce

MAKES About 2 cups | **TIME** 10 minutes

Glossy and smooth, this sauce takes no time to whip up and it keeps, covered and refrigerated, for up to a week so you can make sundaes any day.

1 cup heavy cream
⅓ cup light corn syrup
8 oz. bittersweet chocolate, roughly chopped

1. Mix together cream and corn syrup in a small saucepan and bring to a boil, stirring occasionally, over medium-high heat.

2. Remove saucepan from heat and whisk in chopped chocolate.

Make ahead Up to 1 week, cooled, covered airtight, and chilled; reheat over low heat on the cooktop or in a glass bowl in the microwave, stirring every 20 seconds.

PER 2 TBSP. 140 CAL., 67% (94 CAL.) FROM FAT; 1.3 G PROTEIN; 10 G FAT (6 G SAT.); 14 G CARBO (0.3 G FIBER); 19 MG SODIUM; 20 MG CHOL.

Fresh homemade yogurt

MAKES 3 cups | **TIME** 30 minutes, plus at least 8 hours to set

Making your own yogurt is surprisingly easy. It's just milk with a bit of yogurt stirred in, which, after several hours, turns all the milk into yogurt. It'll have a softer texture than store-bought yogurt. If you want it firmer, boil the milk for 10 to 15 minutes before cooling it to evaporate the liquid (yogurt will have a slightly "cooked" taste) or drain yogurt in a cheesecloth-lined sieve to release water. Swirl in jam for a quick snack or breakfast.

1 qt. milk (full-fat, low-fat, or nonfat)
2 tbsp. very fresh plain regular or Greek-style live-culture yogurt (full-fat, low-fat, or nonfat)

1. Pour milk into a large, heavy pot and bring to a boil, stirring often, over medium-high heat. When milk foams up, pour into a bowl and put bowl in a sink of cold water. Cool milk to 110°.

2. Whisk ¼ cup 110° milk with yogurt in a bowl, then whisk into milk. Pour into 2 large glass jars, cover, wrap jars in towels, and put in a cooler. Add a few jars filled with hot water to cooler to keep milk warm. Cover cooler and let milk sit 8 to 12 hours to set (it will look and taste like yogurt when it's done). The longer it sits, the tangier it gets; putting it in the refrigerator stops the process.

Make ahead Up to 1 week, chilled.

PER ¾ CUP (MADE WITH WHOLE MILK) 154 CAL., 48% (74 CAL.) FROM FAT; 8 G PROTEIN; 8.2 G FAT (4.7 G SAT.); 12 G CARBO (0 G FIBER); 108 MG SODIUM; 25 MG CHOL.

Crème fraîche

MAKES 1 cup | **TIME** 15 minutes, plus at least 8 hours to thicken

Crème fraîche is a cultured product that is similar to sour cream. It came from France originally, but it couldn't be easier to make at home.

1 cup heavy whipping cream
2 tablespoons buttermilk

Pour whipping cream and buttermilk into a small bowl and stir to combine. Cover tightly with plastic wrap and let sit at room temperature until thickened, at least 8 hours or overnight. Stir; keep chilled and use within a week. Stir before serving.

PER TBSP. 53 CAL., 94% (50 CAL.) FROM FAT; 0.4 G PROTEIN; 5.6 G FAT (3.5 G SAT.); 0.5 G CARBO (0 G FIBER); 7.4 MG SODIUM; 21 MG CHOL.

Microwave apricot Grand Marnier jam

MAKES About 1 cup | **TIME** 30 minutes, plus 2½ hours to cool

A quick jam such as this is great to have on hand to flavor yogurt (see opposite), dab on vanilla ice cream (see opposite), or spread on toast. Zapped in small quantities in the microwave, the pieces of fruit retain their shape and fresh flavor better than when boiled for jam.

1 to 1¼ lbs. firm-ripe to ripe apricots, pitted and quartered
2 tbsp. lemon juice
½ cup sugar
2 tbsp. Grand Marnier or other orange-flavor liqueur

1. Put apricots in a 3- to 4-qt. microwave-safe bowl. Add lemon juice and sugar; mix.

2. Microwave until juices boil, 6 to 8 minutes. Stir gently to turn fruit pieces over; let mixture stand until cool, at least 1 hour or up to 3 hours. Microwave again until boiling, 5 to 6 minutes; let stand at least 1 hour or up to 3 hours.

3. Stir liqueur into apricot mixture, then microwave again until syrup forms big, shiny bubbles, 12 to 15 minutes, stirring gently every 4 to 5 minutes to turn fruit pieces over and prevent browning. The syrup around the apricots will be thinner than jam, but it thickens as it cools. Spoon into a jar or dish and let cool slightly. Serve warm or cool.

Make ahead Up to 2 weeks, chilled airtight; discard if you see any sign of mold.

PER TBSP. 39 CAL., 2.3% (0.9 CAL.) FROM FAT; 0.4 G PROTEIN; 0.1 G FAT (0 G SAT.); 9.9 G CARBO (0.3 G FIBER); 0.7 MG SODIUM; 0 MG CHOL.

Preserved lemons

MAKES 8 preserved lemons | **TIME** About 10 minutes, plus at least 2 weeks to cure

Preserved lemons are a classic North African condiment. The salty, citrusy flavor of the fermented peel is wonderful with lamb, grilled fish, and cooked greens such as Swiss chard or kale. You can also preserve Meyer lemons, limes, or oranges using this recipe.

8 lemons
1½ cups kosher salt
Rosemary sprig (optional)

1. Rinse lemons thoroughly; quarter lengthwise into wedges and put in a large bowl. Stir in salt. With a potato masher or wooden spoon, press fruit to extract some juice. Transfer mixture to a wide-mouthed 1- to 1½-qt. jar. Push a rosemary sprig into jar if you like. Press fruit down to immerse in juice.

2. Seal jar and store in refrigerator at least 2 weeks and up to 6 months. In the first few days, press fruit down occasionally to immerse in liquid.

PER SERVING 4 CAL., 0% FROM FAT; 0 G PROTEIN; 0 G FAT; 1.3 G CARBO (0.3 G FIBER); 3,421 MG SODIUM; 0 MG CHOL.

MEASUREMENT EQUIVALENTS

Refer to the following charts for metric conversions as well as common cooking equivalents. All equivalents are approximate.

COOKING/OVEN TEMPERATURES

	Fahrenheit	Celsius	Gas Mark
Freeze Water	32°F	0°C	
Room Temp.	68°F	20°C	
Boil Water	212°F	100°C	
Bake	325°F	160°C	3
	350°F	180°C	4
	375°F	190°C	5
	400°F	200°C	6
	425°F	220°C	7
	450°F	230°C	8
Broil			Grill

DRY INGREDIENTS BY WEIGHT

1 oz.	=	1/16 lb.	=	30 g.
4 oz.	=	1/4 lb.	=	120 g.
8 oz.	=	1/2 lb.	=	240 g.
12 oz.	=	3/4 lb.	=	360 g.
16 oz.	=	1 lb.	=	480 g.

(To convert ounces to grams, multiply the number of ounces by 30.)

LENGTH

1 in.	=				2.5 cm.	
6 in.	=	1/2 ft.	=	=	15 cm.	
12 in.	=	1 ft.	=	=	30 cm.	
36 in.	=	3 ft.	=	1 yd.	90 cm.	
40 in.	=				100 cm.	= 1 m.

(To convert inches to centimeters, multiply the number of inches by 2.5.)

LIQUID INGREDIENTS BY VOLUME

1/4 tsp.	=					1 ml.		
1/2 tsp.	=					2 ml.		
1 tsp.	=					5 ml.		
3 tsp.	=	1 tbsp.	=	1/2 fl. oz.	=	15 ml.		
2 tbsp.	=	1/8 cup	=	1 fl. oz.	=	30 ml.		
4 tbsp.	=	1/4 cup	=	2 fl. oz.	=	60 ml.		
5 1/3 tbsp.	=	1/3 cup	=	3 fl. oz.	=	80 ml.		
8 tbsp.	=	1/2 cup	=	4 fl. oz.	=	120 ml.		
10 2/3 tbsp.	=	2/3 cup	=	5 fl. oz.	=	160 ml.		
12 tbsp.	=	3/4 cup	=	6 fl. oz.	=	180 ml.		
16 tbsp.	=	1 cup	=	8 fl. oz.	=	240 ml.		
1 pt.	=	2 cups	=	16 fl. oz.	=	480 ml.		
1 qt.	=	4 cups	=	32 fl. oz.	=	960 ml.		
				33 fl. oz.	=	1,000 ml.	=	1 l.

EQUIVALENTS FOR DIFFERENT TYPES OF INGREDIENTS

Standard Cup	Fine Powder (e.g., flour)	Grain (e.g., rice)	Granular (e.g., sugar)	Liquid Solids (e.g., butter)	Liquid (e.g., milk)
1	140 g.	150 g.	190 g.	200 g.	240 ml.
3/4	105 g.	113 g.	143 g.	150 g.	180 ml.
2/3	93 g.	100 g.	125 g.	133 g.	160 ml.
1/2	70 g.	75 g.	95 g.	100 g.	120 ml.
1/3	47 g.	50 g.	63 g.	67 g.	80 ml.
1/4	35 g.	38 g.	48 g.	50 g.	60 ml.
1/8	18 g.	19 g.	24 g.	25 g.	30 ml.

INDEX